Redcoats on the River

Southeastern North Carolina in the Revolutionary War

By
Robert M. Dunkerly

Original maps by John Robertson

*Special thanks to LtCmdr. Bob Yankle, USN (ret.). His many photos of Revolu-
tionary War re-enactments throughout the South, taken for the N.C. Society Sons
of the American Revolution, add immeasureably to the richness of this book.*

First Edition 2008
Published in the United States of America by Dram Tree Books.

Publisher's Cataloging-in-Publication Data
(Provided by DRT Press)

Dunkerly, Robert.
   Redcoats on the river : southeastern North Carolina in the Revolutionary war
/ by Robert M. Dunkerly.
     p. cm.
   Includes bibliographical references and index.
   ISBN 978-0-9814603-3-8
1. North Carolina —History —Revolution, 1775-1783. 2. Wilmington (N.C.) —
History —18th century. 3. Cape Fear River (N.C.) —History. 4. Moores Creek
Bridge, Battle of, N.C., 1776. 5. American loyalists —North Carolina. 6. North
Carolina —Politics and government —1775-1783. 7. Whig party (N.C.)—
History. I. Title.

F257 .D86 2008
975.67103—dd22

10 9 8 7 6 5 4 3 2 1

Volume discounts available.
Call or e-mail for terms.

Dram Tree Books
P.O. Box 7183
Wilmington, N.C. 28406
(910) 538-4076
www.dramtreebooks.com
Potential authors: visit our website or email us for submission guidelines

Contents

"The reason why I got no more pay was because the money became to be worth nothing, and I esteemed myself rich for I had helped to free my Country, and my children, which was the principle for which I fought, and was more to me than all gold."

- Militiaman John Moore, recorded
in his pension application

Acknowledgements

Many people assisted with this project, and made it better than it would have otherwise been. I would first like to thank Hattie L. Squires of Moores Creek National Battlefield. More than once she helped me track down some obscure source, and she generously opened her private collection to me. Although she won't admit it, Hattie ranks up there with the area's most knowledgeable, and passionate, historians. Her forthcoming research on Pender County's history will be a welcome contribution for researchers and genealogists. Miss Hattie is one of the Lower Cape Fear's most valuable resources.

Two people welcomed me to the Lower Cape Fear and have provided important guidance in my research: Jack Fryar and Dr. Chris E. Fonvielle, Jr. I thank them both for their friendship, support, and encouragement. Beverly Tetterton and Joseph Sheppard of the New Hanover County Public Library in Wilmington pointed out sources I otherwise would have missed. I want to also thank those who suffered through reading the manuscript or offered advice: Timothy Boyd and Angela Bates of Moores Creek National Battlefield, Brenda Bryant of Brunswick Town State Historic Site, Jim McKee of the North Carolina Maritime Museum, Colonial Surgeon Al Denn, and Jackie Margoles of the Burgwin-Wright House.

Butch Adams and Albert Shaw of the Bladen Militia both shared their vast knowledge of local history, as well as their passion for preserving it. Steve McAllister of McAllister & Solomon Used Books read the draft and generously shared his personal manuscript collection. Bob Yankle of the NCSSAR shared his photos.

Barbara Lewis and Ruth Eakins of the Battle of Rockfish Chapter, DAR, were helpful in researching that little known battle. Linda Rivenbark of the Battle of Elizabethtown Chapter, DAR and Frank Melvin both assisted with research in Bladen County. Thanks also to David W. Paul and Clint North, with whom I spent many enjoyable hours in the woods, looking for old roads, campsites, and earthworks. John Robertson provided the excellent maps. To Nancy Stewart of Guilford Courthouse National Military Park, thanks for the favors... you aren't really keeping track are you? Kitty, they are all here.

As always, thanks to my wife Karen, the most patient person I know. She tolerated hearing about Cornwallis, Craig, Harnett, and other long-dead people, knowing that some day it would finally end.

R.M. Dunkerly
Within the British defenses of Wilmington
December 2007

Introduction

Wilmington, North Carolina sits on the east bank of the Cape Fear River, about thirty miles above where the river empties into the Atlantic Ocean. While Wilmington is famous for its role as a blockade running port during the Civil War, its role in the American Revolution as a supply port was no less vital.

As a port city, Wilmington's role in the Revolution was tied to shipping and naval operations. Through the port came news, linking the area's residents to the other colonies and the world. Essential supplies flowed into the city, and Wilmington would be a major source of material for the Continental Army. This fact is why both sides contended for the city, and why both sides occupied it at one time or another. Its merchant-based economy made it a hotbed of dissention when trade and taxes became issues in the years before the Revolution. Among its small population a considerable number of Loyalists shared space with Whigs vying for independence. This led to considerable tension among the civilian population during the conflict.

This work is by no means the complete history of Wilmington during the American War of Independence, but it is hoped that this awakens interest in this often neglected period of the region's history. While Wilmington is at the heart of this work, it is tied to Fayetteville as well. Cross Creek, as it was known in the eighteenth century, was linked to Wilmington by the Cape Fear River. Cross Creek was the interior head of navigation, where many supplies and settlers arriving at Wilmington eventually ended up. This link was critical to the unfolding of events in North Carolina during the Revolution.

It is important to remember that the Revolution was an interruption for the people of the eighteenth century. When the crisis began with England they wanted compromise above all else. They hoped to solve the problems and move on. No one wanted an independent nation at first. The colonies were experiencing tremendous prosperity: increased trade, higher standards of living, growing families, and acquiring wealth. The war forced all colonists to make a choice, and that choice was not always easy.

It was a long, hard road to war, one that was ten years in the making. Many of the most important pre-Revolutionary events of North Carolina happened in the Lower Cape Fear, at places like Wilmington, Cross Creek, Fort Johnston, and Brunswick Town.

Throughout the pages that follow, readers will encounter various terms like Whig and Loyalist. Whigs refer to the Americans, or Patriots, fighting for independence. Loyalists were colonists who fought for the British. Literature often refers to the two groups as Patriots and Tories, however I prefer the terms Whig and Loyalist, to remove any negative connotations or sense of moral superiority.

Chapter 1
The People and the Land

For Rigdon Brice, he thought this day would never come. It seemed unreal, and hard to believe. When the British captured Wilmington, he and other Loyalists thought they could finally live without fear, because royal government was re-established at last. Now, glancing nervously up the river, he wished the evacuation was moving faster.

British troops were neatly and orderly marching onto the transports docked at the foot of Market Street, with fifes and drums playing. Those civilians who had thrown their lot with the British crowded onto the ships, as well.

In fact, a sea of humanity was bumping and jostling for space on the ships: runaway slaves, female camp followers, wounded soldiers, and Loyalist refugees. A multitude of languages were heard from the waterfront: English and Scottish accents, German, Gaelic, and West African dialects. Many of the refugees had nothing but the clothes they wore; a few had managed to bring some valuables on board.

Loyalists had held sway over Wilmington since January. Now in late November 1781, they were pulling out. The news from Yorktown had convinced higher authorities that the British presence in Wilmington could no longer be maintained. It came as a shock to the city's Loyalist population. When the British left what were they to do? Most chose to flee.

The evacuation was proceeding smoothly when suddenly, two blocks up at the courthouse, a civilian looked up Market Street and saw a cloud of dust rising. The thunder of hooves grew louder, and soon a squad of American cavalry burst into view. They quickly charged down the street, pistols blazing and sabers flashing.

One Loyalist soldier stepped out in front of a cavalryman, and the horsemen swung his saber, taking his head off with one blow. Confusion and panic spread among the British troops still in the street, while civilians ran for cover. Cannon fire from the ships in the river drove the horsemen back, and as quickly as they had come, they were gone.

The British quickly loaded their men and supplies and set sail. The gunfire and artillery barrage had driven many residents into their cellars to hide. As Wilmington faded from view, Brice turned his back forever on the city he had called home.

A few hours later Wilmington civilians looked out from their doors and windows to see American troops marching into the city. Some arrived from the northeast, coming down Market Street, while others, coming from upriver, docked at the waterfront.

Col. James Martin of the North Carolina militia stopped amid the cheering and the swarm of soldiers and civilians around him. Wilmington was now free from enemy occupation, its citizens would no longer live in fear. Martin, too, thought this day would never come.

It had been five years since the residents of the Lower Cape Fear went to war against their Mother Country - and themselves. In fact, the area had only been settled for fifty years when violence erupted in 1776. In less than a generation, the Lower Cape Fear was transformed from fledgling settlements to prosperity, and eventually to unrest and bloodshed.

The Lower Cape Fear Region of North Carolina, that piece of land that juts out to the southeast on a map, is dominated by numerous creeks, swamps, and most importantly, the Cape Fear River. The river is the most essential feature of the area. It is why Wilmington exists at all, and it is why the armies came there over two hundred years ago. The river has always been central to the region's economy and transportation, and remains so to this day. The Cape Fear is the only river in North Carolina that flows directly into the Atlantic, and it stretches far into the interior. This fact first attracted settlers to the region, and it was why the American and British armies occupied the area during the Revolution.[1]

Negro Head Point, where the Cape Fear River splits across from Wilmington.

The Cape Fear drains nearly the entire middle section of North Carolina. Its total length -including the tributaries - is over 500 miles. Its basin encompasses over 9,000 square miles, the largest drainage basin in the state. The river begins at the junction of the Haw and Deep Rivers at Mermaid's Point in Chatham County (north of the town of Sanford). From there it flows over 200 miles to the Atlantic Ocean below Wilmington, at Cape Fear.[2]

The Deep River begins near High Point (below modern Greensboro), and flows for 125 miles. The Haw begins at a spring north of Kernersville, and flows 135 miles, pumping 1,200 gallons daily into the Cape Fear. "Haw" is short for an Indian name, Saxapahaw.[3]

Another important tributary, the Northeast Cape Fear River, begins near Mt Olive. It flows south and makes a sharp bend to the west before flowing into the Cape Fear at Wilmington. The junction of these two rivers is at Negro Head Point, named for the site where slave ships unloaded their cargo. The Northeast is 125 miles long, and its unique course served to cut off Wilmington from the rest of the interior, making maneuver difficult for both armies in 1781.[4]

The rivers flow through areas of flat, bottomland hardwood swamps, full of cypress and pine trees. Acid from decaying vegetation produces tannin, which discolors the water to a black color. This severely limits visibility in deep waters, but an observer near the shore can easily see into the water, revealing that it is not polluted, just dark.[5]

The area's wide and powerful rivers impressed all who saw them. Calm waters belie their strong currents: the rivers hold a mesmerizing quality. During the colonial period, the current Northeast Cape Fear River was considered the main branch, and the modern Cape Fear was seen as a tributary, opposite of how they are viewed today. One observer wrote that "wild fruit trees are in full blossom, the ground under them covered with verdure and intermixed with flowers of various kinds made a pleasing Scene." Rivers were the main routes of transportation as the area developed roads slowly, long after settlements had penetrated the interior.[6]

During the eighteenth century Wilmington was commercially linked to Cross Creek (modern Fayetteville) by the Cape Fear River. While goods were unloaded at Wilmington, many were simply transferred to shallower draft vessels to move up to Cross Creek, eighty miles inland. Cross Creek became the end of the trade link that stretched from Wilmington across the Atlantic to Europe. Moravians (a German religious group) came regularly from Salem, in the western part of the colony, for supplies. They wrote that they were "dependent on what could be secured from Springhill, a storehouse which had been built on the Cape Fear River, to which flat-bottomed boats brought some supplies from the harbor at Brunswick. To Springhill [later known as Cross Creek and then Fayetteville] our wagons took flour, and brought back salt and whatever else could be found there." Coming over two hundred miles without good roads to get supplies from Cross Creek attests to its importance as an inland link to the North Carolina interior.[7]

By the late 1700s Cross Creek had become an important shipping and trade center, with sawmills and gristmills for wheat and corn. It had over forty buildings, including taverns, a brewery, mills, a tannery, the county jail, stores, and warehouses, making it a crossroads for trade and communication. Many craftsmen resided there, including merchants, coopers, blacksmiths, tailors, weavers, shoemakers (known as cordwainers), hat makers, brewers, brick makers, bridle makers, joiners, wagoners, wheelwrights, rope makers, and wool combers. It was the closest to the coast that traders had to come from the interior to purchase goods, and many merchants and farmers from western communities like Salem, Charlotte, Hillsboro, and Salisbury came to Cross Creek rather than having to travel all the way down to Wilmington or Brunswick. Wagon shipments regularly left Cross Creek, headed west on trade routes to these distant but growing communities.[8]

Cumberland County (home of Cross Creek) in the 1700s was much larger than the modern county, with Moore, Harnett, and Hoke having been carved from it after the Revolution. In fact, it was an area twice the size of Rhode Island. By the 1760s and 70s the county's population was booming. Records from 1765 indicate a black population of 366, along with 1,109 whites.[9]

Ships could navigate the Cape Fear as far as Cross Creek, 100 miles from the ocean. Smaller waterways in the Upper Cape Fear region connected settlers to trade, including Lower Little River, Rockfish Creek, and others. Numerous industries sprang up on the various creeks and streams around Cross Creek, including both sawmills and gristmills.[10]

The importance of the rivers is easily lost, as they no longer function as major routes of transportation. Rivers were a more reliable means of travel than roads for residents of the interior. Scottish observer Janet Schaw wrote of the

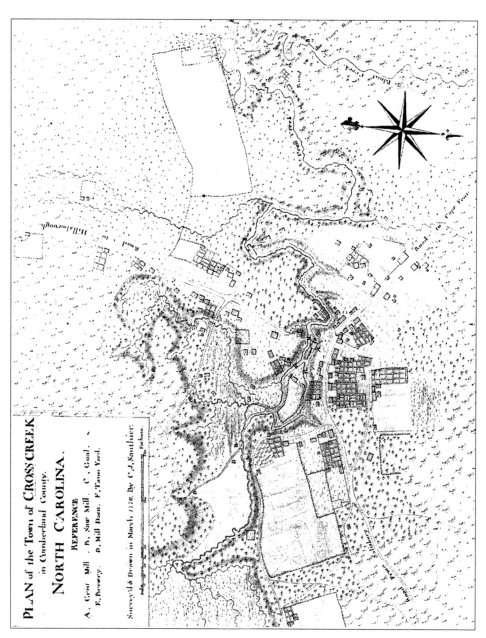

PLAN of the Town of CROSS CREEK in Cumberland County. NORTH CAROLINA.

REFERENCE

A, Great Mill . B, Saw Mill . C , Goal .
E, Brewery . D, Mill Dam. F, Tann Yard.

Surveyd & Drawn in March 1770. By C J. Sauthier.

C.J. Sauthier's map of Cross Creek (modern Fayetteville).

"immeasurable creeks that communicate with the main branches of the river and every tide receives a sufficient depth of water for boats of the largest size and even for small vessels."[11]

The defining feature of the region, and one which would form the basis of its economy, was the longleaf pine. Early explorers and modern scientists who study it were, and remain, amazed at this forest's biological diversity.[12]

Janet Schaw wrote of her observations in a journal. She noted the landscape's lush produce. She saw new fruits like "water mellon," wild grapes, plumb, and peaches. Of the Cape Fear she wrote that "Nothing can be finer than the bank of this river; a thousand beauties both of the flowery and sylvan tribe hang over it and are reflected from it with additional luster." In addition, she noted that "Grapes grow wild and abundant. A large red one bruised and fermented made as good a wine as some imported. Deer plentiful and their meat made delicious soup. The rivers are full of fish. Bears are a problem since they hunted the pigs."[13]

Anne Rutherfurd Schaw, said to closely resemble her daughter, Janet Schaw.

Schawfield Plantation, the home of Janet's brother, Robert, stood on the west side of the Northwest Cape Fear River, along Indian Creek. Robert arrived there in the 1750s and quickly became a successful merchant who was active in local politics. He refused to side with the Whigs (rebels, or Patriots) as the Revolution approached. In 1775 his younger sister Janet visited, and fortunately kept a journal with some of the best observations yet discovered of the land, and the events of 1775-76.[14]

In time the lack of periodic burning (which benefits the longleaf pine trees and the area's plant life), erosion, and extensive harvesting took their toll on these tall, stately trees. In the twenty-first century longleaf pines are rare in the Lower Cape Fear, having been largely replaced by the faster growing loblolly, a tree more suited to the timbering industry.[15]

The forest of longleaf pines formed a massive ecosystem that stretched from southeastern Virginia to eastern Texas, an area of over ninety million acres. Today only about three million acres remain, representing a loss greater than that of the Amazon rainforest or the tall grass prairie of the central United States.[16]

The longleaf pine was the mainstay of the early economy in southeastern North Carolina.

The longleaf forest provided habitat that supported a diversity of plant and wildlife. Some of the more unique plants include the Venus Flytrap, which only grow naturally within a one hundred mile radius of Wilmington.[17]

Other trees growing in this region dominated by swampy land and creeks included swamp oak, cypress, ash, maple, tupelo, gum, poplar, and juniper trees, as well as cane. Gray Spanish moss draped the limbs of the trees. Grassy savannas dotted the landscape, where few trees grew. Wire grass thrived among stands of long leaf pine. In swampy bays (oval shaped wet areas) sweet and black gums, maples, and cypress trees dominated. Settlers also found mulberry trees, and wild berries and grapes.[18]

The region was settled somewhat late by colonial standards, as several earlier attempts had failed. Settlers permanently came to the Lower Cape Fear in the 1720s. Wealthy planters from Charleston (Goose Creek) and Barbados came to this unsettled region that was still claimed by both North and South Carolina. In time, for political and economic reasons, the region aligned itself with the northern colony. By the time the Revolution broke out, it was led by only the second generation of Cape Fear residents.[19]

When originally settled, the Cape Fear region was still part of South Carolina. The area was isolated from both colonies, and for a time it seemed that families like the Moores and other founders might attempt to start their own separate colony there. In time they gravitated to North Carolina's rule. The upper colony had a weak and distant leadership that allowed the early settlers a measure of independence. In fact the region had such a reputation for lawlessness and lack of government that one observer noted in 1729 that "North Carolina...has only been a Receptacle for Pyrates, Thieves, and Vagabonds of all sorts."[20]

In 1729 North Carolina officially claimed the Cape Fear region, creating New Hanover Precinct. Court sessions began meeting at Brunswick Town a few years later. Surveyors did not finalize the boundary between the two Carolinas until 1735.[21]

The region remained sparsely populated, and by the time of the Revolution settlers had only been here for fifty years. Isolation and the endless forests dominated the landscape as one traveled along the area's few roads or its broad waterways. Even today, long stretches of the region's roads like Interstate 40, and highways 421, 76, and 17 run through sparsely settled areas. One observer wrote that he traveled through a region that was "gloomy and dismal, through hot parching sands . . . a few wire grass ridges . . ." Yet the soil was fertile enough for some crops, and the long leaf pines that grew well here became the basis for the area's economy.[22]

In time wealthy planters established tight control over the region's land ownership, politics, and economy. One of the most powerful families included the Moores. In 1725 "King" Roger Moore rebuilt his home at Orton, having lost an earlier one to Indian attack. The Moores, founders of Brunswick Town, would become one of the area's leading families, and formed close alliances with other powerful landowners. In fact, in the 1720s and 1730s, half of all landowners in the area were related to the Moores, an unprecedented statistic.[23]

As the Lower Cape Fear region developed it retained economic ties to South Carolina and the West Indies, and in fact resembled those regions more

The tomb of Roger Moore (left), who built Orton Plantation (right) in 1725.

than the rest of North Carolina. The area stood out as unique: a majority slave population, an economy tied to shipping and naval store production (tar, pitch, and turpentine). These materials were vital in the shipping industry: tar as axle grease on working parts and in machinery, pitch to seal wooden hulls and keep them water tight, and turpentine had a variety of uses, including paint, paint thinner, medicine, and other products. North Carolina's naval stores kept the Royal Navy afloat. The economic dependence on naval store production, which required large tracts of undeveloped land, slowed the growth of traditional food or crop plantations in the area.[24]

In fact, the Lower Cape Fear was the only region of North Carolina with a majority slave population, like the South Carolina lowcountry and the West Indies. Naval stores production here was unique in Colonial America, as it was the only non-agricultural staple in British North America.[25]

The large slave population in the Lower Cape Fear developed the same Gullah cultural traditions that are more commonly associated with lowcountry South Carolina and Georgia. Gullah included West African language dialects and unique ways of cooking with rice, seafood, vegetables, and seasonings. While some came directly from Africa or other colonies, most of the region's slaves arrived from the West Indies.[26]

Slaves worked under what became known as the task system: they did not work all day, but rather were given assignments. When the task was completed, their time was their own. Most owners permitted slaves to raise their own livestock, or hire themselves out for pay. These conditions gave them a measure of independence and control over their affairs. The constant fear of slave insurrection would continue throughout the period, and intensify with the outbreak of war.[27]

As the Lower Cape Fear attracted wealthy planters, large numbers turned to rice, indigo, and naval stores production. The area's longleaf pines were an excellent source of tar, pitch, and turpentine. North Carolina became the British navy's leading supplier of these valuable materials. Wilmington was the largest exporter of those products, shipping more naval stores than the other colonies combined.[28]

North Carolina's intense production of these supplies ensured it an important place in the British Empire's economy. Landowners never bothered to improve the quality or invest in better production, as their focus was always on the bottom line in this volatile industry. North Carolinians easily fell into trade deficits.[29]

Naval stores from the Cape Fear were shipped to Boston and Philadelphia. While the British government created bounties for naval stores and tobacco, they remained risky crops. Prices were often low, and a variety of circumstances beyond the planter's control could affect the market.[30]

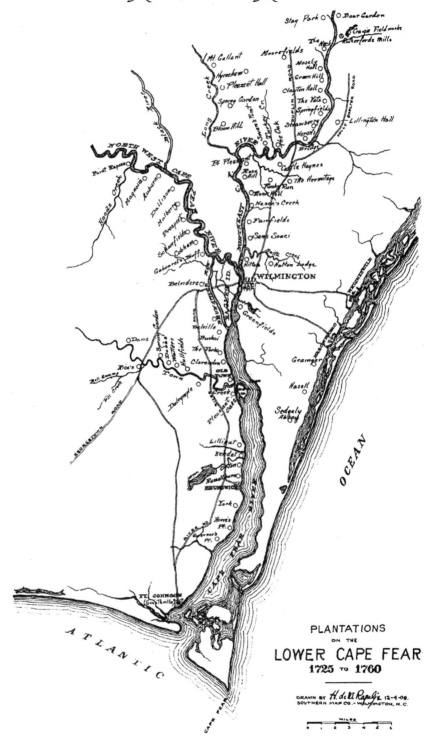

Stag Park ○ ○ Bear Garden
Craigie Field works ○
Rutherfords Mills
The Neck
Moorefields ○
Mosely Hall ○
Green Hill ○
Clayton Hall ○
The Vats ○
Springfields ○
Mt. Gallant ○
Hyrcham ○
Pleasant Hall ○
Spring Garden ○
Strawberry ○
Herons
Long Creek
Bloom Hill ○
Lillington Hall ○
Swann's Point Cr.
One Oak ○
Castle Haynes ○
Ft. Pleasant ○
Rose Hill ○
Roots Run ○
Rock Hall ○
Nesau's Creek ○
Fairfields ○
Sans Souci ○
Smith Creek
Hilton ○
Nutton Lodge ○
POINT Repose ○
Magnolia ○
Auburn ○
Dallison
Mulberry
Prospect
Maryfields
Cobham
Gabourel's Bluff
Belvedere ○
WILMINGTON
Greenfields ○
Spring Garden ○
Davis ○
Dobb's ○
Walters ○
Huffields ○
Rice's ○
Zill Swamp
Town Creek
Dalrymple ○
Belville ○
Bushoi ○
The Forks ○
Clarendon ○
OLD TOWN
Elizabeth Creek
Grange ○
Hasell ○
Sedgely Abbey ○
Lilliput ○
Kendal ○
Orton ○
Russellboro
BRUNSWICK
York ○
Howe's Pt. ○
Governors Pt. ○
RIVER RD.
FT. JOHNSON
(Smithville)

OCEAN

ATLANTIC

CAPE FEAR

PLANTATIONS
ON THE
LOWER CAPE FEAR
1725 TO 1760

DRAWN BY *H. deM. Rapalje* 12-1-08.
SOUTHERN MAP CO.—WILMINGTON, N.C.

MILES
0 1 2 3 4 5 6

The climate and soil of the region also supported rice and indigo production, yet these other crops were never a significant source of income for planters. As with naval stores, various factors like the weather, shipping delays, and a volatile market made rice and indigo crops tough to make a profit on. Thus rice and indigo were grown here but were not major crops like in the South Carolina lowcountry. They did, however, serve as yet another feature that set the Cape Fear Region apart from the rest of North Carolina.[31]

The process of extracting the naval stores products was a labor intensive, smelly, and wasteful one. Plantation slaves cut off strips of the pine tree's bark at the base of the trunk, allowing rosin (crude turpentine) to flow from the exposed area. Each week two fresh cuts could be added above the others. The rosin was scooped out of a box at the bottom of the cut, and ladled into barrels. This was known as "boxing" a tree, named for the box cut into the base where the rosin collected. The rosin was then boiled to produce turpentine.[32]

Trees that no longer produced rosin were cut down and slowly burned for tar. Tar kilns, large piles of logs covered with earth, burned slowly to scorch the wood and force the hot tar out of the logs. Generally the mound of logs was ten to thirty feet wide, and the kiln was packed with earth or clay. An opening at the top allowed air to fuel the fire. Workers ignited the kiln at the edges and had to monitor the temperature and rate of burning. A kiln could burn for a day or two before tar began to flow. The kilns had to be watched constantly, twenty-four hours a day, to maintain the right conditions. Again this was collected into barrels. Tar was then boiled in large kettles to produce pitch. The material had to be stirred as it thickened.[33]

All of this work producing tar, pitch, and turpentine was backbreaking, time consuming and, most importantly, dirty. The gooey mess stuck to everything, and the messy work, done largely by slaves, may be one reason North Carolinians earned the nickname "Tarheels."

Many trees still stand that bear scars from "boxing," evidence of past turpentine production. Some are known to exist in Pender County near Moores Creek, others on the campus of the University of North Carolina at Wilmington, and near New Hanover Regional Medical Center on South 17th Street in Wilmington, to name a few.

The lumber itself was another "crop" fueling the area's economy. By the time of the Revolution there were fifty lumber mills in the Lower Cape Fear. North Carolina was the second largest colonial exporter of sawn lumber.[34]

In time large plantations, most involved with naval stores production, lined the rivers of the Lower Cape Fear. These materials, along with the region's other "crops" like lumber, rice, and indigo, went down river to the ports of Brunswick and Wilmington to be exported.

Founded on the west bank of the Cape Fear River in 1726, Brunswick Town became an official port of entry for shipping in 1731, one of three in the colony. It was here ships had to stop and register their cargo before unloading. A few miles to the north, settlers founded a town in 1732, first as New Liverpool, then New Town or Newton, and finally incorporated the town as Wilmington in 1739. At the mouth of the Cape Fear River, where it empties into the Atlantic Ocean, stood Fort Johnston, protecting entry into the river (at modern Southport), built between 1745-49. Among its commanders would be Robert Howe, and John Collet, who produced an important map of North Carolina. The fort was apparently small and in constant need of repair. Janet Schaw, who passed by it in 1775 recorded that it was not "quite so Tremendous, tho I see guns peeping thro' the sticks [the fort's wooden walls]."[35]

Although founded as the area's principal port and capital, Brunswick grew slowly. One observer noted in 1731 that it was "but a poor, hungry impoverished place, consisting of not above 10 or 12 scattering mean houses, hardly worth the name of a village." He went on to note, however, that "the platform is good and convenient, and the ground high considering the country."[36]

As a port of entry, Brunswick soon became busy with ships unloading supplies and raw materials for export. The town included a tavern, or public house as it was known, a physician, the county courthouse, a church, and also the residence of the royal governor. Soon after its founding a ferry began operation, offering transport across the Cape Fear River to Sugar Loaf, now Carolina Beach State Park, below Wilmington.[37]

Although it never grew into a large thriving town, many prominent Cape Fear families lived or owned lots at Brunswick, including the Moores, Moseleys, William Dry, Cornelius Harnett, Richard Quince, Jonathan Dunbibin, and Dr. John Fergus. Many merchants, ship owners, and plantation owners owned property or conducted business there. The presence of the church, courthouse, tavern, and the fact that the governor resided there all gave the town prominence despite its small size.[38]

St. Philip's Church, begun in 1754 and completed in 1768, had brick walls nearly three feet thick. In this period when there was no separation of church and state, the presence of this large, imposing church was a symbol of stability, law, and order in the region.[39]

Religion was not a separate entity from government in colonial America. The official, or state religion, of the British empire was the Church of England (known today as the Anglican Church). While officially it was the only church legally recognized, North Carolina was lenient on some dissenters. As long as citizens upheld the law and did not threaten the established church, other denominations were generally tolerated.[40]

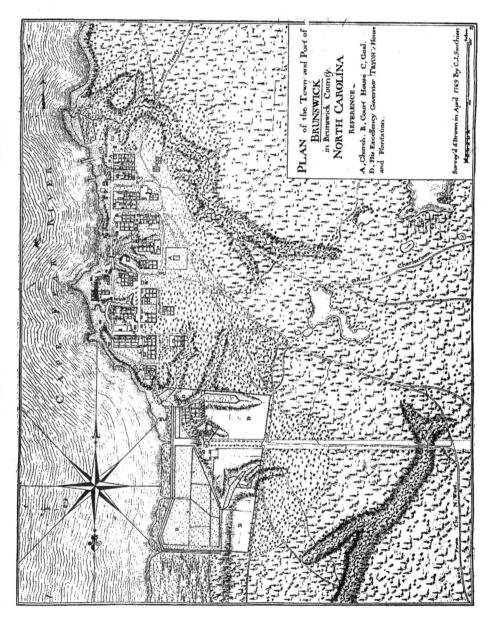

C.J. Sauthier's map of Brunswick Town.

The original St. James Anglican Church in Wilmington.

Despite this, the Church of England was tax-supported and the most prominent members of society attended its services. The only legal weddings were those done by Anglican ministers, although some Presbyterian ministers were allowed to wed couples. The Church was a symbol of authority and British power in Colonial America.[41]

The church often shared a minister with St. James Church in Wilmington. Reverend James Moir also taught a school while stationed at Brunswick's St. Philip's Church. Governor Dobbs was married there and is buried there, as are many prominent, and not so prominent, Cape Fear citizens.[42]

An artist's conception of the finished St. Philip's Anglican Church at Brunswick.

Brunswick sat on a bluff overlooking the river, with streets running parallel to the water. It was never a large town, and observer Janet Schaw wrote in 1775 that it had "a few scattered houses on the edge of the woods, without streets or regularity." Another observer noted, "The little town of Brunswick stands in an exceedingly pleasant situation, but is very inconsiderable, nor does it contain more than 50 or 60 houses."[43]

A combination of things led to Brunswick's decline. A Spanish attack in 1748 showed how vulnerable the site was to raids from the sea. Two powerful hurricanes in 1761 and 1769 further damaged the town. The storms devastated buildings and destroyed many ships in the river. In addition, settlers found Wilmington easier to access by river from the interior, and soon it began to surpass Brunswick for shipping. Perhaps more importantly, Royal Governor George Burrington used his authority to move the seat of government to Wilmington during a dispute with the Moore family. When the Revolution broke out many residents fled Brunswick as the presence of British ships in the river threatened the town. As it was a symbolic target (the scene of early protests), British forces burned it in 1776, and it never recovered.[44]

During the Civil War Confederate forces occupied the site and constructed massive earthworks there. In the 1960s archaeologists excavated much of the town and discovered the foundations of buildings and thousands of artifacts. The site is preserved and its ruins have been stabilized for viewing, although only about half the town is visible to modern visitors. Looking over the quiet ruins makes it hard to imagine the importance of this town two hundred years ago. Just to the north of Brunswick was Russellborough, home to two of the colony's five royal governors.[45]

In 1758 Royal Governor Arthur Dobbs bought Russellborough and made it his home in North Carolina. Next, Governor William Tryon resided there after he replaced Dobbs, and before moving on to New Bern. Tryon gave a detailed description of Russellborough: "This House which has so many assistances is of an oblong Square Builg of Wood. It measures on the outside Side Faces forty five feet by thirty five feet, and is Divided into two Stories, Exclusive of the Cellars the Parlour Floor is about five feet above the Surface of the Earth. Each story has four Rooms and three...Closets. There is a good Stable and Coach Houses and some other Out Houses. The garden has nothing to Boast of except Fruit Trees - Peaches, Nectars, Figgs and Plumbs are in perfection and of good Sorts...Apples grow extremely well here I have tasted Excellent Cyder..."[46]

When archaeologists investigated Russellborough, they discovered its brick floors, with broken jars, teacups, plates, saucers, and wine bottles scattered across the area. Many had the seal of William Dry, Collector of the Port who resided here in the 1770s. Dry led the counterattack that drove Spanish troops out of the town in 1748, and was active in the Stamp Act controversy of the

Royal Governor Arthur Dobbs (left), and his Russelborough home (right).

1760s. Archaeologists also discovered a brick tunnel that ran from the home's basement to the back of the property, used to transport garbage and as a sewer.[47]

In the town of Brunswick, archaeologists found that many home foundations were built using ballast stones from ships, along with a mortar made with limestone extracted from crushed shells called tapia. Many homes were two stories with brick chimneys and large wooden porches. Artifacts at some buildings gave clues to their usage: pins, thimbles, buttons, and buckles identified a tailor's shop. Glass and pottery at another identified a tavern. Clay pipes, coins, and various types of jars, plates, and drinking vessels revealed how people lived. A knife from Malay and porcelain from China illustrate the network of trade that linked Brunswick to the world. Even intact hen eggs were discovered at one site.[48]

One primary reason for the town's location was that it sat below the Flats, which blocked shipping from going above that point of the river. The Flats, a shallow area upriver, prevented ships with drafts above nine feet from going any further inland. Thus ocean going vessels unloaded their cargo at Brunswick, while shallower draft ships could proceed on to Wilmington. The Flats were located about seven miles above Brunswick.[49]

One local landmark that defined the region was the Dram Tree. This sturdy old cypress stood along the river between Wilmington and Brunswick. Upon their return to port, sailors drank to celebrate another safe voyage. The Dram Tree stood until the mid-twentieth century, when it was destroyed due to expansion of the N.C. State Ports below Wilmington.[50]

Despite the presence of The Flats, which barred large ships from moving farther north, Wilmington provided easier access for goods coming from the interior, using rivers like the Cape Fear, Black, and Northeast Cape Fear to bring goods down to the newer town. Brunswick, being more exposed to raids from the sea and severe storms, began to lose population and business to Wilmington. Plantations located along the main rivers and other waterways shipped lumber and barrels of tar, pitch, and turpentine on rafts down to Wilmington. The area's waterways were an existing, constantly flowing highway that enabled goods to be moved easily and cheaply. Eastern North Carolina had no other river system quite like it, with many small tributaries flowing into progressively larger streams. The network reached far inland and enabled trade and shipping to spread far and wide across the colony's southeastern corner.[51]

Wilmington's cemetery stood behind Mrs. Heron's home (widow of Benjamin, who built and operated the draw bridge on the Northeast Cape Fear). It had a brick cellar and a piazza. Her home stood on the east side at the corner of Market and Third, now the site of St. James Church. Across Market Street below the jail were the homes of Duncan and Dry, and farther down was that of George Parker. Dr. Tucker had a shop on Front Street, while Dr. Cobham's home, with a piazza, stood between Princess and Chestnut.[52]

The Dram Tree on the Cape Fear River.

The town jail was located at the corner of Third and Market Streets, underneath the present Burgwin-Wright House. Built in 1769, the jail was a sturdy stone building made of ballast from ships. Nearby stood stocks, a pillory, a whipping post, and a jailor's home. The Burgwin-Wright House would be built on top of the jail in 1771, using it for its foundation.[53]

Only a few remnants remain from colonial Wilmington's past, including the Mitchell-Anderson home (the oldest in the city) at the corner of Orange and Front Streets, the Burgwin-Wright House, and just next to it, the Boatwright House.

Another feature of early Wilmington that remains visible today are a series of hills and valleys. Wilmington's downtown is not flat. In fact, the lower end of Market Street - the main thoroughfare - is in a low depression. Wilmington's streets and homes follow the contours of the land, rising and falling over the landscape. Surveyors superimposed a grid on this rolling landscape.

The courthouse, built in 1740, stood in the intersection of Front and Market Streets, as was not uncommon in some towns. Traffic simply moved around the building in the center of the intersection. The courthouse was the center of business and would be a focal point for protests, meetings, and demonstrations in the 1760s and 1770s.

The town was also built over a landscape that included streams and gullys. As the town grew, these were channeled into underground tunnels, some of which remain to this day. Over this uneven ground surveyors imposed a grid of streets and lots. One observer noted that "The Regularity of the Streets are equal to those of Philadelphia and Buildings in General very Good. Many of Brick, two or three Stories high with double piazzas which make a good appear [ance]."[54]

Resident James Murray wrote of his home and store in 1741, "In my house, there is a large Room 22 by 16 feet, the most airy of any in the Country, two tolerable lodging rooms & a Closet up stairs & Garrets above, a Cellar below divided into a Kitchen with an oven and a Store for Liquors, provisions, etc. This makes one half of my house. The other, placed on the east end, is the Store Cellar below, the Store and Counting House on the first floor, & above it is partion'd off into four rooms, but this end is not plaister'd but only done with rough boards."[55]

Chimney fires remained a constant danger, and records mention many instances of homes catching fire, and residents being fined for carelessness with their chimneys. In 1771 a "dreadful fire" began on the south side of Dock Street below Front Street, burning fifteen homes before it was contained. Fortunately Wilmington had a fire engine and residents responded quickly.[56]

Wilmington's major thoroughfare, Market Street, was 99 feet wide, and the other streets were 66 feet wide. Surveyors laid out the city's grid pattern in the 1730s, and it is still seen today in modern Wilmington. Along Market Street stood shops, houses, and other businesses. A large bakery supplied biscuits (hard bread) for ships in the West Indies.[57]

Completed in 1770, St. James Church stood a block north of the current church's location (where the synagogue now stands on Market and 4th Streets). The original St. James was a square building with brick walls, and no bell tower.[58]

Running out from Wilmington, along modern Market Street and turning into Highway 17, was a post road that ran north to New Bern, and eventually to Boston. North from the town another road ran up to the Northeast Cape Fear River, crossing it at a drawbridge near the modern I-40 bridge. Known as Heron's Bridge, this was a structure unique in Colonial America. (Heron's Bridge was referred to by contemporaries as the Big Bridge, the Great Bridge, Blueford's Bridge, Heron's Bridge, and other names. For sake of consistency, Heron's Bridge will be used from here on to refer to this impressive structure). Known as the Great Duplin Road, it ran all the way to Duplin Courthouse near modern Warsaw. The only other drawbridge in the colonies was in Maine (then still part of Massachusetts).

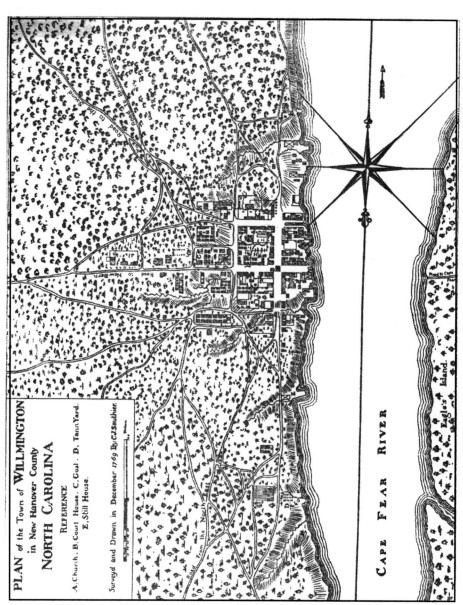

C.J. Sauthier's 1769 map of Wilmington.

Here the Northeast Cape Fear is about 25 feet deep at the center of the river. Sediment and tides vary the water's depth at any given time. The bridge was 403 feet long over the water, and about twelve feet wide. One section was a drawbridge, with two parts drawn up to allow ships to pass. The bridge was built with beams over trestles in the water. It impressed all who saw it, and would be a key strategic point during the war.[59]

Janet Schaw wrote that the bridge, "tho built of timber is truly a noble one, broader than that over the Tay at Perth. It opens at the middle to both sides and rises by pulleys, so as to suffer Ships to pass under it. The road is sufficiently broad to allow fifty men to march abreast and the woods much thinner of trees than where I have seen them."[60]

Archaeological work done in the 1980s at the site has found evidence of its eighteenth and nineteenth century use. Artifacts discovered included two flat bottomed vessels (used for ferrying), an earthenware (redware) crock, a three-leg cast iron pipkin (cooking pot), fragments of a creamware plate (white pottery), green bottle glass, and printed ceramics.[61]

Wilmington gradually became the economic and political center of the region, much like Charleston did in the South Carolina lowcountry, or Philadelphia in southeastern Pennsylvania.

As settlement moved into the interior, other towns sprung up. Settlers founded Elizabethtown in 1773 to host the new Bladen County courthouse (though it still had not been built by 1778). Its streets were laid out over a 100 acre area, and it soon included a tanyard, mills, marketplace, and other public buildings. Located on the Cape Fear and along the road between Wilmington and Cross Creek, the town existed on trade and commerce. The previous courthouse had been located about three miles above the town.[62]

Bladen County, like the rest of the area, thrived on shipping naval stores and lumber to Wilmington via the Cape Fear. Plantations sprung up along the river, focusing on tar, pitch, turpentine, shingles, staves, and boards.[63]

During the 1770s North Carolina experienced tremendous population growth. The colony's population doubled in the twenty years between 1730 and 1750, reaching 65,000 residents. In another twenty years it more than doubled again. By 1776 it had 250,000 people, making it the fourth largest colony. Yet it was a primarily rural population, as only two percent of the population lived in towns. Wilmington was one of those few urban settings. The bulk of the colony's citizens lived in the backcountry, the area west of modern Raleigh.[64]

By 1772 Brunswick County's population (which at the time included modern Brunswick, Bladen, and Columbus Counties) was 947 white residents, and 2,054 black, for a total of 3,001. New Hanover County (which included modern New Hanover and Pender) had over 2,000 white and 3,000 black residents, for a total of 5,000. Thus the Cape Fear region was an anomaly in North Carolina. Economically and ethnically it was much more like Barbados or the South Carolina lowcountry than other regions of its own colony. By way of comparison, the 2006 population of Wilmington was 76,000, and that of a much smaller New Hanover County, 182,591.[65]

A sampling from Pitt County shows that most families (70%) had fewer than five children. None had more than nine, with the average being 3.2 children per household. Only 9% of the families had no children. These numbers are probably representative of the region.[66]

Most of the settlers of the Lower Cape Fear were of English descent, but large numbers of Scottish settlers came through Wilmington and Brunswick to settle the interior. From the ports of entry they traveled to Cross Creek, and from there spread out up and down the region's many creeks and streams. In the twenty years before the outbreak of the Revolution, 5,000 Scots settled in a compact area comprising modern Anson, Scotland, and Cumberland Counties. They were mostly Highland Scots, with some Lowlanders mixed in. Clannish and poor, they remained a distinct ethnic group, separated by language, religion, and custom from the majority of the region's population.[67]

Many Scots came to the region because land was available. Among those settlers were veterans of the latest uprising against English rule: the failed 1745 Jacobite Rebellion. Many fled Scotland for America to escape English oppression. The presence of these Scottish immigrants played an important role in the outbreak of the coming war in North Carolina.

Other ethnic groups that arrived at Brunswick and Wilmington included French Huguenots, Quakers, Welsh, Germans, and a few Jewish families. By far the most numerous were the Scots. Incomplete records suggest that the average family size was 4.5-6.3 people per household, with most having between three and nine.[68]

Slave ownership, while high in the area, was concentrated in the hands of the wealthy. The top one percent of the wealthiest residents held ten percent of the region's slaves. The top one-half percent of the property owners controlled ninety percent of the property. Their wealth was primarily in land and slaves.[69]

Besides population composition and economy, land owning patterns were another factor that distinguished the Lower Cape Fear from the rest of the colony. The largest landholdings of the entire colony were found here. The average property size was greatest in New Hanover County, at 934 acres. Brunswick County was second at 804 acres. The area's primary products of lumber, tar, pitch, and turpentine did not require many improvements to the land, but did require large tracts to clear and extract these products.[70]

Of the many plantations that lined the Cape Fear and Northeast Cape Fear Rivers, Orton is one of the few now open to the public. Founded by Roger Moore, the home has been expanded over the years by descendents and subsequent owners. Here the family cemetery holds the remains of several generations of the region's most prominent family.[71]

Wilmington quickly became a thriving port town with a diverse and cosmopolitan population. The city was North Carolina's only major port; other seaports like New Bern, Edenton, and Bath never attained the level of trade that Wilmington did. Its direct access to the ocean, and its large network of rivers linking it to the interior, gave Wilmington a great advantage. By the time of the Revolution, the Lower Cape Fear region was the colony's shipping leader. By far the greatest volume of this trade was with the West Indies, with England a distant second.[72]

Shipping through the Cape Fear region averaged over 9,000 tons per year in the decade before the outbreak of war. Various types of vessels were seen in the river and docked at Brunswick and Wilmington: sloops, schooners, brigs, and snows. Over three quarters of the ships carrying goods were large vessels, benefiting from the easy access from the ocean to the interior. Ocean going ships could come inland as the Cape Fear lacked the shoals, sandbars, and shallow sounds that restricted trade at North Carolina's other ports.[73]

The types of ships seen in the river included two-masted schooners and single-masted sloops, the smallest that could move far up to Cross Creek and the plantations along the rivers. Larger vessels like two-masted brigs and snows were ocean going ships that could not venture above The Flats at Brunswick.[74]

Between 1768 and 1773 the Lower Cape Fear accounted for over half of the value of all of North Carolina's exports. According to financial records, the area also profited more from exports than the rest of the colony, even more than the middle colonies, and New England- a region renowned for its shipping industry.[75]

A glimpse of the region's exports reveals that in the decade before the Revolution, tar accounted for over half of outgoing products, followed by pine boards, turpentine, tobacco, lumber, deerskins, beef and pork, bread and flour, and rice and indigo last. Indigo exports always exceeded the quantity of rice shipped out. The majority of North Carolina's naval stores were shipped through the Cape Fear River, surpassing all its other ports combined.[76]

Other products produced and shipped out of the area included planks, staves, hoops, barrels, posts, masts, and oars; all part of the naval industry that thrived in colonial North Carolina. Seventy-five percent of the colony's sawn lumber was exported from the Cape Fear. In fact, the largest concentration of sawmills in the colony was along the Cape Fear River. Some of the biggest included mills run by John Rutherford (at Hunt Hill near Holly Shelter), and Joseph Eagles (on Eagles Island opposite Wilmington). Other sawmills operated near Cross Creek, which offered easy access down the Cape Fear to Wilmington.[77]

The river brought materials and news from around the world to the people of the Cape Fear area. For example, a merchant in the February 22, 1766 *North Carolina Gazette* advertised "a compleat assortment of check'd and striped linens," as well as silk petticoats, "satin hats, cloaks, and bonnets...iron pots, frying pans and skillets."[78]

Newspaper advertisements regularly mention Irish linen, rum, sugar, and molasses from the Caribbean (usually Jamaica), tea from Asia, cotton fabric from India, various manufactured goods from England, and Madeira wine from Portugal. Far from a frontier society, the residents of southeastern North Carolina had access to the world marketplace.[79]

Merchant John McDonell advertised oznaburg (a type of cotton), Irish linen, blankets, India cotton prints, gown patterns for women, silk hats and mits, sadlery, and even tools like axes, as well as molasses, sugar, and rum.[80]

John Burgwin arrived in Wilmington from England in the 1750s and quickly achieved success as a merchant. He built a prominent home on Third Street, one that would figure later during the British occupation of the city. Burgwin served as a clerk of court and in the General Assembly. He was also the private secretary to Governor Dobbs. As tensions increased with Great Britain he found himself in a difficult position. He left before the outbreak of war to receive medical treatment in England, and remained there during the duration of the conflict. Afterwards he returned, reclaimed his property, and rebuilt his business, passing away in 1803.[81]

Burgwin imported Irish linen, hats, shoes, carpet, knives, forks, table linen, candlesticks, carpenter's tools, and a variety of maritime supplies, including anchors, mariner's compasses, grapnels (anchors for small ships), cordage, and sail cloth. He also carried swords and pistols, gunpowder, and lead bars (for melting into ammunition). One of the city's wealthiest residents, he accepted raw goods like tar, turpentine, and lumber in lieu of cash.[82]

Robert Kennedy offered oznaburg, women's shoes, hats, blankets, and pipes for sale. Ancrum Forster imported rum and coffee from Jamaica. Business partners Richard Quince and John Burgwin owned ten shipping vessels. Quince was a wealthy merchant who lived in Brunswick, while Burgwin resided in Wilmington. Quince was a justice of the peace for Brunswick County, and served on the Wilmington Committee of Safety as well as with the Sons of Liberty. He died in 1778 and is buried in St. Philip's Church.[83]

Jonathan Dunbibin operated a store near the Market House that carried Barcelona handkerchiefs, white kid gloves, earrings and necklaces, candlesticks, scissors, thimbles, combs, writing paper, sealing wax (for envelopes), china, teacups, umbrellas, nails, a dozen types of cloth, shoemakers hammers, axes, hoes, knives, saws, belts, buckles, sugar, frying pans, iron pots, and skillets. The variety of his goods is an indication of the typical merchant's selection.[84]

He lived on Market Street, and in addition to his store he also operated a saltworks on Masonboro Sound. Dunbibin was clerk of court for New Hanover County and became active in the coming protests, serving on the local Committee of Safety.[85]

During the 1760s and 1770s, merchants Robert Hogg and Samuel Campbell imported rum, sugar, and molasses, while exporting naval stores, wood products, timber, deerskins, and flour. Their trade network included contacts in Charleston and Cross Creek. Campbell was captain of the Wilmington militia but had lukewarm support for the Revolution. When the British arrived in 1781 he assisted with running the city government under their occupation. He evacuated with them and later moved to Nova Scotia.[86]

Wilmington became a center of trade, commerce, and communication. The city had taverns where men met to discuss news and business, and offered services not found in the surrounding area like wig makers, saddlers, physicians, carpenters, goldsmiths, tanners, silversmiths, and furniture makers.[87]

There were several Cabinet makers and furniture makers in the town before the war. Carpenter John Nutt owned property on Princess Street, and William DuBose operated another shop in the town. Their work was for local consumption only, and their goods did not reach the interior.[88]

Several physicians resided in Wilmington, including Dr. Thomas Cobham and Dr. Robert Tucker. Cobham accompanied Governor William Tryon on his expedition against the Regulators in 1771. He remained an ardent Loyalist, and treated the wounded Loyalists who were captured at Moores Creek.

Cobham intended to return to England with the outbreak of hostilities, but was persuaded to stay. When Major James Craig's British troops arrived in 1781 he actively assisted them. With Craig's evacuation, he fled with the British forces, taking his wife Catherine to England.[89]

As with the farmer's planting, the merchant's sales followed a seasonal rhythm. Sales peaked in the fall, when farmers had money after the harvest to buy goods.[90]

Ships brought news from London and Europe, Boston, New York, Philadelphia, Halifax, Nova Scotia, and elsewhere. Wilmington had several newspapers through this period, including Andrew Steuart's *North Carolina Gazette* from 1764-66, and Adam Boyd's *Cape Fear Mercury* from 1769 through 1775. News also arrived on ships, and by post riders from north and south along the mail route (now modern day US 17). Slave auctions, merchant ads, runaway slave notices, auctions, international news, and various local items appeared in the region's newspapers. A colorful example of the latter includes the notice by Morris Connor that his wife Mary had eloped and "otherwise treated me ill" and he would not pay any debts that she incurred.[91]

Wilmington's shipping importance propelled it to the forefront of dissent in the growing crisis with England. Issues of trade and taxation were keenly felt in the port town.[92]

The men who would lead the movement towards Revolution were already the area's elite: Justices of the Peace, members of the Colonial Assembly and provincial council (the colonial government), militia officers, judges, lawyers, and landowners. Most were the upper crust of society: lawyers, planters, land speculators, and other government officials.[93]

North Carolina's government consisted of a Royal Governor appointed by the King, and the Assembly. The Assembly consisted of two houses: the Governor's Council, also appointed by the Crown, who acted as advisors to the Governor, and the lower house, who were elected by voting citizens. It would be these men who led the coming Revolutionary movement.[94]

Justices of the peace and sheriffs managed local government at the county level. These officials were appointed by the Royal Governor. As with the other colonies, North Carolina had a militia system in place for defense and maintaining law and order. Every free male in the colony aged 16 to 60 was automatically in the militia. Exceptions were made for millers, ferry owners, lawyers, court officials, and physicians. Thus the governor could call out the militia to deal with emergencies. Religious officials and Quakers were also exempt from service. Fines and punishments enforced attendance.[95]

Militia also performed public duties like building roads, fighting fires, slave patrols, and assisting sheriffs with maintaining law and order. Militia were expected to train several times throughout the year and men were fined who did not attend. Militia service was seen as a form of taxation and part of the duty of a citizen. By the time violence broke out in 1775, there was a militia system in place, and when the war came it split into Whig and Loyalist groups.[96]

In 1775 North Carolina also created a separate organization of Minutemen. These men were specially trained and equipped to respond to emergencies more quickly than the regular militia companies. They were disbanded by 1776, when the creation of the Continental Regiments made them obsolete.[97]

In the fifty years between 1725 and 1775, a unique regional identity formed along the Lower Cape Fear. While part of North Carolina, its economy (tied to shipping and naval store production), its demographics (with a slave majority), and its political structure (dominated by elite families) all combined to make the area different.[98]

British General Braddock, mortally wounded during the French & Indian War.

Chapter 2
The Road to War

In 1763 Americans were among the most prosperous people on earth. They were proud to be part of a growing British Empire that guaranteed their safety, preserved their rights, and expanded their trade networks. Within ten years it had all changed. Disagreements over taxes, colonial rights, trade regulation, and other issues caused deep division between England and the colonies.

Britain won the French & Indian War that year (also known as the Seven Year's War) by not only harnessing its military might, but also by spending at a tremendous rate. The English defeated the French in Canada once and for all, ending nearly a century of warfare in America between the two world powers. England won Canada and Louisiana from the French, and secured all the land east of the Mississippi River. The British government, led by Prime Minister William Pitt, allowed the colonists a measure of control in waging the war in North America. Pitt also subsidized troops and supplies, spending heavily to assist the colonies in the war effort.[1]

As taxes were the root of the crisis with England that led to Revolution, they deserve further examination here. In 1763 the highest taxes paid by citizens in the British Empire were borne by those in England; the lowest were in America. The English national debt had doubled during the war, and the annual interest alone was staggering. With the war over, Britain now turned to reeling in the expenses of maintaining its empire and finding ways to raise revenue. The cost of maintaining and defending this large, prosperous empire was enormous, and Parliament felt the American colonists should only bear their share of it. Ireland was paying for the maintenance of troops there, so America, it was felt, should do the same.[2]

The British Parliament passed laws soon after the close of the French & Indian War in 1763 to raise revenue for the empire. Traditionally each colonial government collected revenue and paid a portion of that to the British treasury. The British Parliament never directly taxed citizens, and the average person never directly felt the burden of maintaining the empire. In North Carolina, the colonial government collected revenue from quitrents (land taxes), poll taxes (voter registrations), shipping duties, import duties, and liquor taxes.[3]

The Stamp Act of 1765 changed all that: it was a direct tax on the common citizen, and it was felt in ways that no tax had ever been before. The act called for a tax to be paid on any paper product or document. The list was mind-boggling: newspapers, court documents, contracts, marriage certificates, playing cards, shipping documents, deeds, diplomas, magazines, and any other printed item. A stamp on the document showed proof of payment.

The right to be taxed by one's own elected representative was an ancient and sacred right of all Englishmen, and Americans, as citizens of the empire, guarded this right jealously. They felt that taxes imposed by Parliament, where Americans were not represented, were unfair.[4]

As the Americans began to resist this tax and others, the English responded by tightening enforcement and enacting tougher laws. Each side felt slighted and took offense at the other's reaction. Each action by one side led in turn to a reaction by the other. In time mistrust grew and the two sides could not find common ground.

Other issues surfaced as well, including stricter trade regulations. Parliament also cut off the newly won land from France, west of the Allegheny Mountains, from settlement. This was an effort to appease the Indians living there, and prevent warfare between settlers and Native Americans. Both of these developments increased tensions between Britain and America.

These issues were important in every colony and in every town, but were magnified in an area whose livelihood was tied to trade, like the Lower Cape Fear region. Wilmington and Brunswick took the lead in North Carolina in actively protesting the British taxes and regulations.

The leaders of this movement were the second generation of the early settlers of the Cape Fear Region, and came from the area's elite. Samuel Ashe was a judge who served on the Wilmington Committee of Safety and was Governor from 1795-8. He led militia throughout the war in the Lower Cape Fear. His brother John was Speaker of the House of the General Assembly of the Colony, led Stamp Act protests, was a member of the state's first Provincial Congress, and served as Brigadier General of the Wilmington District militia.[5]

The Moore family was also heavily involved in resisting the British. Son of patriarch Roger Moore, James was active in the local militia during the pre-war protests, and would rise to the rank of Brigadier General during the war. His brother Maurice was judge of superior court, Council member, and an assemblyman.

Robert Howe of Brunswick County was also a militia officer who rose to the rank of Major General in the Continental Army, becoming one of the highest ranking North Carolinians of the war. He was the only officer from the lower South to be appointed to the rank of Major General. He became a personal friend of George Washington, and presided over the court martial of Benedict Arnold. Ambitious and energetic, Howe was legally separated from his wife (something extremely rare at the time).[6]

Major General Robert Howe

Howe served as a militia captain, justice of the peace, and represented Brunswick County in the Colonial Assembly before the war. He twice served as commander of Fort Johnston. During the Regulator conflict of the 1760s and early 1770s, he served as quartermaster for Governor Tryon's army.[7]

An observer called him a "brave, prudent, and spirited commander." When the Revolution broke out Howe led North Carolina troops to Virginia to assist in driving out Lord Dunmore's Loyalists. He then was sent to Charleston and helped defend the city from Sir Peter Parker's invasion after the British failed to take Wilmington in the spring of 1776. Howe lost the city of Savannah to the British in 1778 and his reputation suffered. He was transferred north and never again led forces actively in the field. Howe commanded the post at West Point, New York later in the conflict. After the war he helped found the Society of the Cincinnati, an organization of Revolutionary officers.[8]

Perhaps the area's most active, influential, and forgotten person was Cornelius Harnett. He served as a justice of the peace, President of the Council of Safety, delegate to the Continental Congress, representative in the North Carolina Assembly, and in the various Provincial Congresses. He also commanded Fort Johnston for a time in the 1760s.[9]

Harnett was born in 1723, most likely in Chowan County (near the Virginia border), and moved to the Cape Fear region. From 1726 to 1750 he lived in Brunswick Town. He assisted in driving the Spanish from the town during their attack in 1748. In November of 1774 he was elected to be chairman of the Wilmington Committee of Safety, and later was chosen to represent the region in the Provincial Congress. In 1776 he essentially acted as governor, assisting with preparations for war and managing the running of the state.[10]

A colleague wrote of Harnett that he was "about five feet, nine inches. In his person he was rather slender than stout. His hair was of a light brown, and his eyes hazel...His countenance was pleasing, and his figure, though not commanding, was neither inelegant nor ungraceful."[11]

His home, Maynard, was described by Janet Schaw: "in all of my life I never saw a more glorious situation. It fronts the conflux of the north and northwest rivers, which forms one of the finest pieces of water in the world. On this there is a very handsome house." His wife Mary was reported to be industrious and a great cook, making pies, cheese-cakes, tarts, and "little bisketts" to be sold in town. The home stood until the early twentieth century, and was located along the river just north of Wilmington, near the mouth of

Harnett's Wilmington home, Maynard (also known later as Hilton).

Smith Creek. Harnett also owned a rum distillery in what is now the block between Walnut and Red Cross streets in downtown Wilmington.[12]

Harnett's health began to decline as he neared the age of 60 late in the war. Years of active service for his state took him away from personal affairs and family in Wilmington, a sacrifice he willingly undertook. He finally left public service in December 1779. His home was on the Northeast Cape Fear River, now site of the Wilmington water works, just north of downtown. He wrote of his experiences in the Continental Congress, "This has been the most difficult piece of Business that ever was undertaken by any public Body."[13]

Hugh Waddell was another important figure who was actively involved in the colonial protests. Son of a Scotch-Irish merchant, Waddell and his family first settled in Boston. After his father's death he used his important political connections to gain access to Governor Arthur Dobbs of North Carolina. Waddell was appointed lieutenant of militia and fought in the French & Indian War in the campaign that captured Fort Duquesne (at modern Pittsburgh) with a Virginia militia colonel named George Washington. He also fought the Cherokee on the frontiers of North and South Carolina.[14]

Col. Hugh Waddell

Waddell settled at a plantation on the Cape Fear near Bladen Courthouse (Elizabethtown). He led protests against the Stamp Tax in 1766. During the Regulator movement Governor Tryon sent him to raise militia in the western part of the state. With his political connections and military experience, Waddell would have done a great deal more for the American cause had he not passed away in 1773. He remains a forgotten leader during the movement towards independence.[15]

The early British attempts at taxation met stiffening resistance. In October 1764, the North Carolina Assembly wrote that the "Tax on Trade, lately imposed by Act of Parliament on the British Colonies in America must lend greatly to the Hindrance of Commerce, and be severely felt by the Industrious Inhabitants of this Province..."[16]

On November 23rd the Assembly clearly stated its view, asserting "our inherent Right, as British Subjects, that no Tax could be imposed upon us, but where we were legally represented..."[17]

Also that month the Assembly received a letter from Massachusetts inviting them to begin correspondence. This was an important step, for while the colonies seemed to have common cause, in fact they had great difficulty achieving unity. Each colony was jealous of the other: there were disputes over boundaries and trade, and some colonies had been founded by residents of others that fled persecution. Until the start of British taxation, they had little in common to bond them. Separated by great distances, divided by economic, political, ethnic, and religious differences, the colonies rarely cooperated on issues, but that was about to change.[18]

What was happening in North Carolina was occurring elsewhere too, and leaders in Massachusetts decided to reach out to their fellow colonists. By corresponding and keeping up with developments in each region, they could coordinate their efforts and make a stronger case in dealing with the British.

Salt became the subject of trade restrictions, like other goods, and could only be purchased from Britain. Even Royal Governor Arthur Dobbs noted that "The Prohibition of the Trade of Salt from all Parts of Europe except Britain...is a considerable Drawback upon our Trade." Cornelius Harnett agreed, and called it harmful "to the Trade of this Province."[19]

In the fall of 1762 Governor Dobbs, well over seventy (and recently married to a fifteen year old girl, Justina Davis, of Brunswick), suffered a stroke that paralyzed his legs. He requested to be relieved and return to England, which was granted. William Tryon was to be his replacement. While waiting to return to England in 1765 Dobbs died and was buried at St. Philip's Church in Brunswick. His young widow later remarried, becoming the wife of Governor Abner Nash.[20]

In the meantime other developments drew the attention of North Carolinians. The Sugar Act of 1764 had created controversy, but the worst was yet to come. On March 22, 1765, Parliament passed the Stamp Act. Besides the fact that it was a direct tax on the colonists, which had never been done before, the sheer magnitude of how it would affect daily transactions triggered the anger of nearly all colonists, regardless of class or standing.

The new Royal Governor, William Tryon, was 36 years old when he arrived at Brunswick in 1765, amid the Stamp Act controversy. He was from a prominent family and also had some military experience.[21]

Tryon rented a home in Wilmington but spent most his time with his family at Russellborough, the former home of Governor Dobbs. In the meantime construction proceeded on a new Governor's mansion in New Bern, soon to be known as Tryon's Palace and soon to be a center of controversy.[22]

Tryon immediately faced challenges as news of the Stamp Act's passage reached the colony. Tryon attempted to ease tensions by inviting local leaders to a dinner at Russellborough and offering to personally pay for tavern licenses and many legal documents. His gesture was rejected by the colonists, who insisted the taxes were unfair to begin with.[23]

The Stamp Act called for a stamp on every document or paper item, showing that the tax had been paid. Yet that was not the worst of it. The key point that struck Americans was that violators would be charged in admiralty courts (naval courts, not civil courts) in Halifax, Nova Scotia. Thus the act violated two basic rights of British citizens: the right to be taxed by an elected representative, and the right to a trial by a jury of peers. The law was to go into effect November 1, 1765, and from the start colonists geared up for a fight. Governor Tryon asked Speaker of the House John Ashe how North Carolina would react, and Ashe predicted that it "would be resisted to blood and death." It turned out he was right.[24]

The British, quite innocently, felt that every citizen of the empire, whether in America, Europe, or Asia, was virtually represented in Parliament. This body made the laws for the empire, and managed the government for the good of British society. Britain insisted that it had the right to make laws and govern, and that this included the right to tax. Americans disagreed, noting that Parliament could make laws, but not tax them directly.

Maurice Moore wrote a pamphlet in 1765 titled "Justice and Policy of Taxing the American

An example of a British stamp

Colonies in Great Britain Considered" In essence, it stated that the Americans could only be taxed with their consent, through elected representatives, and it criticized the concept of virtual representation.[25]

On the evening of October 19th, about five hundred people gathered in Wilmington and hanged an effigy of Lord Bute, who they incorrectly blamed for passage of the law, and tossed it into a bonfire. The crowd then went door to door, brought men out to the fire, and "insisted upon their drinking Liberty, Property, and no Stamp-Duty." The revelry continued until midnight and then dispersed "without doing any mischief." On October 31st, the day before the Act went into effect, a large mob held a rally in the streets of Wilmington. Again an effigy was burned, this time named "Liberty." Again there was no violence, as the *North Carolina Gazette* reported, "not the least Injury was offered to any

Person." Protests and rallies often happened on Saturdays, which were market days. The population of Wilmington, only about 1200, was swelled by people from the surrounding area, and it was a perfect time for discussion and discontent to ferment.[26]

On November 1st the Stamp Act went into effect, and Governor Tryon suspended any commerce that required stamps, though they were not yet available in the colony. Trade was cut off, goods became scarce, and uncertainty grew among the population.[27]

A confrontation forced the resignation of Stamp Distributor William Houston on November 16th. Houston apparently did not know he had been appointed the colony's Stampmaster, but was about to find out. While in Wilmington on personal business, about three hundred men, with drums beating and flags flying, seized Houston and took him to the courthouse where he signed a resignation of his office.[28]

He wrote that the crowd "assembled about me & demanded a Categorical Answer whether I intended to put the Act...in force. The Town Bell was rung Drums beating, Colors flying and [a] great concourse of People gathered together." The *North Carolina Gazette* estimated three or four hundred and also mentioned the beating drums and presence of colors (flags).[29]

When asked by the crowd if he intended to execute his office, he responded that "He should be very sorry to execute any Office disagreeable to the People of the Province." It was certainly the right answer to give in the face of an armed and angry mob.[30]

After forcing his resignation the crowd placed him in a chair and paraded him around town, then to his lodging where they cheered and toasted him. Along the way they stopped at the *Gazette's* office where they received assurances that the publisher would print the paper without the required stamps.[31]

That night another bonfire lit the sky of Wilmington, in celebration of the people's victory. In Cross Creek and New Bern, news had not yet arrived of Houston's resignation, and citizens of each town prepared an effigy of him that was "try'd, condemn'd, hang'd, and burn'd." Again this occurred on market day, and included typical forms of protest and celebration, such as toasting, vocal protests, bonfires, and oaths. Such protest and anger was unheard of. It was an important step in solidifying resistance to the British and opening the way for more forceful protests. News of the incident spread through the empire, eventually finding its way into the *London Chronicle*. The action forcing Houston's resignation was not violent, and was not targeting law and order or authority. That time would soon come, however.[32]

A physician who resided in Duplin County along the Northeast Cape Fear River, Houston also served as Justice of the Peace on three separate occasions. He was a well respected member of the community and probably no one was more surprised by his appointment than Houston himself. He proved himself loyal to the Americans during the war, serving on a committee that punished militia deserters and Loyalists.[33]

Two days later, Governor Tryon, in an effort to appease the citizens who were upset over the Stamp Act, arranged for an ox to be barbecued and several barrels of beer to be served as the militia gathered to drill. The people came, but threw the ox into the river and poured out the beer onto the ground. Several days of rioting followed.[34]

A tragic event followed. Charles Berry arrived in Wilmington as the new Chief Justice for the colony. An argument between two British seamen during the recent riot resulted in a duel. A sailor named Simpson shot and killed another named Thomas Whitehurst. Both were from the crew of the *Diligence*, and Simpson had stated he sided with the Americans, while Whitehurst disagreed. Simpson was tried for murder but was acquitted by Berry. Governor Tryon accused Berry of favoritism, and planned to remove him from office. Devastated by the governor's lack of faith, Berry committed suicide with his pistol just before Christmas of 1765.[35]

On November 28, 1765 the *Diligence* arrived in the Cape Fear with the dreaded stamps. Wilmington merchants refused to use them, and no ships had left the harbor by December, a serious statement from a port city. The stamps sat unused, and trade came to a halt. Militia officers Hugh Waddell and John Ashe spearheaded the effort to prevent the stamps from being landed.[36]

Waddell's Brunswick and Ashe's New Hanover County militia stood onshore watching over the ship. They informed the ship's commander, Captain Phipps, that they would fire on anyone attempting to unload the stamps. The militia took one of the *Diligence*'s small boats, mounted it on a cart, and took it

Militia line the Wilmington riverfront to prevent British ships from landing the stamps.

CONTINUATION OF

(November 20.)   THE   (Numb. 58.)

NORTH-CAROLINA GAZETTE.

WILMINGTON, November 20.

O N Saturday the 19th of laft Month, about Seven of the Clock in the Evening, near Five Hundred People affembled together in this Town, and exhibited the Effigy of a certain HONOURABLE GENTLEMAN; and after letting it hang by the Neck for fome Time, near the Court-Houfe, they made a large Bonfire with a Number of Tar-Barrels, &c. and committed it to the Flames.—The Reafon affigned for the People's Diflike to that Gentleman, was, from being informed of his having feveral Times expreffed himfelf much in Favour of the STAMP-DUTY.——After the Effigy was confumed, they went to every Houfe in Town, and bro't all the Gentlemen to the Bonfire, and infifted upon their drinking, LIBERTY, PROPERTY, AND NO STAMP-DUTY, and Confufion to Lord B-TE and all his Adherents, giving three Huzzas at the Conclufion of each Toaft.——They continued together until 12 of the Clock, and then difperfed, without doing any Mifchief. And,

On Thurfday, 31ft of the fame Month, in the Evening, a great Number of People again affembled, and produced an Effigy of LIBERTY, which they put into a Coffin, and marched in folemn Proceffion with it to the Church-Yard, a Drum in Mourning beating before them, and the Town Bell, muffled, ringing a doleful Knell at the fame Time;—But before they committed the Body to the Ground, they thought it advifeable to feel its Pulfe; and when finding fome Remains of Life, they returned back to a Bonfire ready prepared, placed the Effigy before it in a large Two-arm'd Chair, and concluded the Evening with great Rejoicings, on finding that LIBERTY had ftill an Exiftence in the COLONIES.—Not the leaft Injury was offered to any Perfon.

On Saturday the 16th of this Inft. WILLIAM HOUSTON, Efq; Diftributor of STAMPS for this Province, came to this Town; upon which three or four Hundred People immediately gathered together, with Drums beating and Colours flying, and repaired to the Houfe the faid STAMP-OFFICER put up at, and infifted upon knowing, " Whether he intended to execute his faid Office, or not?" He told them, " He fhould be very forry to execute any Office difagreeable to the People of the Province." But they, not content with fuch a Declaration, carried him into the Court-Houfe, where he figned a Refignation fatisfactory to the Whole.

As foon as the STAMP-OFFICER had comply'd with their Defire, they placed him in an Arm-Chair, carried him firft round the Court-Houfe, giving three Huzzas at every Corner, and then proceeded with him round one of the Squares of the Town, and fat him down at the Door of his Lodgings, formed themfelves in a large Circle round him, and gave him three Cheers: They then efcorted him into the Houfe, where was prepared the beft Liquors to be had, and treated him very genteely. In the Evening a large Bonfire was made, and no Perfon appeared in the Streets without having LIBERTY, in large Capital Letters, in his Hat.—— They had a large Table near the Bonfire, well furnifh'd with feveral Sorts of Liquors, where they drank in great Form, all the favourite AMERICAN Toafts, giving three Cheers at the Conclufion of each. The whole was conducted with great Decorum, and not the leaft Infult offered to any Perfon.

B   ¶ Immediately

——Its Brow's the Title Page,
That fpeaks the Nature of a TRAGIC Volume!
Shake.

This is the Place to affix the STAMP.

An issue of the **North Carolina Gazette,** *with a space reserved for the hated stamp.*

to Wilmington where it was paraded around the town as a trophy. This took protests to a new level: directly confronting the British.[37]

Governor Tryon wrote to Britain that "all Civil Government " was at a standstill: no shipping, no business activity. The breakdown in trade had a ripple affect, hurting merchants inland at Cross Creek as well. One report from the town declared, "The trade of this river is at present entirely ruined!" Far from being innocent protests led by men cherishing liberty, who plotted their activities accompanied by the clinking of mugs of ale, these activities were determined and deliberate acts of subversion against British authority.[38]

On December 20, 1765, Governor Tryon was officially inaugurated in Wilmington as the colony's new royal governor. The pageantry of the event, along with its free food and spirits, drew a large attendance, including 2,000 local militia. Tryon arrived in a barge from Brunswick, and landed at the foot of Market Street.[39]

All went well until Tryon mentioned the Stamp Act, requesting the assembled citizens to accept and use the stamps. Captain Phipps of the *Diligence* further aggravated the situation when he saw a ship in the river flying an Irish flag (only English flags should have been flying at the royal governor's ceremony).[40]

He ordered his sailors to seize it, which "exasperated not only the sailors but the Townsmen and Militia." The citizens seized it back, but in another round of this tug of war the sailors retook it. The militia then took two of the *Diligence's* boats and hauled them up to the courthouse. They were about to become fuel for another bonfire, when some of the mob decided to exchange them for the flag from Phipps.[41]

After fifteen minutes of discussion they reached a compromise. The crowd then proceeded to trade insults with Phipps and the Governor at his home (which stood at the corner of Market and Front Street). They poured the punch into the river and gave the roasted ox to the town's slaves, a calculated insult. This last act infuriated Tryon the most.[42]

On January 14, 1766 two merchant ships, the *Dobbs* and the *Patience*, dropped anchor at Brunswick but were seized by the commander of the British warship *Viper*, Captain Jacob Lobb. The two arriving vessels did not have the stamps affixed to their shipping papers. Angry citizens of Wilmington reacted by refusing to sell supplies to the British ships, causing them to run low on food. When sailors came ashore to get bread, citizens seized them and threw them into jail. This first enforcement of the Stamp Act had infuriated the colonists.[43]

Led by John Ashe, Alexander Lillington, Hugh Waddell, and Col. Thomas Lloyd, a group of men boarded the *Diligence* and demanded the surrender of the two ships seized for lack of stamps. The Americans were able to seize the *Dobbs* but the British held onto the *Patience*. Governor Tryon wrote that, "...the detaining of the *Patience* became a point that concerned the honor of the government and...I found my situation very unpleasant, as most of the people by going up to Wilmington in the sloops would remain satisfied and report through the province that they had obtained every point they came to redress."[44]

His statement illustrates an important point: neither side could back down now. The British had to maintain the position of authority, and found it difficult to compromise without losing respect or surrendering control. The Americans, insisting they were only defending what they believed were their rights as citizens, refused to back down. The stakes were too high for either side to give in.

William Dry, the customs collector for Brunswick, received letters from

The seal of William Dry

citizens instructing him not to allow the quarantined ships to be taken to Halifax for trial, threatening to "come down in a body" and that if he did, "very Ill Consequences...will attend this affair." Dry had been an early settler to the region, and led the counterattack that drove off the Spanish invasion in 1748. He served in the Colonial Assembly and was also on Governor Dobbs' Council. He was no friend to the British, but was caught in a difficult position as a royal official.[45]

On February 15, 1766 Attorney General Robert Jones officially ordered the vessels sent to Halifax, Nova Scotia for trial before an admiralty court. The dreaded events that the Americans feared most were now unfolding: the loss of their right to a trial by a jury of their peers.

Merchants in Wilmington signed an agreement on February 18th, stating "We...detesting Rebellion yet preferring Death to Slavery, Do with all Loyalty to Our most Gracious Sovereign, with All deference to the Just Laws of Our Country...here mutually and Solemnly plight our Faith and Honor that We will at any risqué...unite...in preventing entirely the operation the Stamp Act." They called themselves the Sons of Liberty and stated that they "detest Rebellion" and hoped for a "Redress of their Grievances."[46]

The next day one thousand men led by George Moore descended on Brunswick to meet with royal officials there regarding the stamps and trade issues. After two days they forced the collector of customs and the naval officer there to agree to not enforce the Stamp Act. William Dry had refused to negotiate, but the mob broke into his home, rummaged through his desk, and seized the official papers. He then had no choice.[47]

Another group of 300 men under Col. Hugh Waddell marched on Fort Johnston, which only had a garrison of five soldiers. The small force stationed there was not uncommon, as the British often reduced fort garrisons in peacetime, knowing they could beef them up when needed. Yet it made the many forts, with their stashes of weapons, tempting targets for colonial militias.[48]

That night Tryon sent a message to one of his naval officers, Captain Jacob Lobb, asking him to assist the garrison at Fort Johnston and "repel with force" any attempt to seize the fort or its weapons. The British were now mobilizing for defense. The time was nearly past for negotiation.[49]

On the 20th, a delegation rowed out to Captain Lobb on board the *Viper* and demanded the release of the seized ships. Lobb requested the Governor's presence for the negotiations, and they met again at noon with Tryon. This round of talks hammered out an agreement that opened the port and released the ships. The colonists had gotten their way.[50]

The next day, still unsure that Tryon was as good as his word, area residents invaded Governor Tryon's home and boarded the *Viper*. They sought out the comptroller - William Pennington - who was seeking shelter at Tryon's home. Between four or five hundred militia gathered, led by Col. James Moore, but the governor refused to see them at first. They requested the comptroller come out, and their spokesperson insisted that they would otherwise be forced to enter the home. Pennington emerged, and the crowd marched him into town, where, surrounded by the protestors, he took an oath swearing he would not enforce the Stamp Act. Mob action had won the day yet again.[51]

Tryon, enraged by the audacity of the Americans, had Pennington resign his position before going out to meet the crowd. It probably made no difference to the assembled militia, but Tryon could claim that the mob did not force the resignation of a royal official; he had resigned before meeting the mob.

According to the *North Carolina Gazette*, "It was about 10 o'clock... when a body of men in arms from four to five hundred moved towards the house [Russellborough]. A detachment of sixty men came down the avenue, and the main body drew up in front in sight and within three hundred yards of the house. Mr. Harnett a representative in the Assembly for Wilmington, came at the head of the detachment and sent a message to speak with Mr. Pennington.[52]

"The Customs-House Officers [Pennington and Dry]...made oath, that they would not, directly or indirectly, by themselves, or any other person employed under them, sign or execute in their several respective offices, any stamped Papers..." Pennington then resigned, but Tryon had him resign to him as governor, so as not to appear to give in to the mob. The upshot, however, was that mob violence had forced British officials to violate their orders, and had forced them into backing down.[53]

The activities of the residents of the Lower Cape Fear in resisting the Stamp Act reached other colonies. The *Virginia Gazette* reported on their actions and wrote that they acted with "decency and spirit" in defending American rights.[54]

During this time the entire colony felt the effects of the crisis. There were no courts, and cases were backlogged for months. There was also no trade, and a scarcity of goods combined with a bad harvest made life miserable for the common citizens.[55]

Due to unprecedented outrage from all of the colonies, Parliament repealed the Stamp Act on March 18, 1766, and the news reached North Carolina in June. It was only in effect for five months, and not one stamp had been issued in the colonies. On June 26th, after receiving word of the Act's repeal, citizens of Wilmington expressed their gratitude to the governor, Parliament, and the King for its repeal. But it was not that simple. While repealing the act, the British stated that they maintained their right to tax. For the moment there was relative calm in the aftermath of the Stamp Act turmoil.[56]

The British were determined to assert their authority, and maintain their right to legislate and collect revenue. Americans would dispute this, arguing Parliament could make laws and had authority as the empire's ruling body, but could not tax them. In the aftermath of the Stamp Tax crisis, other events closer to home began to draw the attention of North Carolinians.

In 1768 St. Philip's Church at Brunswick was finished. With its tall, sturdy, brick walls, the Anglican church was one of the most imposing in the entire colony, and was a focal point in Brunswick. The church represented stability, and was a symbol of British authority in the area. It was also a welcome sign of peace and progress during these turbulent times.[57]

Despite the relative calm, there was still tension in the air, and Americans continued in their efforts to protest British taxes. In November 1769 Governor Tryon dissolved the Assembly before it could join in non-importation agreements with other colonies, known as the Continental Association. Most delegates went to the courthouse for their own meeting, where North Carolina became the last colony to adopt the Continental Association.[58]

In Wilmington Cornelius Harnett urged the Committee of Safety to enforce non-importation of British goods, and threatened to publish the names of merchants who violated this. It was hoped economic pressure would force the British to back down.[59]

On November 24, 1769 the *Cape Fear Mercury* published a petition to the King from North Carolina:

"We your Majesty's most loyal, dutiful, and affectionate subjects, the house of Assembly of this your Majesty's colony of North-Carolina, now met in General Assembly, beg leave, in the most humble manner, to assure your Majesty, that your faithful subjects of this colony ever distinguished by their loyalty and firm attachment to your Majesty and your royal ancestors, are far from countenancing traitors, treason...and ready at any time to sacrifice ourselves and fortunes in defense of your Majesty's sacred person and government.[60]

"It is with the deepest concern, and most heartfelt grief that your Majesty's dutiful subjects of this colony find, that their loyalty has been [questioned] and that those measures, which a just regard for the British constitution (dearer to them than life) made necessary duties, have been misrepresented as rebellious attacks upon your Majesty's government."[61]

By the 1770s most Americans wanted compromise, and very few were speaking out yet for total separation from England. It was hoped that the Continental Congress, meeting in Philadelphia, could produce such a resolution.

Yet another crisis was brewing closer to home that distracted North Carolinians temporarily. The backcountry of the colony, that area west of modern Interstate 95, was growing rapidly in population and far outpaced that of the older, established eastern counties. The region suffered from lack of good infrastructure, needing roads and other internal improvements. Most importantly, the region's settlers felt neglected by the eastern government and its wealthy plantation owners.

While the eastern counties (small in size and population) dominated the colonial assembly, the large western regions had less representation. Wealthy planters, who owned large tracts of land and slaves, held the true power in the colony. The majority of the colony's settlers were small farmers with little say in the colony's government. In 1760 the makeup of the Lower House illustrated this disparity: the twenty-two eastern counties had 66 representatives, while the four western counties had eight. The population of the western territory was double that of the east.[62]

Corruption and crime were also rampant in the backcountry, especially in Anson, Orange, and Granville counties. Sheriffs charged excessive fees, taxes were high, and what made it worse was that payments had to be made in specie (in actual coins rather than paper notes). There were also fees for court proceedings as well as high lawyer's expenses. Most backcountry farmers had little cash - their limited wealth was in land, crops, and animals. Trade and barter were used in their frontier exchanges, and they had little hard currency for official transactions.[63]

Tryon Palace, in New Bern.

Taxes were also uneven, falling heavily on backcountry farmers. North Carolina's taxes were higher than those in other colonies. Those who fell behind on tax payments had their property auctioned.[64]

One resident wrote that "as soon as counties were organized...sheriffs, clerks, registers, and lawyers swooped down upon the defenseless inhabitants like wolves." Many of these men held multiple offices, like sheriff, clerk of court, and representative, thus concentrating power in a tight knit web that outsiders could not penetrate.[65]

Increasing backcountry anger even more was the new governor's home, known as Tryon Palace. In 1766 New Bern became the permanent capital of the colony. As part of this move, an elaborate home was constructed for the royal governor. As Tryon was the first to occupy it, the home became known by his name.[66]

Small farmers were outraged as the legislature enacted new taxes to pay for its construction. They were primarily on liquor and a new poll tax (for voting). Backcountry settlers generally did not have much cash for paying taxes, and felt that the colony's government did not do much for them anyway.[67]

Tensions boiled over into what was called the Regulator Movement. Backcountry settlers formed groups of "regulators" to maintain law and order. They were vigilantes that took justice into their own hands: they made official protests to the colonial assembly, and hoped to have their grievances addressed.

In May 1768 the Regulators first petitioned the colonial government to address its concerns. Not all protest was peaceful, however, as 300 men burned the Rowan County jail in Salisbury. Closer to Wilmington, a mob tried to prevent the Johnston County court from meeting in August .[68]

Two men chosen to represent the Regulators met with Governor Tryon at his home in Brunswick. The governor, not knowing the full extent of the problem, told them that the situation did not justify their violent actions, and ordered them to stop resisting authority. Tryon was willing to punish corruption and correct injustices in the system, but underestimated the extent of discontent in the interior.[69]

The Regulators claimed to "to assemble ourselves for conference, for regulating public grievances and abuses of power, in the following particulars...we will pay no more taxes until we are satisfied they are agreeable to law, and applied to the purpose therein mentioned...we will pay no officer any more fees than the law allows...we will attend all our meetings of conferences as often as we conveniently can...we will contribute to collections for defraying the necessary expenses in attending the work..."[70]

On September 22nd over 3,000 Regulators gathered at the opening of the court session in Hillsboro. They broke several men out of the jail there, and otherwise threatened and intimidated the court officials.[71]

No central leader rose amid the Regulator movement, although there were several prominent men who were outspoken for the Regulators. A newcomer to North Carolina, Governor Tryon was unaware of the issues that caused the unrest, but did try to crack down on corruption, and punish those guilty of abusing their power. He traveled to Hillsboro in July 1768 to negotiate with Regulators and investigate charges of corruption. Yet it was not enough to correct the many problems or satisfy the widespread discontent of the backcountry.[72]

Gov. William Tryon confronts the Regulators.

In 1769 Tryon dissolved the colony's Assembly and called for a new one in an attempt to root out representatives who supported the Regulators. Orange, Anson, Granville, and Halifax Counties all re-elected their old delegates, who were sympathetic to the Regulators. Tryon was angered by this and dissolved the Assembly again.[73]

In September 1770 another mob broke into the Hillsboro jail to free imprisoned Regulators. They also assaulted lawyer William Hooper, dragging him through the streets, harassed other court officials, and looted and damaged property in the town. While the Regulators claimed that they had no voice in the local government and court system, it seemed that they had gone too far in attacking officials and taking the law into their own hands.[74]

That same year Captain John Abraham Collett at Fort Johnston published a map of the colony. It was so accurate that many others were based on it. Swiss by birth, Collett served in the British army and would be an aide to Tryon in his campaign against the Regulators.[75]

With events spiraling out of control in the colony, Tryon declared the Riot Act in 1771, which gave him the power to try a defendant in any county, not just the county where he resided, and also authorized him to use military force if necessary. The first provision violated a basic right of English citizens: the right to a trial by jury of peers. The second was a clear message that Tryon had had enough and was ready to use force.[76]

That spring Tryon called out the militia from the eastern counties. At the Johnston County courthouse over 1,000 men gathered from Craven, Carteret, Orange, New Hanover, Beaufort, Onslow, Dobbs, Johnston, and Wake Counties. In the meantime the Regulators had assembled their own army in the Hillsboro area.[77]

The Regulator army and the governor's militia met in battle at Alamance, near modern Burlington, on May 16, 1771. The discipline and firepower of the militia prevailed, and the Regulators were routed. Both sides lost about 150 total, most of the casualties being Regulators. In the weeks that followed leaders were rounded up, and some were hung in Hillsboro, a small but growing town.[78]

While Tryon marched from the eastern part of the state, he had sent Colonel Hugh Waddell to Rowan County in the west to secure that area and raise militia. Waddell was marching east to join Tryon and attack the Regulators from both sides when the Battle of Alamance occurred.[79]

Tryon had his surgeons treat the wounded prisoners, and pardoned most of the rest. News soon arrived that he had been appointed as Royal Governor of New York, and he departed North Carolina at the end of May. Later during the Revolution, he recruited and commanded Loyalist forces in the New York City area. His most successful exploits during the war were raids on Westport and

An enlargement of Capt. John Abraham Collet's map of N.C. showing the southeastern part of the colony.

Danbury, Connecticut that destroyed valuable supplies. He was promoted to Major General, but poor health forced his return to England, where he died in 1788.[80]

The significance of the Regulator movement was that it made the later conflict more bitter than it would have otherwise been. Lingering unrest from the Regulator movement triggered violence later when people chose to support either Loyalists or Whigs during the Revolution. Often the decision was based more on settling old scores or taking revenge than abstract political issues. Many former Regulators, always fearing what the eastern dominated government did, refused to go along with the Colonial protests against England and sided

Royal Governor Josiah Martin

with the Loyalists. Whatever the wealthy planters did, they were opposed to in principal. Not a first war of independence, it was an internal colonial struggle, but one that would affect the coming war greatly.

The Regulator War also provided valuable military experience for men of both sides. Many officers who fought on both sides in the Revolution first experienced field command of troops and combat in the Battle of Alamance. Among those who marched with Tryon were Robert Howe, James Moore, Needham Bryan, Cornelius Harnett, Hugh Waddell, and Samuel Ashe.[81]

The Regulator War temporarily distracted colonists from the tensions with England, and bound colonial leaders to Royal Governor Tryon. On August 12, 1771 Josiah Martin became the next Royal Governor of North Carolina. It was not an enviable position, as Martin faced many issues as the colony's new executive. Regulator unrest, anger from the Stamp Act, internal debates over taxes and corruption, land ownership and tax problems, a currency shortage, skyrocketing debt, boundary problems with South Carolina, and debt from raising the militia all faced Martin when he arrived.

A former British military officer, Martin had been stationed in New York and was well acquainted with the current crisis in the colonies. Martin was hard working but lacked political experience, especially when dealing with such a volatile situation as now existed in North Carolina. He quickly chose to take a hard line with his dissatisfied colonists.[82]

In news of more local importance, the town of Wilmington received a new fire engine in 1772. Chimney fires were a constant danger, so much that city leaders levied fines for those whose chimneys caught fire due to poor cleaning and upkeep.[83]

Other improvements to the town included filling in low ground on Princess Street and along Market Street. Much of this was done with ashes and trash, though it was stipulated that garbage used in the fill must "not be offensive."[84]

In the meantime important events had occurred while North Carolina had its internal civil war in the early 1770s. The Boston Massacre, in which British troops opened fire on a mob that had surrounded them, occurred in March 1770. Three years later another mob held the Boston Tea Party, dumping hundreds of chests of tea into the harbor. As Massachusetts took the lead in resisting English authority, its political leaders gained respect among citizens in the other colonies.

From March 27-30, 1773 Josiah Quincy Jr. of Boston visited the Lower Cape Fear in an effort to get North Carolina to join in the Committees of Correspondence with the other colonies.

William Hooper (right), and his Wilmington home (below).

He wrote that he "Dined with about twenty at Mr. William Hooper's, find him apparently in the Whig interest...Spent the night at Mr. Harnett's - the Samuel Adams of North Carolina (except in point of fortune)."[85]

Hooper indeed was in the Whig interest, and became one of the region's most outspoken and active leaders of the Revolution. He is the Cape Fear Region's only signer of the Declaration of Independence. Educated at Harvard, he moved to Wilmington in 1764, and owned a small home that stood in the center of the block bounded by Second, Third, Market, and Princess Streets. It survived until it was destroyed by fire after the Civil War, and it was the oldest in Wilmington at the time.[86]

Hooper was a lawyer and was also involved with shipping. In 1773 he

purchased a home on Masonboro Sound known as "Finian." During the Regulator crisis Hooper was harassed by vigilantes in Hillsboro, and was firmly behind Governor Tryon's use of force to suppress the Regulators.[87]

Contemporaries described him as "ingenious, polite, spirited, and tolerably eloquent." Hooper first served on Wilmington's Committee of Safety, and later in the Continental Congress. He found his time in Philadelphia demanding and unrewarding. He returned to Wilmington prior to the British invasion in 1781.[88]

Hooper evacuated his family when the British came, and ironically, American militia looted Finian while his slaves fled to join the British. By this time he was

The site of Hooper's Wilmington home, near Third and Princess Streets.

suffering from malaria as well. After the British evacuation he urged leniency on Loyalists. As an example of how the war divided not only communities but families, Hooper's own brothers, George and Thomas, were Loyalists.[89]

Josiah Quincy, Jr. spent five days in the Cape Fear, mostly in Brunswick, and established important contacts with leaders of colonial protest in the region. This was a vital step in the process of establishing a network of friendship and support among the colonies, who were separated not only by distance but often by rivalries from trade disputes and boundary issues. During his stay Quincy also met with Robert Howe and other important figures from the area.[90]

The visit soon produced results. After the port of Boston had been closed as punishment for the Tea Party, Parker Quince, son of prominent merchant Richard, gathered supplies and shipped them to Boston to assist the citizens there. Among the foodstuffs were corn, wheat, and pork. Parker was a Commissioner for the Town of Brunswick, Chairman of Superior Court, church warden of St Philip's Church, Justice of the Peace, and served on the local Committee of Safety.[91]

In January 1774 articles published in the *Cape Fear Mercury* protested England's taxes. Governor Martin wrote to the Earl of Dartmouth in England, "I inclose herewith, a weekly paper printed in Wilmington in this Province, under which head, in the last page, your [Lordship] will see what disingenuous representations are made to inflame the minds of the People."[92]

On April 6th, after the Colonial Council passed new regulations related to the colony's courts, Martin wrote that the Council's actions were "to my great surprise...it contained Provisions expressly contrary to His Majesty's instructions..."[93]

Later that month William Hooper wrote "I anticipate the important share which the Colonies must soon have in regulating the political balance. They are striding fast to independence, and ere long will build an empire upon the ruins of Great Britain." This was three years before the Declaration of Independence.[94]

On May 5th Governor Martin wrote that "The maintenance of Fort Johnston is of great importance to the security of the Cape Fear River, the great channel of commerce of this country." Both sides were now gearing up for conflict. There was less effort at discussion and compromise, and more effort towards military preparation.[95]

A week later voters elected representatives for the General Assembly. From the Lower Cape Fear Region, New Hanover County sent Col. John Ashe and William Hooper. Wilmington's representative was Cornelius Harnett; Duplin County sent Thomas Gray and Thomas Hicks; Bladen County elected William Salter and James White; Brunswick County sent Col. Robert Howe and John Rowan; and from Brunswick Town, Parker Quince.[96]

On July 21st "At a General Meeting of the Inhabitants of the district of Wilmington..." citizens supported the call for a Provisional Congress and Continental Congress. They produced the following decision: "Resolved that Col. James Moore, John Ancrum, Fred Jones, Samuel Ashe, Robert Howe, Robert Hogg, Francis Clayton, and Archibald Maclaine Esqrs be a Committee to prepare a circular letter to the several Counties of this Province expressive of the sense of the Inhabitants of this district with respect to the several acts of Parliament lately made for the oppression of our Sister Colony of Massachusetts Bay for having exerted itself in defense of the constitutional Rights of America." Deputies were to attend a general meeting at the Johnston County courthouse on August 20th to "adopt and prosecute such measures as will most effectually tend

to avert the miseries which threaten us...in order to effect an uniform Plan for the conduct of all North America that it will be necessary that a General Congress be held and that Deputies should there be present from the several Colonies..."
The men hoped "to produce an alteration in the British Policy and to bring about a change honourable and beneficial to all America." From all over southeastern North Carolina came endorsements for a Continental Congress.[97]

On August 25th the First Provincial Congress met in New Bern, the beginnings of North Carolina's state government. This event was significant as it laid the groundwork for an organized system of resisting British authority. Now the Americans were beyond protest, there was less talk of compromise and little discussion of a solution. While the royal governor still sat in New Bern, the colonists had formed a dissenting governing body.[98]

Two days later on the 27th the Provincial Congress elected delegates for the Continental Congress in Philadelphia. On September 5th William Hooper, Joseph Hewes, and Richard Caswell took their seats to represent North Carolina.[99]

Enough cannot be said about Caswell. Born in Maryland, he moved to North Carolina in 1746. He resided near Kingston (now Kinston), served as President of the Provincial Congress, and was the state's first Governor from 1776-80, and again from 1785-87. Living in New Bern, he helped lay out that town and also served as deputy surveyor for the colony, clerk of court for Orange County, served in the colonial assembly, and even commanded the right wing of the army at the battle of Alamance in 1771. All of these experiences prepared him for a leadership role during the Revolution.[100]

Caswell served his state with distinction until the Battle of Camden, South Carolina, in 1780. His militia panicked, and he tried every exertion to rally them, to no avail. The disaster, though not his fault, diminished his reputation. Much later, through continued hard work and sacrifice, he recovered his good standing in the minds of the state's people.[101]

Prior to the Revolution he was elected to the first Continental Congress in 1774, representing North Carolina in Philadelphia. John Adams wrote of him, "We always looked to Richard Caswell for North Carolina. He was a model man and a true Patriot." He then served in the second Congress that met in 1775. He returned to North Carolina in time to raise troops and fight at Moores Creek Bridge.[102]

Caswell was the state's first elected governor, serving two separate terms. In between he was state treasurer. Among his little known achievements

are changing Kingston's name to Kinston, a move intended to remove
tie to England. After the war he effectively dealt with the state of Franklin, in
which western settlers tried to break away from North Carolina (in modern
Tennessee). Caswell also pushed for adoption of the Constitution in 1787. He
died of a stroke at age 60 in 1787.[103]

Also in August 1774, most of the men serving in the colony's Assembly
met in a body known as the Provincial Congress in New Bern. The Congress
issued a Declaration that summed up colonial views on the crisis:

*"...our most essential rights are invaded by powers unwarrantably
assumed by the Parliament...We claim no more than the rights of Englishmen...it
is the very essence of the British Constitution that no subject should be taxed but
by his own consent, freely given by himself in person or by his legal
representative...as the British subjects resident in North America, have nor can
have any representation in the Parliament...any act of Parliament imposing a tax
is illegal and unconstitutional..."*[104]

An important step in securing the Lower Cape Fear took place on
November 23, 1774 when the Wilmington Committee of Safety organized in the
Courthouse at the intersection of Front and Market Streets. Its members
consisted of Cornelius Harnett, John Quince, Francis Clayton, William Hooper,
Robert Hogg, John Ancrum, Archibald McLaine, John Robinson, and James
Walker. Their expressed purpose was to carry out the wishes of the Continental
Congress. Events now began to sever family, economic, and political ties:
Archibald McLaine, named above, was a business partner with John Burgwin,
who seems to have had Loyalist leanings. William Hooper's two brothers,
George and Thomas, remained loyal to the crown.[105]

A slow and gradual division was forming among the population through
the 1760s and into the early 1770s. The Revolution did not start in 1776. By
then it was already underway. The military and political conflict began that year,
but in the preceding years both sides had come to the point of no return:
stockpiling weapons, establishing spies, making plans for conquest, and
otherwise preparing for war.

Throughout the 1760s, each event brought a reaction from the other side.
Each reaction in turn brought charges of foul play from the other. Mistrust grew,
and by the 1770s neither side could find common ground, and negotiation was
no longer possible. Violence became the only alternative.

At the meeting of the First Provisional Congress in New Bern in August
1774, delegates adopted a resolution that echoed the actions of the First
Continental Congress that had met earlier in Philadelphia. The North
Carolinians, agreeing in principal with the Continental Congress, declared "That
we will not directly or indirectly after the first day of January 1775 import from
Great Britain any East India Goods, or any merchandise whatsoever, medicines

excepted, nor will we after that day import from the West Indies or elsewhere any East India or British Goods or Manufactures..."[106]

The boycott was a peaceful protest, and by interrupting trade, the intention was to cause British merchants and shippers to put pressure on Parliament to back down from its efforts at taxes and trade regulation. Colonial leaders realized that price controls were necessary during this tumultuous time, and the First Provisional Congress also dealt with that issue: *"That the Venders of Merchandize within this province ought not to take advantage of the Resolves relating to non-importation in this province or elsewhere but ought to sell their Goods or Merchandize which they have or may hereafter import, at the same*

Penelope Barker and the ladies of Edenton sign their Tea Protest.

rates they have been accustomed to..." Efforts to control prices and inflation were a losing battle, and only got worse once the war began.[107]

Merchants who ignored non-importation were subject to public censorship. It was fairly easy to violate the law, and many actively did so because of poor enforcement. Of forty-five merchants in the Lower Cape Fear, about half were indifferent to the protests or outright hostile to the movement.[108]

In October 1774 about fifty women in Edenton, North Carolina demonstrated their support for the American cause by holding their own "tea party." The ladies signed a boycott refusing to purchase English tea. It was a bold statement at a time when women were not permitted to be involved with politics, and the event was widely publicized in both England and America.[109]

Wrote one observer, "It would be injustice to the Ladies, not to add, that they have entirely declined the use of Tea. Such a sacrifice by the fair sex, should inspire ours..."[110]

North Carolina's tea party, though not as large or as famous as Boston's, showed that public opinion in the Southern colony was aligned with that of New England. A statement from inhabitants of Wilmington noted that, "we consider the cause of the Town of Boston as the common cause of British America and as suffering in defense of the Rights of the Colonies in general."[111]

The closing of the port of Boston was a serious issue that was felt even in the Lower Cape Fear. Residents here knew if it could happen there it could happen anywhere, and there was no greater fear in a port town than the loss of trade. The closure of Boston, in fact, led to the First Continental Congress in Philadelphia, the largest city in the colonies. This meeting resulted in an agreement to not import British goods after December 1, 1774.[112]

On December 8th North Carolina's leaders created a Committee of Correspondence, thus linking North Carolina into the communication network with the other colonies. This was an important step in coordinating unified efforts to resist the British.[113]

1774 saw resistance stiffen against British rule. North Carolinians had established a network of communication and mutual support with the other colonies, were actively participating in the Continental Congress, and at home were organizing a new, if not yet official, government to act in place of the royal governor. Militia were training and stockpiling arms, and citizens were no longer wondering if a break with England was coming, but when.

The foregoing association being determined upon by the Congress was ordered to be subscribed by the several Members thereof and thereupon we have hereunto set our respective names accordingly.

In Congress Philadelphia October 20th 1774.

Peyton Randolph President

New Hampshire: Jno. Sullivan, Nathl. Folsom

Massachusetts Bay: Thomas Cushing, Saml. Adams, John Adams, Robt. Treat Paine

Rhode Island: Step. Hopkins, Sam: Ward

Connecticut: Eliphalet Dyer, Roger Sherman, Silas Deane

New York: Isaac Low, John Alsop, John Jay, Jas. Duane, Phil. Livingston, Wm. Floyd, Henry Wisner

New Jersey: Wil: Livingston, John De Hart, Richd. Smith

Pennsylvania: Jos. Galloway, John Dickinson, Chas. Humphreys, Thomas Mifflin, E. Biddle, John Morton, Geo: Ross

The Lower Counties New Castle &c.: Caesar Rodney, Tho. McKean, Geo. Read

Maryland: Mat. Tilghman, Th. Johnson Junr., Wm. Paca, Samuel Chase

Virginia: Richard Henry Lee, G. Washington, P. Henry Jr., Richard Bland, Benj. Harrison, Edmd. Pendleton

North Carolina: Will Hooper, Joseph Hewes, R. Caswell

South Carolina: Henry Middleton, Tho. Lynch, Christ. Gadsden, J. Rutledge, Edward Rutledge

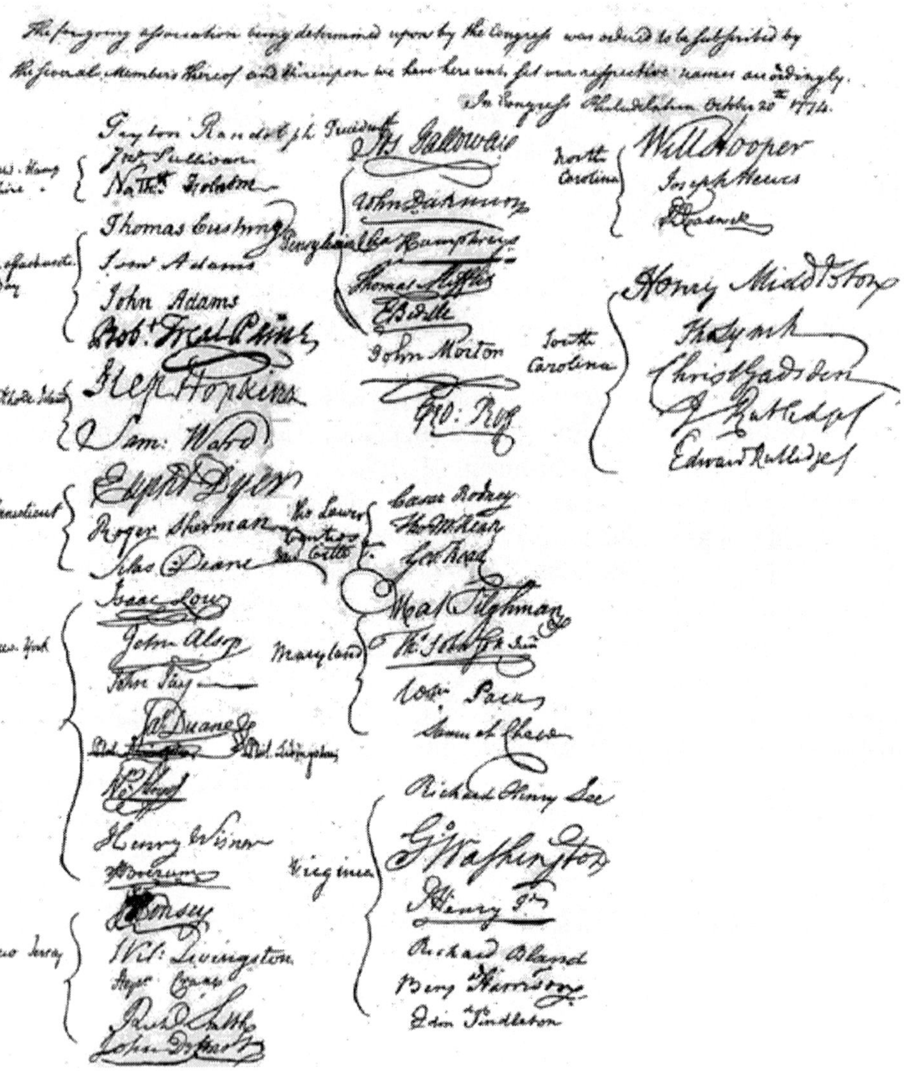

Hooper, Hewes, and Caswell's signatures as North Carolina's representatives to the early Congress are at the top right of the document pictured here.

Chapter 3
Wilmington Prepares

The year 1776 stands out in the minds of Americans as the year the Revolutionary War began. While the nation declared independence in that year, in fact the fighting had begun nearly a year earlier in April of 1775. Yet the Revolution really began in 1774, as local groups like the Sons of Liberty and Committees of Safety seized power and stockpiled weapons. At the local level, real power was taken out of the hands of royal officials and seized by colonial leaders who then formed de facto governments. Revolution was in fact underway long before the shooting started, and before the official break with England.[1]

This transfer of power occurred at different times in each colony. It happened earlier in Massachusetts and Virginia than it did in North Carolina. But by 1775 royal government was no longer functioning in the province. Citizens had forcibly, though not violently, taken control.[2]

On January 4, 1775 New Hanover County's leaders formed a Committee of Safety. These organizations, now being formed across the state, took on the role of local government, and began to function in place of the governor, courts, and colonial assembly. They developed rules for conducting business, and elected positions like chairman, vice chairman, and secretary. They varied in numbers, from New Hanover County's twenty-five members to Wilmington's nine, to Rowan County's thirty-seven.[3]

They also began to go beyond the issues of public safety, using coercion and force to mold public opinion and push for consensus. When leading a political movement, dissent cannot be tolerated, and the image of unity is crucial in such a major movement. The Committees of Safety also began regulating various things like censuses, collecting taxes, road maintenance, fiscal affairs, and slave patrols. These local organiations took power out of the hands of the royal governor and took control over matters of daily life for common citizens.[4]

The Wilmington Committee of Safety soon merged with the New Hanover Committee of Safety, as their functions overlapped. Among its first acts was to begin checking on the amount of gunpowder in the city, and forbidding merchants to sell it. The new Committee of Safety worked with those in Duplin, Brunswick, and Bladen Counties to share news, send messengers, and to hold joint meetings.[5]

The New Hanover County Committee of Safety was fairly successful at preventing merchants from trading with England, as part of the boycott set by the Continental Congress. They also began implementing price controls on important items like salt. One violator, Jonathan Dunbibin, was censured, and forced to revise his inflated prices. Throughout the year the Committee of Safety made repeated efforts to have it imported, along with weapons and ammunition.[6]

It is hard today to appreciate importance of salt. It is essential for health, and was used to preserve food in a time before refrigeration. Farm animals require it for digestion. No household, farm, or plantation could operate without it.[7]

In the last half of 1774, Brunswick Town imported over 33,000 bushels of salt, with some ships bringing in 5,000 bushels at a time. Firms like Hogg and Campbell in Wilmington had agents in Cross Creek for its distribution. The cargo went upriver on shallow draft vessels, or by land in wagons, and from there it moved further inland to Anson, Rowan, Guilford, and other western counties.[8]

Bedsides Robert Hogg and Samuel Campbell's store on Princess Street in Wilmington, they also had one in Cross Creek and in Hillsboro. The Hogg-Anderson house still stands on the corner of Front and Orange Streets (it is the oldest in Wilmington). Hogg was a member of the Committee of Safety in 1774, but sided with the Loyalists and left the area in 1775 for New York. He died in 1779, before the end of the war.[9]

Trade was not the only thing regulated by the Committee of Safety. On January 21st they set prices for merchants and banned billiard tables. A few days later the Committee announced that there would be no more balls or dancing at "Public Houses." Visitor Janet Schaw noted that she was going into Wilmington to attend the last of the balls, and that even card games were forbidden as part of the effort.[10]

More aid left North Carolina for Boston's citizens in February. The Pitt County Committee of Safety sent supplies, as did merchants from New Bern. The suffering of Boston became a symbolic common cause for all the colonies.[11]

On March 6th the Committee of Safety endorsed the Test of the Continental Association, requiring everyone in Wilmington to sign it. The Association outlined trade restrictions with England, voiced support for the Continental Congress, and outlined grievances against Parliament. Those who refused risked punishment. In time the regulations, known as Test Oaths, would only get tougher, until people were forced to make a choice, and could no longer stay neutral.[12]

On April 2nd the North Carolina Provincial Congress, meeting in New Bern, officially approved the Continental Association. Now the colony was in line with the others in not importing goods and refusing to export to England.

Janet Schaw wrote that "The ports are soon to be shut up, but this severity is voluntarily imposed by themselves, for they were indulged by parliament and allowed the exclusive privilege of still carrying on their trade with Europe..." She also noted that, "European goods begin to be very scarce and will daily be more so."[13]

Sometime in late March or early April the women of Wilmington held a tea party in protest of the taxes. Nearly every city in America witnessed tea parties, not just Boston. The list also includes New York, Chestertown, MD, Charleston, SC, Yorktown, VA, and Edenton, NC. Janet Schaw observed that the "Ladies have burnt their tea in a solemn procession, but they delayed till their gesture was not very considerable." Unfortunately she does not give more details of the event, and no other accounts of it have surfaced.[14] A letter from late March indicates that a Brunswick merchant threw his tea stock into the Cape Fear River, and refused to receive any more shipments.[15]

In May the North Carolina Provisional Congress took a bold step by declaring that, "unless American Grievances are redressed before the first day of October 1775, We will not after that day directly or indirectly export Tobacco, Pitch, Tar, Turpentine, or any other article whatsoever, to Great Britain..." This was a strong statement from the British empire's leading supplier of naval stores.[16]

North Carolina also began organizing a state navy. This may seem odd, but it is important to remember that just as the war began with no national, or Continental Army, there was no Continental Navy either. Each colony prepared for its own defense, and only in time did a national, or Continental Navy, form. Initially North Carolina planned to arm five ships. Every state but Delaware and New Jersey had state navies.[17]

The clash at Lexington & Concord .

On May 8th news of the Battles of Lexington and Concord, (fought April 19th near Boston) reached Brunswick by ship, and was quickly conveyed to Wilmington and other towns. Now residents of the Lower Cape Fear knew that violence had started and the war had begun. Most felt it was only a matter of time before it would come to North Carolina.[18]

Also that month rumors began circulating that Governor Martin was going to free and arm the slaves. There was no greater fear among the area's residents than that of a slave revolt, especially given the demographics of the Lower Cape Fear, which had a majority slave population.[19]

On May 19th in Charlotte, local leaders signed a document that has become known as the Mecklenburg Declaration (Charlotte being in Mecklenburg County). The document called for resisting British authority. While some historians have argued that it was the first declaration of independence, the document did not take so bold a step. Nor has it survived, and the only version of it is one recited from memory. Nonetheless it did signify the growing discontent of other regions of North Carolina.

Janet Schaw, who was becoming more sensitive to the tension every day, wrote "my tongue is not always under my command" and she tried to avoid political discussion. This was difficult for her as she was in contact with

Wilmington's elite, many of whom were leaders of the Revolutionary movement.[20]

While she may have held her tongue in public, she recorded her feelings openly in her diary, writing on the various people and events that she observed. Her journal is a wonderful view of events and people from a Loyalist perspective. Of Robert Howe she wrote, "This Gentleman has the worst character you ever heard thro' the whole province," referring to his reputation as a womanizer. When she met him in person, she noted that she was not impressed.

She wrote that Cornelius Harnett "is at best a brute by all accounts and is besides the president of the committee and the great instigator of the cruel and unjust treatment of the friends of government." Of James Moore she wrote that he has an "unblemished character, has amiable manners, and a virtuous life." Despite their political differences, she respected him, noting that "He acts from a steady tho' mistaken principle." She no doubt appreciated that he did not criticize her brother for refusing a command with the militia. Despite this, the growing tension caused her to fear for him.[21]

By the end of May Royal Governor Josiah Martin no longer felt safe in the capital at New Bern. On the 24th he fled, and arrived at Fort Johnston (at the mouth of the Cape Fear) on June 2nd. He sent his family on to New York City, which was more firmly in control by British forces.[22]

With the Governor gone Revolution was now a fact. For all practical purposes the Provincial Congress was running North Carolina, now with no interference from the Governor. At the local level, Committees of Safety were overseeing law and order and improving military defenses.

In June 1775 the Committee of Safety urged local governments to employ gunsmiths in repairing and building weapons. They were also to stockpile gunpowder and place it in safe keeping under trustworthy persons. They also had boats sunk in the channel of the Northeast River, fortified the shoreline, and ordered a boom put over the Cape Fear at Mt. Misery, northwest of Wilmington.[23]

Despite these efforts the Committee was not entirely effective at controlling the movements of Loyalists. In June several Highland leaders traveled from Cross Creek to meet with Governor Martin at Fort Johnston, passing through Wilmington itself.[24]

On June 16th Governor Martin issued a proclamation that stated, *"Whereas...ill disposed persons have been...industriously propagating false, seditious and scandalous reports, derogatory to the honor and justice of the king and his Government...I do most earnestly exhort and advise all His Majesty's... Subjects within this Province, firmly and steadfastly to withstand and resist all attempts of the seditious to seduce them from the duty and allegiance they owe to His Majesty..."*[25]

A few days later the Wilmington Committee of Safety wrote its sister organization in Cumberland County requesting gunpowder, and recommending that all inhabitants sign the oath of loyalty. Pressure was building to monitor those suspected of being Loyalists and aiding the royal governor and the British military.[26]

The Wilmington Committee also began to monitor the activities of James Hepburn a lawyer from Cumberland County who was a suspected Loyalist. Hepburn was in fact communicating with the governor, and would play a very prominent role in the coming Loyalist uprising, but the Whigs were unable to contain his movements or activities.[27]

Despite being heavily Loyalist in sentiment, on June 30th, citizens held a rally in Cross Creek, signing an association known as the "Liberty Point Resolves." The crowd met at a tavern known as Liberty Point, and vowed to defend their rights against the British. Robert Rowan of the local militia led the rally.[28]

Liberty Point, in modern Fayetteville.

In the meantime, Alexander McLeod and Allan MacDonald traveled from Cumberland County to meet with Governor Martin on July 5th, and discussed his plans to retake the colony by force. The two men accepted the ranks of Captain in the Royal Highland Emigrants Regiment, which they intended to organize from among the Scottish population of the interior. The Wilmington Committee of Safety got wind of the meeting and tried to stop the men, but could not find them. Allan is not as famous as his wife, Flora.[29]

Among the recent Scottish immigrants to the region were Flora and Allan MacDonald, who arrived in Wilmington in the autumn of 1774 with five children. Allan and Flora, now 55 years old, moved inland, eventually settling on Cheeks Creek in the lower part of modern Montgomery County. There they lived near her daughter's family, the McLeod's. As was typical, they settled with family groups in close proximity.[30]

Flora earned everlasting fame among the Scots when she assisted Prince Charles Edward Stuart in escaping the British after his failed uprising in Scotland in 1746. The Jacobite Rebellion was ruthlessly crushed, and many Scots fled to America for a new start. Reluctant to challenge British authority again, many signed oaths of allegiance to the Crown in order to obtain land in North Carolina. They primarily settled in modern Scotland, Cumberland,

North Carolina's counties in 1775.

Robeson, Moore, and Harnett Counties. Although she is well known in North Carolina, Flora and her family experienced troubled times during their stay here, and eventually fled back to England.

In June 1775, John Ashe marched into Wilmington with several hundred militia (though he had just resigned as colonel of the New Hanover County militia) and demanded that merchants take the oath of allegiance to the Committee of Safety. When some asked for his authority in making such a demand, he pointed to his assembled troops.[31]

That summer Cumberland County held two militia musters: one for the Whigs and one for the Loyalists. Throughout the Lower Cape Fear the Whigs held the upper hand, as they largely kept control of the pre-existing militia system and local government, and forced out any opposition.[32]

Flora MacDonald

On July 7th the Wilmington Committee of Safety began organizing the militia, stating that "every white man capable of bearing Arms, resident in Wilmington, shall on or before Monday the 10th...enroll himself in One of the two Companies there..." They went on to state that "every Man...who has not signed the Association...be considered" a threat. Intimidation and force were now being used to achieve consensus.[33]

Janet Schaw observed a militia muster from Dr. Cobham's home at the north end of Wilmington. She wrote of the "constant draughts of grog" consumed by the men and observed them practice a battlefield maneuver, writing "I cannot say whether they performed it well or not; but this I know that they were heated with rum till capable of committing the most shocking outrages." They were "in their shirts and trousers, preceded by a very ill beat-drum and a fiddler, who was also in his shirt with a long sword and a cue at his hair who played with all his might. They indeed make a most umartial appearance." Men wore their long hair tied in back in what was called a queue. She may have found the fact that they were only in their shirts surprising, since men generally wore coats or waistcoats (vests) when out in public.[34]

The militia seized a man from the crowd and threatened to tar and feather him. Tarring and feathering was no laughing matter, for the tar had to be hot to be poured, and the victim often suffered severe burns. Janet Schaw feared for his life, but the militia officers interceded, and they let him off with standing on a table and begging forgiveness. The man was then drummed and fiddled out of camp, and told never to return. His offense: he had smiled at militia, no doubt enjoying their motley appearance as much as Schaw.[35]

On July 10th the Committee of Safety forbade correspondence with the Governor at Fort Johnston without "first applying to this...Committee." This was an effort to cut him off from Loyalists in the interior. A week later Governor Martin evacuated the fort for the warship *Cruzier*. He had the fort's commander, Collet, withdraw the guns, garrison, shot, and supplies to the British ships in the Cape Fear River. Collet eventually joined British forces in Boston, where he tried to raise Loyalists with no luck. He then disappears, having created one of the most important maps of colonial North Carolina.[36]

Martin wrote to Lord Dartmouth in England that the fort "is a most contemptable thing, fit neither for a place of Arms, or an Asylum for the friends of Government, on account of the weakness and smallness of it." He added that North Carolina was in a state of "Revolt and Anarchy." In another letter he wrote that the "Scotch Merchants at Wilmington who so long maintained their loyalty have lately been compelled ostensibly to join in sedition by appearing under Arms at the Musters appointed by the Committees."[37]

Despite the effort of the Wilmington Committee of Safety, Governor Martin remained able to communicate with Loyalists not only in Cross Creek, but in Wilmington itself. That summer he corresponded with Alex McLean, Samuel Campbell, Robert Hogg, William McTier, and John Slingsby. McLean coordinated communication with Highland leaders in the interior, while Campbell and Hogg were providing Martin's ship with supplies. McTier, another merchant, was able to relay messages for the governor. Not only could the Committee not prevent communication with the Loyalists at Cross Creek, but supplies flowed upstream as well.[38]

McLean was such an outspoken supporter of the King that Elizabeth DeRossett, wife of another Loyalist, noted that he spoke "such things as are disagreeable to the people," and said that his friends wished he would leave.[39]

On July 18th Martin held a meeting of his Council on board the *Cruzier* in the Cape Fear River, forming a plan of action. In the meantime, 500 militia under Col. Ashe gathered at Brunswick to keep an eye on the governor's ship.[40]

The first armed resistance of the Revolution in North Carolina occurred in July. The local militia under Cols. Ashe, Howe, and Moore planned to take Fort Johnston, and Martin learned of the plan. On the 17th he ordered sailors and

marines to remove the supplies and dismount the fort's artillery. On the morning
of the 19th about eight hundred militia arrived and burned the fort's buildings. It
was a direct assault on royal property.

From the river the British warships fired on the militia and the
harassment continued for several days afterwards. Governor Martin watched
from onboard the *Cruzier* and was outraged at the act. There had now been open
fighting, though still no official break between England and America.[41]

The torching of Fort Johnston was a key turning point for both sides.
The British felt outraged that the colonists had openly destroyed royal property.
The Americans knew they had taken a bold step and that there would be no
turning back now that the stakes had been raised. Writers on both sides
remarked on the significance of the act.

On July 21st news arrived from the New Bern Committee of Safety to
Wilmington's that two British officers had arrived in the area. Donald
MacDonald and Donald MacLeod had been sent by General Thomas Gage,
British commander in Massachusetts, to organize Scottish Highlanders in North
Carolina. Thus by the summer of 1775 both sides began gearing up for war,
knowing that the time for negotiation was over.[42]

Both MacDonald and MacLeod had fought at Bunker Hill in June, and
were also veterans of Culloden, where a Scottish army met defeat in 1745,
during the Jacobite Rebellion. MacDonald began his career as a colonel of
Marines in 1763. MacLeod entered the army as a lieutenant in the 42nd
Regiment, and had been wounded at Bunker Hill. Both men had relatives
among the Scottish settlers of the Lower Cape Fear.[43]

The Wilmington Committee of Safety next learned that James Hepburn
of Cumberland County had tried to help Governor Martin raise Loyalists against
"the Noblest Struggles of Insulted Liberty." The Committee called him "a false,
Scandalous Incendiary...who...favours Tyranny and oppression." They also
urged "Friends to American liberty" to avoid "such a wicked and detestable
Character." We will meet him again later, as Hepburn plays a critical role in the
Loyalist uprising.[44]

In the meantime the Provisional Congress in New Bern attempted to put
the state on a footing to wage war. It reorganized the militia, authorized local
militia captains to drill their troops, and issued orders to inspect and repair
weapons. Local governments were also increasing security. That July fears of
slave revolt spread across Pitt, Beaufort, and Craven Counties. The Pitt County
Committee of Safety began aggressive slave patrols, rounding up over forty men
and jailing them. Most were whipped, receiving eighty lashes, though there was
no definite evidence of a planned uprising.[45]

In August the Provisional Congress also authorized the raising of two
Continental Regiments - the first to be commanded by Col. James Moore, the
second by Col. Robert Howe. Unlike the militia, the Continental troops were to

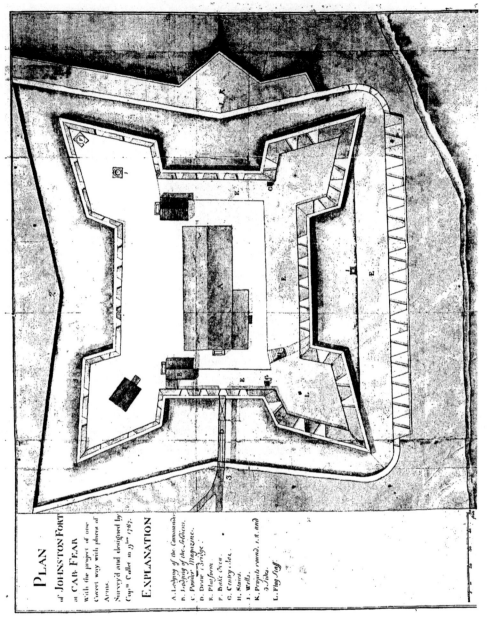

Plan of Fort Johnston, N.C.'s first fort, dating from 1748. Located at the mouth of the Cape Fear River, the modern town of Southport grew up around it.

join the newly raised American army. In June the Continental Congress had authorized George Washington to take command of the New England militia surrounding Boston, thus creating the American national army. Each state was assigned a quota of regiments to contribute to the Continental Army. Also, unlike the militia, these men were to enlist for longer periods, be better supplied, receive uniforms, and could leave their home state on military assignments.[46]

The following month North Carolina also organized its militia into Minute Man companies. These troops were to keep weapons and supplies ready, and were chosen to respond to emergencies rapidly. Each of the colony's military districts had a battalion of Minute Men.[47]

The Minute Men were instructed to train every two weeks at a central place. Officers were ordered "That in case of Insurrection, Invasion, or other Emergency such Captain or Captains, as may be nearest to the Scene of Action or first informed of the danger, shall have power to order all or part of his or their men as may be necessary into Immediate Service..." Legislation set rates for pay, established that weapons could be seized to arm the men so long as receipts were issued for them, and instructed ferry operators to transport them without charge.[48]

Now North Carolina had taken the bold step of forming an army. It was not just for home defense; these two Continental Regiments were authorized to serve outside the state and assist other states in resisting the British. In addition, other troops were to be organized in each county for home defense.[49]

The Wilmington Committee of Safety assumed responsibility for fortifying the city, stockpiling weapons and ammunition, and supervising the activities of those felt to be a threat to their authority. One of the biggest fears among the committee, most of whom were elite planters and landowners, was of slave insurrection (the region's population was over half black). Rumors of slave revolt circulated over the summer, but were unfounded.[50]

Rumors of slave rebellion hit close to home as Virginia's Royal Governor Dunmore had tried to enlist slaves to fight for him. Josiah Martin was accused of forming "a design of Arming the Negroes, and proclaiming freedom to all such as should resort to the King's Standard." On June 20th the Wilmington Committee of Safety organized militia patrols to "Search for, and take from Negroes, all kinds of arms whatsoever."[51]

The Committee reported that Captain John Collet, commander at Fort Johnston had "given encouragement to Negroes to Elope from their Masters" and that he had "declard openly that he wuld excite them to an Insurrection." Both rumors were untrue but they fed the fears of a slave uprising.

Whigs were not the only ones organizing. Loyalists opposed to the violence and intimidation used to force Revolution were gathering as well. James Cotton of Anson County, a planter, surveyor, and office holder, found out

By His Excellency the Right Honorable JOHN Earl of DUNMORE, His Majesty's Lieutenant and Governor General of the Colony and Dominion of Virginia, and Vice Admiral of the same.

A PROCLAMATION.

AS I have ever entertained Hopes, that an Accommodation might have taken Place between GREAT-BRITAIN and this Colony, without being compelled by my Duty to this most disagreeable but now absolutely necessary Step, rendered so by a Body of armed Men unlawfully assembled, firing on His Majesty's Tenders, and the formation of an Army, and that Army now on their March to attack His Majesty's Troops and destroy the well disposed Subjects of this Colony. To defeat such treasonable Purposes, and that all such Traitors, and their Abettors, may be brought to Justice, and that the Peace, and good Order of this Colony may be again restored, which the ordinary Course of the Civil Law is unable to effect; I have thought fit to issue this my Proclamation, hereby declaring, that until the aforesaid good Purposes can be obtained, I do in Virtue of the Power and Authority to ME given, by His Majesty, determine to execute Martial Law, and cause the same to be executed throughout this Colony: and to the end that Peace and good Order may the sooner be restored, I do require every Person capable of bearing Arms, to resort to His Majesty's STANDARD, or be looked upon as Traitors to His Majesty's Crown and Government, and thereby become liable to the Penalty the Law inflicts upon such Offences; such as forfeiture of Life, confiscation of Lands, &c. &c. And I do hereby further declare all indented Servants, Negroes, or others, (appertaining to Rebels,) free that are able and willing to bear Arms, they joining His Majesty's Troops as soon as may be, for the more speedily reducing this Colony to a proper Sense of their Duty, to His Majesty's Crown and Dignity. I do further order, and require, all His Majesty's Leige Subjects, to retain their Quitrents, or any other Taxes due or that may become due, in their own Custody, till such Time as Peace may be again restored to this at present most unhappy Country, or demanded of them for their former salutary Purposes, by Officers properly authorised to receive the same.

GIVEN under my Hand on board the Ship WILLIAM, off NORFOLK, the 7th Day of NOVEMBER, in the SIXTEENTH Year of His Majesty's Reign.

DUNMORE.

(GOD save the KING.)

Lord Dunmore's proclamation.

the price for his Loyalty. Cotton refused to sign the Association, and the Anson County Committee of Safety allowed him two weeks to reconsider.[52]

When time ran out a mob broke into his home at night and seized him from his bed, with his terror stricken wife at his side. Cotton managed to escape his captors and hid in the woods for several days until he was able to make his way down to the Cape Fear River. He visited Governor Martin onboard his ship and was influential in the Governor's decision to recruit Loyalists from the interior. In the meantime the Anson County militia threatened to burn his home and take his slaves, his most valuable property.[53]

Lord Dunmore.

Scottish visitor Janet Schaw once again witnessed important events when at the home of a friend in Wilmington. She noted that there was a secret meeting held in one room, though she did not know any more than that. It seems they were ambassadors on way their way from the interior settlements to meet Governor Martin on the river. Later that summer her brother Robert snuck out to a British ship with letters from Governor Martin to officials in England. Janet was glad to see him leave and reach safety.[54]

Local militia had set up camp at Jumping Run in Wilmington's modern Greenfield Park, as well as at Cato Spring. Here they constructed earthworks to defend the town and began drilling for combat. A sawmill here provided a convenient source for lumber. A fort was also built along the river below the city, where modern Northern Boulevard ends. Batteries of artillery were placed around the town, including one battery of 9 pound guns, another of 5 and 12 pound guns, and one of two field guns. Nothing remains of these defenses today, though Greenfield Park's location along the creek shows how it formed a natural defense line below the town.[55]

On July 21st, the Edenton Committee of Safety wrote to that of Wilmington that "...a vessel from New York to this place brought over two officers who left at the Bar to go to New Bern, they are both Highlanders, one named McDonnel, the other McCloud. They pretend they are on a visit to some of their countrymen on your river, but I think there is reason to suspect their errand of a base nature...”[56]

In fact, the two men were Donald McDonald and Donald McLeod, who had arrived in North Carolina and made their way to Cross Creek to recruit an army to march on Wilmington. Had the Whigs been able to stop them at Edenton or New Bern the Highlanders might not have organized for their march to the sea.

The British belief in large numbers of Loyalists in North Carolina rested on shaky ground. A number of citizens were willing to resist the Revolutionaries, but not in the numbers that London believed. They also lacked organization, weapons, and means of self support. The British consistently overestimated Loyalist capabilities, yet the hope remained that Loyalists could help win the war, thus prompting the British to return again to the South later in the war.

In the meantime, on August 3rd the Provincial Congress established a provisional government for North Carolina: the Provincial Council. They also created six district Committees of Safety to oversee military preparations in each region of the colony. There were now Committees of Safety in twenty-six of the colony's thirty-five counties. North Carolinians had now non-violently taken control of their province and were running it as their own.[57]

A week later in Wilmington the Committee of Safety ordered weapons collected from among the residents, “whether the property of the Public or private persons.” They also rounded up artillery pieces to be used in the town's fortifications. All available weapons were badly needed for the militia and the forming Continental troops.[58]

That same day the *Cape Fear Mercury* reported the first news of the fighting at Bunker Hill in Massachusetts. The paper's brief article reveals how slowly news traveled and how problematic verifying its accuracy was. The paper reported that “We hear a captain of a vessel, arrived from the northward...has reported, that the Americans and ministerial troops have had a general engagement, which proved fatal to the latter. We do not know what foundation there is to this report; but from many circumstances, it appears probable such an engagement has happened and we daily expect an account of it.”[59]

While the colonists made great efforts to build an army, it was slow going. Janet Schaw observed that “every man is ordered to appear under arms” to drill. She felt that “Two regiments just now would reduce this province, but...in a little time four times four would not be sufficient.” She could not have been more right. At the beginning the British had a chance to retake North Carolina, but with time the Americans would become better organized and establish better infrastructures for waging war.[60]

On August 21st the 3rd Provisional Congress met in Hillsboro, feeling that this interior location was safer than Halifax or New Bern. All the counties of North Carolina were represented. For the Lower Cape Fear were Cornelius Harnett, Archibald Maclaine, Robert Rowan, William Hooper, Walter Gibson, Robert Howe, Samuel Ashe, Maurice Moore, and John Ashe.

Seeing his colony slip away from his control, Governor Josiah Martin sent a message to his superiors in England indicating that he could retake North Carolina if he were supported. Martin asked for weapons with which to arm the Highland Scots of Cumberland County. He insisted that there were enough Highlanders, former Regulators, and other loyal civilians to stop the Revolutionaries.

Frederick Lord North

In London on October 15th Prime Minister Lord North met with King George III to discuss the plan proposed by Governor Martin. The next day the King agreed to furnish troops and weapons for the Loyalists.[61]

While nearly every royal governor in the American colonies was asking London for help, Martin's proposal had special merit. He only asked for weapons, not men. In claming he could raise several thousand Loyalists and easily re-take his province, his plan was more appealing than those of other royal governors. As events would show, however, Martin overestimated Loyalist support among his citizens.

Martin would be pleased when he learned that he had official support, yet things quickly became complicated when the King authorized troops and a fleet as well. Now Martin would have to coordinate his uprising of Loyalists with the arrival of British forces. He was getting more than just weapons, he was getting an armada.

Sir Peter Parker was chosen to lead the expedition. From a naval family, Parker had fought in the West Indies under Admiral Edward Vernon (for whom George Washington's Potomac River plantation was named). Parker had a solid reputation and began the laborious process of assembling officers, ships, and supplies for his fleet. Slowly but steadily, the cumbersome British war machine churned into motion, trying to shake off its peacetime lethargy.[62]

Back in North Carolina, the situation had now become too volatile for an outspoken Loyalist, and by October Janet Schaw had fled to the *Cruzier* with family and friends. She wrote that "I at present require all of my sprit to carry me thro' many difficulties."[63]

In November 1775 the Committee of Safety directed militia to go door to door in Wilmington confiscating weapons, leaving one per white man, and giving receipts for those taken.[64]

Throughout that fall Loyalists had been making their way from Cross Creek and points west to meet with Martin on his ship in the Cape Fear. Allan MacDonald (Flora's husband) met with the governor at Fort Johnston. Alexander MacLean visited Martin in November to assist with planning for raising the army.[65]

Admiral Sir Peter Parker

On November 7th British Secretary of State for the American Colonies Lord Dartmouth wrote to Royal Governor Martin that his plan had been approved, and he was now to do his part to raise men for the invasion. The Royal Governor would not get this news for a few months. In the meantime Parker was assembling his fleet and the troops were preparing equipment. For this expedition sixty female camp followers accompanied each regiment, along with twelve servants. The camp followers performed important tasks like sewing and nursing. In addition, each regiment was alotted twenty tons of equipment.[66]

It took time to assemble this massive amount of men, supplies, ammunition, and food. General Charles Lord Cornwallis assembled troops stationed in Ireland for the trip across the Atlantic. They were to join British troops from Boston for the invasion of North Carolina. In the meantime the British also shuffled regiments in England and Ireland to ensure enough remained for defense of the home islands. Unfortunately, Parker's fleet did not even set sail until February 12, 1776, when the Loyalists were already on their way to Wilmington. Communication between London, Boston, and the Cape Fear was difficult, and timing was impossible to coordinate.[67]

Martin made a convincing case to his leaders in London. All of the Royal Governors of the Southern Colonies had by now been forced from their capitals and were each on warships offshore. The governors of Virginia, both Carolinas, and Georgia all appealed to England for help to retake their colonies, and were in communication with each other as well.[68]

Martin estimated he could raise about 30,000 men, principally from the Scottish Highlanders and former Regulators. The former were bound by oath to the King, and the latter were dissatisfied with the colonial government. Both groups had suffered recently and would take advantage of the opportunity for revenge. Martin's number was wishful thinking, for reality would prove it was entirely unrealistic.

Joseph Hewes

On November 9th Joseph Hewes, one of North Carolina's delegates to the Congress in Philadelphia, wrote Samuel Johnston about the lack of weapons, ammunition, supplies, and pay issues for the soldiers being raised. "I hope you have fallen on some method to furnish your Soldiers with Arms and Ammunition; those articles are very scarce throughout all the Colonies...all the Gunsmiths in this Province [Pennsylvania] are engaged and cannot make Arms near so fast as they are wanted. Powder is also very scared not withstanding every effort...to make and import."[70]

A few days later Josiah Martin wrote to Alexander McLean that it was time to gather the Loyalists, and asked how many he could raise. Across the Scottish settlements of the Upper Cape Fear region, families began to assemble and prepare for the gathering.[71]

On November 13th the Committee of Safety ordered John Forster, Peter Mallet, William Wilkinson, and Charles Jewkes to take inventory of the weapons of families in Wilmington, reserving one for each white man in the house. The rest were collected for the 1st North Carolina Regiment, camped at Barnard's Creek, about three miles below the town.[72]

On the 16th the Committee of Safety told all white male residents to meet at the courthouse in four days to form into companies of militia. By now over 300 men of the 1st North Carolina were camped at Barnard's Creek.[73]

On November 20th the Committee ordered artillery sent from Wilmington to Col. Moore at Brunswick, where it was felt he might be attacked. They also ordered that no provisions be sent to Martin's ship, and had several vessels chained and sunk in the river to block access to the town harbor. Lastly, they sent a plea to the New Bern Committee for gunpowder.[74]

Days later, on November 24th, fearing the British would attack Brunswick and Wilmington, the Committee again ordered all weapons in the county collected for the use of the troops. They also wrote to the Salisbury District for troops, and asked to purchase lead for ammunition. In case of bombardment by the British, property in Wilmington was to be valued and recorded.[75]

In November 1775 the Committee of Safety also adopted a resolution agreeing with one passed by the Continental Congress: *"We will, in our several stations, encourage frugality, economy, and industry, and promote agriculture, arts, and the manufactures of this country, especially that of wool; and will discountenance and discourage every species of extravagance and dissipation, especially all horse-racing, and all kinds of gaming, cock fighting, exhibits of shows and plays, and other expensive diversions...on the death of any relation or friend, none of us, or any of our families, will go into any further mourning-dress, than a black crepe ribbon on the arm or hat, for gentlemen, and a black ribbon and necklace for ladies, and we will discontinue the giving of gloves and scarves at funerals."*[76]

On December 6th Cornwallis's troops prepared to depart Cork, Ireland. They were to first sail to Boston to meet up with a force under General Clinton, then proceed on to North Carolina.[77]

On December 19th the Wilmington Committee of Safety ordered Ralph Millar to begin manufacturing gunpowder, and also ordered supplies furnished to him. The next day the Provincial Council noted that "this Province may soon be invaded by British troops." They continued to order supplies and tried to cut off communication between Governor Martin and his supporters. Samuel Ashe, William Campbell, and James Kenan were appointed to buy supplies and organize gunsmiths to mend weapons, make bayonets, and purchase gun parts, lead, and flints. Weapons of the day required a good sharp flint to ignite the gunpowder, and the many small pieces of the lock mechanism could break and wear down. Replacing spare parts was problematic with the American's lack of industry.[78]

The next day the Provincial Council appointed Richard Quince, Samuel Ashe, Robert Ellis, and John Forster to outfit a ship on the Cape Fear, to aid in defending the river.[79]

War preparations did not cease for the Christmas holiday, and on December 24th the North Carolina Provincial Council, meeting at the Johnston

County courthouse, voted to pay for three ships for its state navy. One each was to be stationed at the Cape Fear, New Bern, and Edenton. In the Cape Fear the *General Washington* was purchased in January 1776, but estimates were that it would be six months until it was ready.[80]

By December 29th, about 500 soldiers were camped near Wilmington and busy building defenses around the town. Little did they know that the enemy would materialize not from the sea, as expected, but from behind them, in the interior.[81]

Chapter 4
Moores Creek

At his headquarters near Boston on December 23, 1775 General George Washington received news that a British fleet was assembling for a strike on the Carolinas. Unfortunately for Governor Martin and General MacDonald, the American intelligence network could accurately and quickly obtain and relay information on British movements.[1]

Violence had broken out in New England, but negotiations were still underway as the Continental Congress, meeting in Philadelphia, was hoping for a compromise. In North Carolina both sides had made threats and prepared for action but had not yet come to blows. Yet the war was about to come to North Carolina.

The focus of most histories of the Moores Creek Bridge Campaign naturally have been on the battle itself, yet the campaign began and ended at Cross Creek (modern Fayetteville). From there the Loyalist army assembled for their march to the sea, and there the remnants retreated, where most were captured.

By January 1776 the American militia had fortified Wilmington and seized Fort Johnston. Royal authority was gone in the colony, and both Whigs and Loyalists were seizing arms and ammunition. Governor Martin, onboard the *Cruzier,* was attempting to rescue a situation that was fast spiraling beyond his control.

Martin learned on January 3rd that his proposal had been approved by
Lord Dartmouth, Secretary of State for the colonies. With a plan now in place,
he acted quickly.[2]

He wrote loyalist leaders in the interior, "...you are hereby required
immediately & with all possible secrecy to concert a general place of rende-vous
thence to march in a body to Brunswick by such route as you judge proper..."
They were to meet the British fleet on the river "by the 15th of February next."
From the beginning a crucial breakdown had occurred, as the timing of the
Loyalists and British fleet could not be coordinated from such widely separated
distances.[3]

On January 5th the Wilmington Committee of Safety ordered all river
pilots taken into protective custody to prevent the British from capturing and
using them. They also decreed that all militiamen must take the Test Oath,
thereby binding the loyalty of the militia to the Committee. The oath required
allegiance to the cause, and was used to control suspected Loyalists. Also in
preparation for hostilities, they established a hospital.[4]

With the start of the new year it was clear to both sides that it was a
question of when, not if, violence would break out in North Carolina. The
situation had deteriorated to the point that people had to choose. Martin and the
Loyalist leaders of the interior, and the Committees of Safety across North
Carolina, were demanding allegiance. Hesitating or sitting on the fence could no
longer be tolerated.

The Wilmington Committee of Safety further tightened its control of the
Lower Cape Fear on January 6th when they began to appraise the value of houses
and buildings in Wilmington, in case of British attack. They also ordered that no
vessel could clear the port without permission.[5]

That same day in Boston, Sir Henry Clinton got word to ready troops for
an expedition to the Cape Fear, and to prepare officers to form the Royal
Highland Emigrant Regiment (later numbered the 84th Regiment), which was to
be raised from the Scottish settlers around Cross Creek. His orders further
stipulated that once finished in North Carolina, he was to return back to New
England in time to begin a campaign against Washington's forces there. This
was entirely unrealistic given the distances and difficulties involved, yet
planners in London could not fathom the distances or complexities of waging
war in North America.[6]

On January 10th Josiah Martin wrote to Alexander MacLean, a key
leader among the Scots, to start raising men and to commission and assign
officers to every fifty men. Martin also issued a proclamation denouncing the
growing rebellion.[7]

Although the Committee of Safety was firmly in control at Wilmington,
there were voices of dissent. On January 15th a note was found posted on the
courthouse, addressed "to those who have a true sense of...Justice &...Liberty."

It went on to condemn the actions taken by the Committee of Safety. The Committee quickly reacted, claiming it had "false & Scandalous reflections on this Committee tending to inflame the mind of the people, to create divisions & dissentions among us." Doctor James Fallon was found to be the author and promptly jailed, where he refused bond for good behavior.[8]

The next day Dr. Fallon again refused to give bond for good behavior, and was subsequently order to be kept under guard. Colonel James Moore was requested to "refuse admittance to any person but such as he or the Officer on Guard may think proper." Dr. Fallon was not allowed to write letters, and guards searched any visitors.[9]

In an even more important development, though the Committee would not realize it at the time, Captain Alexander MacLean visited Governor Martin onboard the *Cruzier*. Afterwards MacLean was captured, fined, and jailed. The colonists released him on a promise of good behavior. MacLean claimed "he had not any design of offending the Committee," but his visit was only to "expedite his business" as his personal affairs were in the "utmost confusion." Unknown to the Americans, he was the man Martin designated to recruit Highlanders in the Cross Creek area. In letting him go, the Committee of Safety lost a golden opportunity to foil the mobilization of the Loyalists.[10]

Col. James Moore.

On January 17th the Committee of Safety named a select group to again "call Respectively on the Inhabitants of the Town tomorrow & borrow from them such Guns as they can spare, to supply Col. Moore as soon as possible with the Number of Guns he wants – they having such Guns Value demand giving proper Receipts for them to the Owners."[11]

In the meantime, Colonel Moore wrote that Dr. Fallon was an "insinuating & dangerous Person among the Soldiers" and he could no longer keep him in the guard house. In response, the Committee ordered him to the town jail with "strict orders that the Soldiers shall not converse" with him. No one was allowed to speak to him but with orders from officer of the Guard.[12]

On January 20th the Committee of Safety granted the request of residents of Lockwoods Folley and Shallotte to have gunpowder to defend themselves. This precious and valuable material was in limited supply and had to be rationed carefully to where it was needed. Also this day Sir Henry Clinton finally set sail from Boston harbor with several ships for the Cape Fear, stopping at New York on the way.[13]

A week later at the end of January, the Committee of Safety reported that the earthworks were nearly completed below Wilmington. The defenses included works at Smith Creek, Burnt Mill Run on the east side of town, and at Jumping Run below Wilmington (at modern Greenfield Park).[14]

A few days later on February 5th, the Committee of Safety received news from Col. Moore at Ft. Johnston that the British warships in the river "had committed hostilities on the Continental Troops under his command by firing on them at the said Fort." As the ships had been regularly requesting supplies, specifically food, the Committee decided to cut them off. The Committee resolved that "the Ships of War now lying in the River have Actually committed hostilities against the Inhabitants of this Province and therefore this committee in Obedience to the said Resolve of the committee of Safety cannot suffer any more provision to go down to the Men of War for the future." Hostilities had begun, although only on a minor scale. The important fact was that the shooting had started. Both sides now waited to see where the major action would take place. Also that same day Dr. Fallon agreed to "good behavior" and was finally released.[15]

One hundred fifty miles to the west on that same day, leaders of the Highlanders and former Regulators held a meeting at David Shanes's home on McLendon's Creek (near modern Carthage in Moore County). The Regulators claimed that 3,000 would join them on the march, and some reports even said 5,000 were willing. It was heartening news but it should have also been suspect. Many of the Scots agreed that they should not assemble their army until March 1st, when the British would definitely be on the Cape Fear, but the leaders of the former Regulators insisted that they gather immediately, and the Highland leaders "gave way" to their opinion.[16]

A few days later Donald McLeod went through the countryside among the former Regulators, hoping to build support. He received a cold reception, and could not even get a guide to lead him back. It should have been a sign that support was lukewarm among the former Regulators of the central part of the colony.[17]

Back in Wilmington, the Committee of Safety clearly stated their grievance against England a few days later on February 9th, when they ordered the Oath taken by every militia soldier. The Oath stated that the person taking it had a "sincere belief neither the Parliament of Great Britain nor any Member or

Constituent branch thereof have a right to impose taxes upon the American Colonies to regulate the internal Policys thereof and that all attempts by fraud or force to establish and exercise such claims & powers ought to be resisted to the utmost and that the people of this Colony singly & collectively are bound by the Acts of the Continental & Provincial Congresses because in both they are freely represented by persons chosen by themselves..." It went on to state that they agreed to "support Maintain & defend all & every" act of the Continental Congress and colony's Provincial Congress.[18]

A further example of the Committee of Safety enforcing cohesion came on February 9th when they ordered the militia to visit "every Man in Wilmington without exception, & whoever shall refuse or decline Voluntarily to take the said Oath shall by the Militia Officer aforesaid be disarmed..." Seizing weapons and forcing conformity was important in building consensus and support for the Revolutionary movement, as well as preventing dissention and aid to the enemy.[19]

In the meantime aboard his warship, trying to run the colony from afloat, Governor Martin continued to communicate with his contacts among the Scots near Cross Creek. Many of those Scottish settlers had fought at Culloden, while others were former British army officers. It was an area ripe for recruiting soldiers with military experience, and those who hoped to regain some of their former military glory.[20]

The former Regulators were another group who were lukewarm to the colonial government. Many of those now in control of the colony had been part

The 1748 Battle of Culloden, the results of which led to the mass emigration of Scots to America.

of Tryon's army that crushed the Regulators at Alamance five years earlier.
They inherently mistrusted any leadership from the eastern part of the colony.
Yet, as dissatisfied as they were with the colony's leadership, many were
unwilling to risk another armed confrontation. During the war former
Regulators supported both sides, and they did not as a whole support one over
the other.

On February 9th a large force of Loyalists camped at Campbell's home
on McLendon's Creek. The next day they rendezvoused nearby at Mr.
Morrison's at Cross Hill. These initial meetings were held in Moore County,
near modern Carthage. Most were Highlanders, but Col. John Cotton brought
150 country born: men who were born in America. One observer noted "no
dependence was to be had on the Regulators as they were all dispersed never to
meet as he supposed." In fact, some officers tried to "revive the drooping spirits
of their friends by spreading a report that the Regulators had now taken a second
thought and that three thousand of them were on the march to join us." This
rumor had the "desired effect" and recruits continued to turn out for General
MacDonald.[21]

On the 10th Col. Thomas Rutherford called on the Cumberland County
militia to appear at Cross Creek in two days and join the Loyalists. On the 12th
many had gathered "but not near so many as was first expected." Men were
encouraged to turn out and fight the "illegal usurpation of wicked and designing
men" according to one Loyalist.[22]

At Cross Hill, Donald MacDonald met with Highland leaders and
instructed them to start recruiting for his army. It was now time to chose sides,
as Col. Thomas Rutherford found out. He had been appointed as Cumberland
County's militia commander, but now switched sides. He tried to bring his men
over to the Loyalists, but few joined him.[23]

The Americans were aware that Loyalists and former Regulators were
organizing, but did not know what their intentions were. As it became clear that
a confrontation was coming, local commanders called out their militia. Among
other places, some militia assembled at the Black River Chapel on Ivanhoe Road
in modern Sampson County, others at Matthews' Old Field in Sampson County.[24]

All across southeastern North Carolina the Whigs were organizing:
gathering supplies, seizing weapons, and mustering the troops. People
contributed various supplies to the cause: flour, peas, turkeys, ham, bacon,
cornmeal, oats, salt, beef cattle, blankets, pots and kettles, horses, wagons, hay,
picks, axes, shovels, spades, and other goods.[25]

The stirring of the armies disrupted normal life in the region as
foodstuffs, horses, and wagons were seized for use. Roads became unsafe, and
commerce and communication came to a standstill. As militia commanders
organized their men, leaders often paid for supplies and transportation costs out
of their own pocket. The rush to organize men, supply them, and move them

The only known portrait of General Donald MacDonald.

came so quickly that the militia system was overwhelmed in trying to coordinate it. The provisional government kept records to reimburse men who supplied food, paid for ferry transportation, and loaned wagons, carts, and horses to the armies.[26]

Wheelwrights and blacksmiths worked overtime to repair wagons, carts, gun carriages, and tools. Bolts of material were collected: oznaburg for clothing and tents, flannel for artillery ammunition bags, and wool for militia flags.[27]

Intelligence traveled fast for both sides. On February 10th the New Bern Committee of Safety learned that Cumberland, Anson, Bladen, and Guilford County Loyalists had met at Cross Creek and were preparing to march.[28]

In the meantime British officers on the ships in the Cape Fear made plans to attack and burn Brunswick Town, as it harbored the local militia. Before the raid was launched a ship ran aground, and it was learned the town had been abandoned anyway. Yet Brunswick would not be spared from violence for long.[29]

Virtually a prisoner on a ship in the river, Governor Martin was not allowed to land or communicate with anyone on shore, but he was still able to get letters out to his superiors in London. Martin wrote to England that "I daily see the Sacred Majesty...insulted...His Government trampled upon... officials...abused." He was more determined than ever to retake his wayward colony.[30]

On February 12th Clinton left New York City, as ice and contrary winds delayed him from leaving any sooner. His next stop would be off the Virginia coast, where he would meet with another deposed royal governor, Lord Dunmore. Winds would again delay their travel to the North Carolina coast for several days.[31]

Two days later as the Loyalists began to assemble at Cross Creek, some were disappointed that Governor Martin himself was not there. There were also rumors that British regulars would greet them. More serious was the fact that there were few weapons for those arriving.[32]

Now appointed to the rank of general, Donald MacDonald issued a proclamation inviting "every well wisher of that form of Government under which they have so happily lived," the "best birth-right of Britons and Americans" to "repair to His Majesty's Royal standard" and implored the Scots to support "the rights and Constitution of their country."[33]

By February 15th nearly 1,400 men had gathered at Cross Creek (of which only 200-300 were former Regulators, a far cry from the 3,000-5,000 promised). Of those 1,400 Loyalists under General MacDonald, only 520 had arms. Consequently, he sent men to scour the countryside, which brought in 130 more. They also took weapons from the Cumberland County Committee of Safety, as well as 1,000 pounds of gunpowder. The Loyalist army left on the 18th and camped four miles below Cross Creek, on the road to Wilmington that crossed Rockfish Creek. The same day Col. James Moore with 650 men of the 1st North Carolina marched out of Wilmington headed to Rockfish Creek, a natural barrier just south of Cross Creek.

MacDonald organized his army into four divisions: the Cumberland County militia, led by Colonel Thomas Rutherford, the Anson County militia under Colonel Hugh MacDonald, former Regulators from the Hillsboro area under Major Donald McLeod, and Colonel James Cotton's Loyalist militia. The men were further organized into companies, and each received a cooking pot (though most companies, while supposed to be fifty men, had closer to thirty).

Nor were the divisions equal in size. MacDonald's division consisted of two battalions of twelve companies each, roughly 720 men in all. McLeod's force had about 130-160 men, and Cotton's militia brought about 500 men in fifteen companies. Small groups from Bladen County and Cross Creek fell in under Rutherford's division.[34]

The gathering of the Loyalist army brought widespread support from the families of the men who volunteered. Nearly everyone contributed weapons, clothing, and supplies: barrels of flour, pork, flints, bed tick, cloth, wagons, shoes, leather, beef, thread, bridles, fodder for horses, venison, hams, horses, sheep, beef, cattle, and corn. It was an immense contribution from many who did not have much to spare.[35]

Merchant George Myline of Cross Creek, a partner with Hogg and Campbell of Wilmington, gave MacDonald's army the Cumberland County Committee of Safety's gunpowder, a significant addition to their meager supplies. Hogg and Campbell had been supplying the Highlanders of Cross Creek all winter in anticipation of the coming violence.[36]

Among those actively supporting the raising of troops was Flora MacDonald, the Scottish immigrant who was famous for saving the life of Prince Charles Stuart in the aftermath of the failed Jacobite Rebellion in Scotland. Flora had been

The Highlanders gather at Cross Creek.

arrested by the British but was eventually released.[37]

Flora witnessed the marshalling of the troops at Cross Creek, and noted their lack of good weapons. She recalled that nearly 1,600 men had assembled, and that they had "no arms but 600 old, bad firelocks [firearms] and about 40 broad swords."[38]

Lack of weapons was a persistent problem, and one participant estimated that only one man in six had a firearm. Before leaving Cross Creek MacDonald divided his army into four divisions, and organized his men into companies. He also appointed a quartermaster for supplies and a wagon master to oversee transportation.[39]

The organizing of the army brought out Scottish national pride among a downtrodden people who had long been oppressed. After a failed revolt against English rule in 1745 (the Jacobite Rebellion), the Scots were not allowed to wear their traditional plaids, bear arms, or play bagpipes. Now Loyalist commanders fed on this enthusiasm for recruitment. Bagpipes, dirks, swords, kilts, flags, and other symbols of Scottish pride, many of which had been banned in Scotland by the English, resurfaced.[40]

Among those active in recruiting former Regulators for the Loyalist army was Dr. John Pyle of Chatham County. He was captured after Moores Creek and taken to New York. After returning to his home in 1781, he again actively supported the Loyalists. He is best remembered for leading a group of mounted troops to join the British army when they were attacked by Col. Henry Lee's cavalry, an action known as Pyle's Defeat. He later treated the American wounded after the battle of Lindley's Mill. The action at Pyle's Defeat remains controversial and hotly debated to this day (for more information on Pyle's Defeat in 1781, see Chapter 7).[41]

The night after leaving Cross Creek, two companies of Regulators ran away with their arms after learning that yet another force, under Col. Richard Caswell, was closing in on them as well. They were called "Base Rascals" who chose not to participate in the "Glorious cause...in serving their King" or "relieving this country from the Tyrannical oppression it now groans under." Later at an assembly, the men were asked "if any amongst them there was so faint hearted as not to serve with that resolution of conquering or dying, this was the time for such to declare themselves, upon which there was a general huzza for the King except from about 20 men" who "declared their courage was not war proof." These men were allowed to leave.[42]

Below Cross Creek, blocking the road to Wilmington at Rockfish Creek, was Colonel James Moore with his troops. He was soon joined by Col. Alexander Lillington with 150 New Hanover County Minutemen, Col. James

Kenan with 200 from Duplin County, and Col. John Ashe with 100 militia, for a total of 1,100. Moore also had five artillery pieces, a formidable deterrent to direct assault, as MacDonald had none.[43]

John Ashe served on the Council of Safety, and had marched on Fort Johnston and burned it in 1775. Ashe raised a unit of militia and commanded them during the Moores Creek Campaign. In 1779 he commanded the Americans at the Battle of Briar Creek in Georgia, where he was badly defeated. His two sons, Samuel and William, also served in the war. Samuel was captured and sent to a prison ship in Wilmington, which debilitated him. John Ashe died of illness in October 1781.[44]

Moore's troops dug earthworks and prepared for an attack from the Loyalist army. In the meantime other troops were closing in as well. Col. Richard Caswell's militia was marching from New Bern, and militia from Rowan and Guilford Counties were coming from the west.

Wilmington got a scare on the evening of February 14th when the Committee of Safety got news that the *Cruzier* had passed Brunswick and was on the way up to the town. "General Confusion" resulted, and one observer reported that "the Town is now almost cleared of all kinds of Goods, and of women & Children."[45]

By this time Duplin, Onslow, and Brunswick County militia had arrived to bolster the town. They had built "Breastworks on the principal Streets & Wharfs and the hills above & below the Town" to "prevent the landing of any men for the Ships." The *Cruzier* tried to avoid the city and its defenses by going around Eagles Island but the river was too shallow. A shore party landed at Mr. Ancrum's plantation and took several livestock, vegetables, and attempted to capture his slaves but they fled. They also took books, clothes, and other personal items before returning back down the river. Panic had spread through the town, but more ominous news would soon be coming to keep people on edge.[46]

Back at Rockfish Creek, seven miles below Cross Creek, the Loyalist army prepared to encounter Moore, who had blocked the road to Wilmington. Moore's troops had prepared defenses with tools borrowed from local residents or contributed by various commanders. In what seemed to defy military logic, Moore's earthworks were above the creek, not behind it - thus he had the creek behind his men. This was a problem since he was not using the creek for defense, and it would force him onto a bottleneck if he had to retreat and cross at the bridge. The earthworks there were still visible in the 1890s.[47]

Hoping to avoid battle, McDonald sent a messenger, Lt. Donald Morrison, to Moore with an offer for them to "join the royal standard." Moore replied by sending the Test Oath, which essentially gave allegiance to the Continental Army. Each side was trying to win the other over, and neither commander budged.[48]

At the suggestion of Farquard Campbell, MacDonald decided to abandon the direct road to Wilmington which was blocked by Col. Moore's troops. The Loyalists could cross the Cape Fear River and march down the other side along the Negro Head Point Road, a lesser used road and one that was still open. Thus on the 20th they marched back to Cross Creek and Campbelltown and crossed, and began a series of moves and counter moves that tested the nerve and skill of each commander.[49]

Farquard Campbell had served in the colony's Provincial Congress but was secretly a Loyalist. During the winter he had visited Martin on his ship and relayed messages between the Governor and Loyalist leaders at Cross Creek. It was a dangerous game he was playing, and eventually he was found out and banished from the state. After the war, he was able to return, and even served in North Carolina's Senate. He is a rare example of an enemy allowed back into society after the war.[50]

In the meantime the Loyalists moved south unopposed on the Negro Head Point Road. Realizing he had been fooled, Moore fell back towards Wilmington to Elizabethtown, where he could get on transports in the Cape Fear River. Encumbered by wagons and artillery, he sent a smaller force ahead under Alexander Lillington to move by water on the Cape Fear River and occupy Moores Creek, another crossing site further south. He also sent dispatches to Col. Richard Caswell, marching from New Bern, to block the Negro Head Point Road at Corbett's Ferry, near modern Ivanhoe.[51]

Militia converged on the area from all over: Black River Chapel, Wilmington, Long Creek, New Bern, Kingston, and Duplin, Sampson, Bladen, and Brunswick Counties. Large numbers of militia gathered at Wilmington, then marched to Rockfish Creek.[52]

Marching from New Bern, Caswell's force was supplied with local pork, corn, flour, and fodder for their horses. Citizens loaned the men axes, iron pots, and other equipment. Others "hired" their horses, wagons, and even muskets and rifles. Thousands of gunflints were needed, and most militia detachments had several hundred with them. Weapons needed a good sharp flint in order to create a spark and set off the gunpowder. Firearms were useless without them.[53]

While most militia were turning out readily, some needed convincing, or at least good enticement. Col. Needham Bryan recruited his men from Johnston County with the help of rum, brandy, toddy, grog, and cider.[54]

A trap was gradually closing in on MacDonald's army. Lt. Col. Alexander Martin with the 2nd North Carolina and Lt. Col. James Thackton of the 4th North Carolina were coming up in the rear of the Loyalists, preparing to occupy Cross Creek, and squeeze the Loyalists between them and Moore's forces to the east. Col. Richard Caswell, with 850 militia from New Bern, was also marching toward Rockfish Creek.[55]

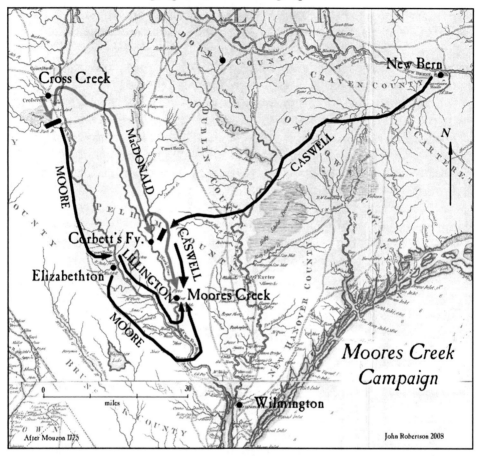

Moores Creek
Campaign

After Mouzon 1775

John Robertson 2008

On the 21st the Loyalists crossed the Cape Fear River in a "drisly rain." They then took the Negro Head Point Road to the south. Desertions were a continuing problem. The next day the army marched ten miles and the "Rain continued" making it "very uncomfortable." "Heavie rain continuing all night" wrote one soldier, as the army camped at Capt. Williamson's plantation, an officer with the Whig army. On the 23rd MacDonald marched ten miles and halted at Dismal Bay (between the modern towns of Roseboro and Garland), where he learned that Col. Richard Caswell was in front of him. On the 24th MacDonald marched to within four miles of Corbetts Ferry, where he halted and prepared for battle, collecting broadswords for eighty men of Capt. John Campbell.[56]

Morale among the Loyalists plummeted as desertions continued. The lack of weapons caused fear, supplies were slim, and the weather was miserable. Many of the Scots no doubt accompanied the army out of a sense of duty because of their oath, rather than conviction for the cause. Their courage and perseverance were admirable.

According to naval records of the *Cruzier* and *Scorpion*, it rained from the 17th to the 19th, again on the 21st and 22nd, and continuously from the 24th to the 26th, including "strong gales" on many days. The conditions were miserable for both sides marching on the poor roads. Creeks were high, low areas flooded, and men were outside for two weeks in cold, damp weather.[57]

Writing from Wilmington on February 23rd, an officer wrote that, "I have got in confinement several Tories and suspected Tories. Many of those still here had inrolled themselves with Col. Ashe, in order, as is believed, to screen themselves from duty, but when the day of the trial came, they shrunk back... The neutrals, as they call themselves, have been forced greatly against their inclinations to work at the breastworks."[58]

The next day the Americans fortified two key positions above Wilmington at Herons Bridge and Mount Misery. A cannon bolstered the defenses at Heron's Bridge. Troops also constructed a boom over the Northeast Cape Fear River at Mount Misery. These preparations shielded Wilmington from attack from the north as well as from the Cape Fear River. Col. William Purviance, overseeing the construction, also noted that he expected to take in more Loyalist prisoners soon.[59]

A small sampling of militia statistics from Duplin, Sampson, Brunswick, and New Hanover Counties reveals that the bulk of the men serving in the militia in 1776 were between the ages of 17 and 36, with the vast majority between 21 and 27 years old. Most were natives of the region.[60]

At Corbett's Ferry on the Black River General MacDonlad found himself facing another water obstacle. Camped four miles above Col. Caswell, MacDonald again preferred maneuver to attack. Scouts went out in search of a way around Caswell's force. To hold Caswell's attention, McDonald had some of his soldiers march back and forth, play bagpipes, shout orders, and fire shots occasionally to give the impression the army was preparing to attack straight across the ford in an effort to "amuse Caswell."[61]

In the meantime, Capt. Donald McLeod led a force of cavalry up the river in search of a way across. They luckily found a slave who told them of a submerged boat on their side of the swampy river and helped them raise it. Here they crossed over at Devane's Plantation, about six miles above Corbett's Ferry. Once on the other shore, McLeod began marching down the road towards Caswell's position. Along the way they encountered two supply wagons and twenty cattle destined for the American camp, and thus managed to gain much needed supplies. It was a stroke of good fortune for an army that had not found much to cheer them.[62]

How Caswell learned that the Loyalists had crossed above him is unknown, but he quickly pulled up stakes and retreated south on the Negro Head Point Road towards Moores Creek, where Lillington's force had already arrived on the afternoon of the 26th. Moores Creek was now the last obstacle between the Loyalist army and Wilmington.

Thomas Corbett's home and grounds, located near the ferry at modern Ivanhoe, suffered as the armies moved through. His apple, peach, and plumb trees were damaged, as was a potato patch. Corbett also lost kettles, pewter plates, and a punch bowl. The soldiers took fence rails from his farm and neighboring homes for firewood.[63]

On the night of the 25th the Loyalists camped at James Rogers' sawmill as the main force and McLeod's flanking party reunited. Here they took twenty-four prisoners from an American patrol sent out to spy on them. On the morning of the 26th they left for Moores Creek from Rogers' mill.[64]

Later that day they came to Caswell's old camp site, where they found forage, hogs, and other supplies. They also captured six prisoners who had been cutting down the bridges to delay their march. A "heavie raine" fell this day, making the trek miserable. That night the army camped at Colvin's Creek, seven miles from the Moores Creek bridge.[65]

After settling into their camp, the Loyalist officers convened a meeting, having learned that Caswell's force was in front of them at Moores Creek. McDonald did not attend this council "by reason of his having contracted a cold brought on by sleeping in the damp night air" and went to the home of John Colvin to rest. It is hard to imagine MacDonald would miss this crucial meeting, but an eyewitness reported it. During the council of officers it was decided to send James Hepburn with a message to Caswell.[66]

The Colvin home stood about three miles from modern Atkinson, near the old Caswell Church in Sampson County, along Slocumb Trail (then the Negro Head Point Road). The family was not home, having gone to visit relatives, but the servants were. Colvin was active in local politics and had served on the Wilmington Committee of Safety.[67]

Upon arriving at Moores Creek earlier that day, Caswell's force set up camp on the west side of the creek, above the bridge. The location of this campsite remains unknown, and most likely lies outside the boundaries of the present National Battlefield. Lillington's forces occupied the east bank, and continued work on their defenses. Wagons, tents, and supplies filled the encampment area.[68]

There has been considerable debate concerning who actually commanded the American forces. Gen. James Moore was in overall command, but Lillington and Caswell were on the field when the attack came. Both men were colonels, and their commissions dated the same day, so they were equals. Lillington, however, was in his home district, while Caswell's force had traveled from New Bern.

Caswell received considerable publicity after the fight, including from General Moore and the North Carolina Congress. Historical records are not clear on the issue, and it remains unresolved whether Caswell and Lillington commanded jointly, whether one was in overall charge, or even what Moore's intentions were when he issued orders for the two forces to link up.

Among the American militia were drummers and fifers, key people in relaying messages on the battlefield. Two cannons under Captain John Vance made their position a formidable one. The guns included a Dutch three pounder named "Mother Covington" and a smaller swivel gun nicknamed, "Mother Covington's Daughter." The three pounder was a big morale booster for the defenders, and it could fire a solid shot or shrapnel, with lots of musket balls that would do terrible damage. The swivel gun was a small, mobile gun mounted on a post, that could be easily moved and loaded by the men.[69]

The troops had rations of pork, bacon, and cornmeal that evening. Within the earthworks the men were cleaning weapons, checking their ammunition, and making last minute preparations. Militiaman James Isaac and his comrades shook hands and pledged to defend the bridge or die trying.[70]

Hurrying towards the American camp was General MacDonald's secretary, James Hepburn, with a message for Col. Caswell. Although MacDonald had not attended the conference with his officers, the message attempted to continue his strategy of avoiding battle and getting the army to Wilmington intact. Hepburn was a lawyer from Cross Creek and had been a liaison between the Loyalists of the interior and Governor Martin over the preceding winter. After Moores Creek he was captured, later paroled, and joined British forces in New York. Following the war he moved to the Bahamas.[71]

That evening Hepburn arrived at Caswell's camp with the message from McDonald. He was taken before Caswell and presented his note. The ultimatum

Old Mother Covington (left), and her swivel gun daughter (right).

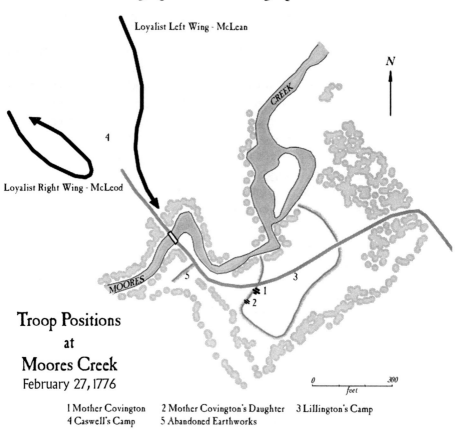

Troop Positions
at
Moores Creek
February 27, 1776

0   300
feet

1 Mother Covington   2 Mother Covington's Daughter   3 Lillington's Camp
4 Caswell's Camp   5 Abandoned Earthworks

After NPS   John Robertson, 2008

urged the militia to lay down their arms and join the King's forces. Refusal meant that McDonald would have no choice but to "conquer, and subdue you." Caswell politely declined and sent Hepburn on his way. As with the earlier exchanges, both sides maintained that they were in the right, and represented the true government, claiming legitimacy for their cause, and insisting they were defending the rights of the citizens.

    While in Caswell's camp, Hepburn made some important observations. First, he did not note any artillery. Unknown to him, however, was the fact that there were many more soldiers and two guns beyond his vision on the other side of the creek. More importantly, Hepburn noted that the militia was camped on the same side of the creek, with the bridge behind them. Thus Caswell was not using the creek for defense. It was instead an obstacle to him, as it blocked any chance for a quick retreat. In front of their camp the Americans had no defenses.[72]

    In the meantime the Americans had been busy preparing a near perfect defensive position on the other side of the creek. They enclosed their entire campsite with earthworks, and those facing the bridge were strongest. Here the defenses included a ditch two feet deep, and an earthen wall four feet high and about seven feet wide. It provided good protection to anyone hiding within the defensive trench. The two artillery pieces were placed to fire on the bridge.[73]

Earlier that day Lillington's men had begun a trench close to the bridge, but soon abandoned it for the higher ground farther back. It is not recorded why they did so. Perhaps the ground was too wet near the creek due to recent rains, but it would serve a useful purpose in a few hours.[74]

Another visitor also arrived in Caswell's camp. That night Felix Kenan, once the sheriff of Duplin County and now a soldier under MacDonald, deserted, and told Caswell that the Loyalists would attack at dawn. Thus Caswell and Lillington's forces were on alert, knowing that the attack would come in the morning. This was crucial, since the Loyalists were unaware that they could not surprise the Whigs.[75]

With an attack clearly coming, Caswell pulled his men back across the creek and united them with Lillington's within the well-built earthworks. In addition, they pulled up the planks from the bridge, greased the girders with soft soap and tallow, and placed guards there to watch for the Loyalist approach.[76]

The position could not have been more appealing to a defender. The Loyalists would have to cross the bridge and then charge up a narrow road into the front of the earthworks. In the words of one soldier, "we had erected strong breastworks having previous taken up the planks from half of the bridge"[77]

When Hepburn returned to MacDonald's camp six miles away at Colvin's home, a heated debate ensued among the officers. It is unknown if MacDonald attended this conference, but if he did he did not say much. Hepburn himself gave his opinion that the army should attack before Caswell got away or destroyed the bridge. Here a series of critical breakdowns began for the Loyalist army. Feeling unwell, MacDonald relinquished command to Donald MacLeod. Nearly seventy years old and on the march for a week in poor weather, the stress of the campaign was getting to him.[78]

The change in leadership now disrupted the army's movement. A change of command in the midst of a campaign is usually not good. One observer wrote that MacDonald "could not stir from his bed or even give the least advice." It was not a good situation for an army that faced a critical decision.[79]

The army left that night, "among the darkest that could be seen." The troops began to march at 1 am, now down to about 900 men. Along the way they had to pass through "a very bad swamp" which " took us a good deal of time to pass." The creek was "raised above its ordinary bounds" by heavy rain. As many of the men were unfamiliar with the area, many got a "severe drenching." It must have been miserable on a cold February night. It took five hours to march those six miles, and it was almost "break of day" when they finally approached Caswell's campsite.[80]

Upon arriving they separated into two groups to attack the camp. Captain Donald McLeod took the right wing himself, while Colonel Thomas Rutherford and Captain Alexander McLean led the left. Captain McLeod and his men saw fires burning in the distance. He halted his detachment and scouted ahead to investigate.

McLeod soon reported back with the news that the Americans had left, and cut the bridge down. With a group of officers, McLeod and the commanders of the Right Wing agreed that the Americans must have retreated during the night, and they should now fall back to inform General MacDonald of the new development. The troops were promptly marched back to a house a short distance in the rear until the other division came back. This may have been the home of James Rogers, who lived near Moores Creek Bridge and claimed that McLeod stopped at his home the night before the battle. As the men retired to the rear to take cover in the woods, they passed the word that in the event of an attack, their rallying cry would be "King George and Broadswords!"[81]

At this point another critical breakdown occurred, as things began to spiral out of control for the Loyalists. In the dark, separated, and without the means to communicate, the two wings went in different directions. While the right wing fell back to regroup in the woodline and await further orders, the left arrived at the bridge ready to attack.

As one participant noted, the "left wing did not know that the right wing had marched back." Literally the right hand did not know what the left hand was doing, and there was no way for the two elements to communicate now.

The left wing had entered Caswell's old campsite from the other side, and managed to advance all the way down to the bridge. McLean with some of his men accidentally came to the span. Ahead in the distance they could see the silhouette of an American sentry.

The sentry challenged McLean, who answered he was a friend. "A friend of whom?" shot back the guard, to which McLean answered "the King." At that point the sentry squatted down. This should have been sign that something was not right, but McLean was not sure that some of his own people had not crossed the creek and were on the other side.

McLean next called out a question in Gaelic (the native Scottish language), which went unanswered. At that point, McLean raised his musket and fired, and ordered those with him to do the same.[82]

When McLean met the sentry, "at whom he imprudently discharged his piece," he alerted the entire American camp with the firing. It also drew the attention of the Loyalist's right wing, now formed farther back up the road. Confused, the men "could not conceive of what it meant," and McLeod quickly rushed down from the rear to investigate.

A reconstruction of the stripped bridge at Moores Creek National Battlefield.

Here events took on a life of their own, and the situation got out of control. Excited, and still in the dark, everyone now thought that the order for attack had been given, which was "three cheers the Drum to beat the Pipes to play."[83]

It takes more time to describe the events than it did for them to unfold, and surely Campbell and McLeod acted on instinct and adrenaline that morning. Quickly McLeod and McLean consulted and decided to send Captain John Campbell's' force of eighty broadswordmen over on the girders of the bridge. One participant noted that it "did not occur to Capt McLeod that they had an ambuscade or that they had time to raise entrenchments."[84]

Thirteen year old Hugh McDonald recalled the assault party and his description did not inspire confidence. "In our Tory party was a Captain, John Campbell...who commanded Broad-swordmen, consisting principally of McRae's strong, resolute men, ignorant untutored and untrained to the use of arms, but every one of that company had his broad-sword drawn and marched in front..." They may have been brave, but they were about to attempt something foolish.[85]

The assault party consisted of broadswordmen who marched up to the bridge in two columns, McLeod on the left and Campbell on the right. They shouted their battle cry, "King George and Broadswords!" as they stepped up to the greased girders. At the bridge each officer took a sleeper and made his slow way across, using the points of their swords to find purchase on the slippery runners. They were followed by the men behind them. The rest of the Loyalist troops converged on the bridge. Donald Morrison was among that group waiting to cross, carrying their battle flag.[86]

Once on the other side, the Loyalists broke into a charge. Still too dark to see clearly, they did not know what waited for them around the bend. From the bridge's eastern side to the American earthworks is a distance of about 120 yards, out of effective musket range but easily covered by artillery.

Moreover, with the creek to their left and swampy ground to their right, the attackers were forced to remain in a small tight group as they advanced. Where the road curves, at about thirty yards from the earthworks, Caswell gave the order to fire. Rifles, muskets, and the two artillery pieces opened fire at point blank range. The Loyalists never stood a chance.

An observer noted that McLeod "said 'Come on my boys, the day is our own' when he was instantly shot down, and all those on the sleepers coming over were fired upon and shot, falling off into the creek. That they attempted three times to come over, but all being killed who came on the sleepers, they did not attempt it a fourth time." McLeod fell, hit by twenty-four balls. Col. James Moore wrote of McLeod that "he was a brave soldier and would have done honor to a good cause."[87]

An American militiaman observed that the Loyalists attempted to cross "on the sleepers of the bridge" and that "artillery...swept the Tories off the bridge. Many of their officers were killed on the Bridge and fell in the water."[88]

A diorama depiction of the Highlanders' suicidal charge at Moores Creek.

Militia gunners fire Old Mother Covington into the charging Scots.

The abandoned earthwork near the bridge may have inadvertently inspired their confidence as the Loyalists gained the east bank. Colonel Moore wrote that, "finding a small entrenchment next the Bridge, on our side empty, concluded that our people had abandoned their post, and in the most furious manner advanced within thirty paces of our breastworks and artillery, where they met a very proper reception."[89]

Militiaman Richard Harrell described what he witnessed, placing himself in the third person:

"When they first came in sight, advancing through the open pine woods on the long slope of descending ground, their officers well dressed in gay regimentals, banners and plumes waving in the breeze, and all marching in good order, but with quick step, to the sound of their pibrochs [bagpipes], while the thrilling notes of the bugle were heard in the distance, they made quite a formidable appearance and he felt a good deal of trepidation. He had never before heard the din of war, nor seen an army ready to engage in the work of wholesale destruction. He had never been called to shoot down his fellow men, some of them his neighbors and acquaintances, nor had he ever seen them shot down by scores at a time; and no wonder if his nerves were a little excited. The firing commenced with the small arms, and continued for a round or two; but...he could neither load nor fire with a very steady hand. They had two pieces of artillery, one of which had by some means or other, got the sobriquet of MOTHER COVINGTON, and for that or some other reason, was rather a

favorite with the men. Not wishing to act cowardly, or be suspect of doing so, he kept trying to do his part, but was all the time wishing most heartily he could hear what Old Mother Covington had to say. At last she let out, and with terrible effect. From that moment, he said, his fear was all gone, and he could load and fire with as much composure, as if he had been shooting squirrels."[90]

American accounts note that nearly everyone who crossed the dismantled bridge was killed or wounded. Col. Donald McLeod, Capt. John Campbell, and privates Duncan McCrary, William Stewart, Kenneth Murchison, Laughlin Bethune, Murdock McRae, Alexander Campbell, and John McArthur, were all known to have gotten over the bridge. Of this list, the last three were captured and taken to Wilmington. A few managed to scramble back to the other side of the creek and join the retreat.[91]

Duncan McCrary, mentioned above, was hit with seven shot and made prisoner. He spent the next two years recovering from his wounds, and was unable to work again. After the war he moved to England. His is the only account by a survivor of the bridge crossing.[92]

Laughlin Bethune, who was wounded on the bridge, managed to recross and escape. He died a few days later. Alexander Campbell, also wounded on the bridge, was captured and taken to Wilmington, where he died a week later.

The earthworks where Caswell and Lillington positioned their militiamen at Moores Creek.

William Stewart, wounded on the bridge, recrossed and escaped. He was left in a home in Duplin County, and died there ten days later. Kenneth Murchison, also wounded on the bridge, recrossed but was captured. He also died soon afterward.[93]

Kenneth Stewart fought at Moores Creek with his two brothers and his father, a surgeon. His father and one brother were killed, and Kenneth spent time in prison in Philadelphia. He managed to escape to British-held New York.[94]

Colonel James Moore (who was not present but arrived soon after) wrote to Cornelius Harnett of the "most furious manner" in which the Loyalists charged. Immediately the Loyalist army retreated from the bridge. One participant wrote that, "most of the country born began to run away and could not be made to stand their ground."[95]

In the quick action Private Edmund Pearce's gun burst, a dangerous accident that left him unwounded. After firing, the Americans charged over the earthworks and the few surviving Loyalists on that side of the creek scrambled to get back over to the west bank and rejoin their comrades. Neil Colbreath was not fast enough, and an American militiaman named Little caught him just short of the bridge. They engaged in a brief hand to hand fight until Little bit Colbreath on his legs and lips. The Highlander surrendered and was taken prisoner.[96]

Standing side by side in the trench were friends Ben Lanier and Abraham Newkirk, both of the Watha District. The men both fired and clearly hit McLeod in the open ground in front of them. After the Loyalists retreated they both raced over the earthworks towards McLeod's body. Newkirk won the race and claimed the officer's watch. Newkirk's sword is currently on display in the museum at Moores Creek National Battlefield.[97]

It was a short and stunning victory. Most accounts reckon that it all happened in less than three minutes. Not only was it fast, but it was also very lopsided. Estimates of Loyalist killed and wounded range from thirty to fifty. Only two Americans were lost, one killed and one wounded. The sole American fatality, twenty year old John Grady, was the first North Carolinian to die in the American Revolution. One soldier wrote that, "There was but one of our men killed and he was unfortunately shot in the back of the head." Apparently John Grady was shot while standing on the earthworks to take better aim.[98]

The wounded man may be James Foy, a wealthy plantation owner who lived near the modern town of Jacksonville (who owned the land that is now Poplar Grove Plantation). According to testimony given by later descendents Foy was wounded in the wrist. He also fought at Kings Mountain, Cowpens, and Guilford Courthouse.[99]

Another candidate for the wounded man is Jesse Goodwin, who in April was receiving compensation for wounds he received while serving in the militia. The identity of the wounded man at Moores Creek may never be known.[100]

It was an unfortunate, and unwise, decision by McLeod to charge over the bridge. That spur of the moment decision affected events for the next few years in North Carolina. The Loyalists would get a second chance, but the situation was never more favorable for solid British support. By nipping the rebellion in the bud in 1776, the British and Loyalists could probably have retaken the colony. Everything that happened afterwards hinged on that charge at Moores Creek.

Col. James Moore and his troops arrived at Dollison's Landing on the Cape Fear the night before the battle. Delays forced him to spend the night there, and march for Moores Creek the next morning. He arrived only a few hours after the battle ended.[101]

On the morning of the battle, Governor Martin, aboard the *Cruzier*, was anchored off Wilmington awaiting the arrival of McDonald's Loyalists. While there, he demanded supplies of flour and beef from the town. The Committee of Safety refused, complaining that Martin's naval forces had been harassing the local population: "property of the inhabitants had been seized...slaves seized, live stock killed and property plundered."[102]

Joseph Foy, whose ancestor James may have been wounded at Moores Creek.

After the battle, as the defeated and disorganized remnants of the Loyalist army fled back to their previous night's campsite, terror set in. Panic is contagious in an army and hard to stop. Upon returning to their campsite, the Loyalists found only two barrels of flour in camp, a sign of their desperate situation. The men could not be kept together, and "officers had no Authority over the men." A council proposed retiring to Cross Creek to wait word from Governor Martin.[103]

The "Country bourn would not proceed a foot further" and in vain officers tried to keep order. Upon arriving back at their camp, the Highlanders found that the former Regulators got there "long before" and many had taken the wagons. MacDonald was in a hut and taken to a house where he was left, too sick to travel. The remnants of the army got to Corbett's Ferry that evening, only to find no boats to cross with. The boat sunk at Devanes (where McLean had crossed) had been sunk so the enemy could not come behind them. The retreat continued to Seven Runs, forty miles from Corbett's Ferry and well off course for Cross Creek. On the morning of the 30th they reached the Cape Fear River opposite Cross Creek. They learned the crossing was guarded, so the Loyalists moved north to the next crossing point, at Smith's Ferry. Here some managed to get across, but the bulk were captured.[104]

MacDonald was captured at Colvin's by the pursuing Americans. One account says he was "drawn out of a lurking hole, where he had been concealed by a free negro." Another that he was "dragged from his sickbed." Wagon master Longfield Cox took MacDonald's horse, saddle, pistols, and sword. The General was taken to Halifax and later Philadelphia.[105]

Although Moores Creek was a small battle and the Loyalist army still had over 800 fighting men, the rout had taken its toll on their morale. One Revolutionary War soldier wrote that "He who has never seen the effect of a panic upon a multitude can have but an imperfect idea of such a thing. The best-disciplined troops have been enervated and made cowards by it. Armies have been routed by it even where no enemy appeared to furnish an excuse. Like electricity it operates instantly and...it is irresistible where it touches."[106]

The bulk of the Loyalists fled back towards Cross Creek, others made their way to Fort Johnston to join up with the British, and still others separated and hid in the woods or tried, singly or in small groups, to make it back to their homes.

A great exodus took place as Loyalists fled, some to as far as Florida or New York. James Cotton, who we met earlier from Anson County, hid for six months after the defeat. Joseph Mercer was able to get to a British warship in the Cape Fear. Daniel Ray hid for four years, and joined the British when they arrived in South Carolina in 1780. For those forced to hide away from home, everything in their life was turned to chaos: personal finances and property. It is difficult to imagine traveling through hostile territory with few roads, crossing rivers and doing it with little money and few extra clothes.[107]

A Brown Bess musket. More than 1,000 of them were captured after the battle at Moores Creek.

Militia from Guilford and Surry Counties, advancing down behind the Loyalists from Cross Creek, took many prisoners in the days and weeks after the battle. There was literally no where to run, and no where to hide.[108]

All told, the Americans captured a cache of supplies that was staggering: 1,850 firearms, hundreds of shot bags and cartridge boxes, 150 swords and dirks, two medicine chests, thirteen wagons with their teams of horses, and 15,000 pounds sterling. It was a tremendous loss to the Loyalists, especially given the difficulty with which the supplies had been assembled in the first place. Many families contributed clothing, food, animals, weapons, and supplies, only to see them disappear. It may seem odd that so many firearms were taken in the battle's aftermath given the shortage beforehand. Most of these were probably seized from Loyalist homes as the Americans swept through the region to disarm them that spring.[109]

One Loyalist described his ordeal at Cross Creek. He writes they were "robbed of all our horses and strictly searched for secreted arms powder [gunpowder] or any papers." They were fed tainted pork and bad water, crammed into small rooms without beds or any other necessaries, and led through the American camp where they were met with "insults and epithets." Their guards "seemed to feel as little for us as carters commonly do for the unfortunate animals they become masters of."[110]

At Smith's Ferry (also known as Devo's Ferry), on the Cape Fear River near Averasboro, the bulk of the Loyalists were surrounded and captured. Here about five hundred were taken by the American militia. Among the Whig officers who led the militia here was Nathaniel Rochester, who later founded the city of Rochester, NY.[111]

He wrote, "In disarming the prisoners at Devo's Ferry, the Scotch gave up their dirks with much reluctance, these having as they said been handed down from father to son for many generations." For many it would only be the first such depredation.[112]

Thirteen year old Hugh McDonald, who survived the assault at the bridge, wrote "The surviving party of the company retreated...about eight miles back to camp, where they found General MacDonald asleep in his tent, to whom their defeat was a melancholy story, and not being willing to try a second attack, we retreated to Smith's Ferry."[113]

As the Loyalists were captured and disarmed at Smith's Ferry, Malcolm Morrison tried to hide a powder horn in the seat of Hugh McDonald's buckskin breeches. In disarming and searching them, their guards discovered the hidden powder. The site of Smith's Ferry was fought over in March 1865 during the battle of Averasboro, a delaying action as outnumbered Confederates tried to slow down Sherman's Union army.[114]

It must have been a miserable march back to Cross Creek, low on supplies, wounded men struggling to keep up, and all the while not knowing what was in store when they finally arrived. The four Field brothers, Robert, William, Joseph, and Jeremiah, were all taken prisoner in the aftermath, and all

Halifax jail, where prisoners from Moores Creek were held.

were banished from North Carolina. After the war Robert's wife Ann petitioned the state for their land, and after two attempts, it was granted.[115]

Moores Creek was the first major American victory of the Revolutionary War in the South. It was important because afterwards North Carolina was in common cause with the northern colonies; the war was spreading and a feeling of unity was slowly taking root. The rebellion was suddenly a reality, and it was no longer just a New England phenomenon but now a colony-wide, or Continental as they would have said, conflict.

Moores Creek also spotlights an important issue that plagued both sides throughout the war: prisoners. The Whig militia rounded up hundreds of men in the wake of the battle, and authorities did not know quite what to do with them. There was no official break or state of war, yet these men were clearly dangerous to their cause and could not be simply let go. Moores Creek brought in the first large number of prisoners that either side would have to deal with during the Revolutionary War.

The common soldiers were paroled, meaning they signed an agreement to not fight until officially exchanged. At the time of their exchange, they were free to go. This was a convenient and efficient way to deal with prisoners. Officers, however, received a different treatment.

They were first taken to Halifax, the temporary capital of the state. Next the most dangerous of them were sent on to Philadelphia, to be the concern of the Continental Congress. Some were still there a year later. Many of these prisoners were eventually exchanged. As the first major battle that produced a sizable number of prisoners, dealing with them became a pressing issue, and one that the Americans were unprepared for. Sending prisoners to the Continental Congress was a unique solution, one that did not happen with captives from any other battle of the war.[116]

With a war to run and heated political debates about independence to deal with, Congress had little time to deal with prisoners from rural North Carolina. They lingered in a kind of legal limbo for several years. Some prisoners were transferred to other locations, like Baltimore and Frederick, Maryland, Reading and Philadelphia, Pennsylvania, or even the backcountry settlements of Staunton, Virginia and Sharpsburg, Maryland. Many were released or exchanged by the middle of the war, by which point their personal affairs had fallen into ruin.[117]

The sheer number of prisoners put a strain on North Carolina's legal system. Most jails in the eastern counties were small structures and were now overflowing with captured Loyalists. One official from Halifax complained to the state government that they had to be moved, as the volume of prisoners interrupted normal court operations and hindered regular legal proceedings, saying that they had "scoundrels enough of our own."[118]

The North Carolina Provisional Government created four classes of prisoners. First, those who had served in Congress; second, those who had taken a Test Oath; third those who had taken up arms; and lastly, a catch all category, "prisoners under suspicious circumstances."[119]

One prisoner wrote that they were "...dragged through the country in triumph, in the most distressed miserable condition, destitute even of common necessaries, and were at last distributed in prisons and wretched places of restraint..." In Philadelphia General MacDonald, who was "near seventy years of age...was most ignominiously and inhumanly treated, being rigidly and cruelly confined in a closed room, secured with iron doors and bars, along with nine gentlemen besides, in the most sultry weather, and hot climate, during the summer."[120]

In late May a frustrated MacDonald wrote to the Congress, "what crime has he since been guilty of, deserving his being recommitted to the jail of Philadelphia, without his bedding or baggage, and his sword and servants detained from him...The other gentlemen prisoners are in great want for their blankets and other necessities."[121]

MacDonald was eventually exchanged in December, along with General Augustine Prescott, for two American Generals: John Sullivan and Adam Stephens. He rejoined British forces in New York and remained there until

1780, when he returned to North Carolina with Cornwallis' army. After the war he returned to London, spending his time assisting other exiled Loyalists with their claims for losses.[122]

Allan MacDonald wrote that they were sent from "Jail to jail," unsure of their fate. In the meantime family and friends knew nothing of their whereabouts, and their personal affairs fell into ruin. One son, Alexander had also been captured, and was imprisoned with his father. Another son, James, escaped from Moores Creek.[123]

Flora was left on their farm while Allan spent time in jails in North Carolina and Pennsylvania. In 1777 the state confiscated their property, and her family was harassed wherever they went. In 1779 Flora took her family and left for New York, where she was reunited with her husband. They then returned to Scotland, after a brief stint in Nova Scotia, having spent only a few turbulent years in America.[124]

Alexander Morrison reported that while he was held as a prisoner for these years, his family back in North Carolina suffered. Militia raided their farm and took nearly all their food.[125]

Mary McCaskle, whose husband Murdo was a captain under MacDonald, also suffered in the battle's aftermath. A few days after the battle she delivered a child, and wrote that, "when confined to her bed was stripped by the rebellious robbers of all her household furniture, shopgoods, and even the bed whereon she lay, by means of which she had nearly lost her life..." Later her husband died, and in "the greatest poverty and distress" she fled to Charleston later in the war to join the British garrison there.[126]

Many who fled from Moores Creek hid in the woods and swamps, some for years, avoiding American patrols. Others, seeing that the Americans were firmly in control of the state, fled to join British forces in the north. Many made their way to Philadelphia which the British occupied in the late summer of 1777. Loyalist Captain Daniel Ray hid in North Carolina's swamps for four years in the aftermath, finally emerging when the British arrived.[127]

Governor Josiah Martin used his influence to ensure that those held captive were still paid, noting that their service was ongoing despite being held prisoner and not actively serving. Most still needed to file claims for losses and reimbursement after the war.[128]

In the meantime, other events of importance were transpiring. On April 4th the Provincial Congress abolished district Committees of Safety, replacing them with a Provincial Council and a Council of Safety for whole state. At the same time, the power of local Committee of Safeties, like those of Wilmington and Brunswick County, began to fade. Power was being concentrated in the state as efforts to gear up for war were now in full swing.[129]

On March 1st two Cape Fear leaders received promotions for their role in securing the region. Col. James Moore and Col. Robert Howe were both promoted to the rank of Brigadier General.[130]

Many other leaders, men of importance at the local level, fought at Moores Creek or otherwise contributed to its outcome. Thomas Hicks, who fought at Brunswick Town when the Spanish attacked in 1748, and also served in the Colonial Assembly, fought at he creek with the Duplin County militia. Maj. James Kenan, sheriff of New Hanover County at age twenty-two, and member of the Colonial Assembly and Provincial Congress did as well. Kenan later served in the North Carolina Senate and at the state's Constitutional Convention in 1789.[131]

Loyalist Duncan McNicol escaped from Moores Creek and made his way down to Brunswick where he was able to flag down the *Scorpion* and get onboard. He informed Martin of the disaster, the first official confirmation of what had transpired. McNicol wrote of the treatment of the prisoners taken after the battle that, "such treatment of prisoners of war I never saw or heard of."[132]

Governor Martin tried to hide his disappointment in the fiasco, writing that it was only a "little check" and that he doubted it "will have any extensive ill consequences." He could not have been more wrong. Moores Creek inspired the Americans to take bolder steps to suppress Loyalists, and forced those willing to fight for the British into hiding.[133]

The event also made it clear to the Revolutionaries that they had to gear up for a military conflict. North Carolina established gunworks in each region of the state to produce arms. In April the state authorized a "public Gun works, near the Black River in the upper part of New Hanover County."[134]

The gunworks was run by Richard Herring, John Devane (who fought at Moores Creek), and James White. The state gave startup funds for the operation, and the owners recruited local men to work it. Its precise location is unknown, though it was thought to be near the bridge over the Black River at Clear Run in Sampson County. Since 1,000 Pounds of public money was committed to start it up, the state insisted that muskets be produced and sold to the state for under five pounds each. It produced 100 muskets and bayonets, three rifles, and six guns before Loyalists destroyed it.[135]

Small-scale industries sprung up all over eastern North Carolina to meet the demand for war material. In Halifax workers produced uniforms, blacksmiths repaired wagons, and other craftsmen labored to keep up with the soaring demand for tools, weapons, and supplies.[136]

It has been a persistent inaccuracy that 1,000 American militia defeated 1,600 Loyalists at Moores Creek. The mistake probably takes root from MacDonald's first report of his numbers in Cross Creek before starting the march. While the army began with about 1,600, by the time they reached Moores Creek desertion had reduced their strength by half, down to about 900.

It appears that low supplies, poor weather, lack of weapons, and uncertainty about their mission all contributed to a lack of confidence.

Not all the Loyalist forces had joined General MacDonald on his march. About one hundred under Col. Reid and Capt. Walter Cunningham arrived at Cross Creek after the army departed. Upon hearing news of the defeat, all but fourteen men decided to return home. The remainder moved on hoping to catch up with MacDonald.

Reid's force came upon a group of Whig militia in a mill and captured them, giving the impression he had a larger force. With their prisoners the small group of Loyalists made their way south, eventually reaching Fort Johnston and getting on board British ships in the river.[137]

The attack from above Wilmington had been foiled at Moores Creek, but a greater threat remained from below, as the British fleet began to arrive in the Cape Fear River. This invasion brought seventy warships and several thousand British troops, professionals who were well trained and armed, unlike the Loyalists who had fought at Moores Creek.

Chapter 5
British on the Cape Fear

lthough the Loyalist tide had crested and receded at Moores Creek, the British were unaware of this until they finally arrived in the Cape Fear. As the Loyalists were dispersed in the interior, the British fleet began drifting into the river, and it seemed likely that there would be other battles fought for control of Wilmington.

In March, about twenty British ships were in the river, waiting for the fleet's arrival. Captain John Abraham Collett, mapmaker and former commander of Fort Johnston, wanted revenge for the loss of his fort. He sent troops ashore to burn Bellfont in Brunswick, home of Col. William Dry, as well as William Hoopers' new home, three miles below Wilmington. In fact, Hooper escaped at the last minute, as the warship was not spotted until it was only one hundred yards away.[1]

When the rest of the British fleet finally arrived in the Cape Fear River, it was too late. The Loyalist army had been defeated and scattered in the aftermath of Moores Creek. Some refugees from the army did manage to make their way to Fort Johnston where they joined British forces, but as news of the disaster reached Martin and British commanders, they realized they had few options left on the Cape Fear.[2]

American militia redeployed after Moores Creek, with various groups moving through the southeastern part of the state rounding up suspected

Loyalists. Some moved down towards South Carolina and the Pee Dee River, Lumber River, and Drowning Creek, with still others scouring out the Scottish regions of Cumberland County. Their operations were to "disarm and disperse the Tories," as one participant wrote. In that region "the Tories were numerous and active."[3]

In the meantime other militia marched through Moore, Cumberland, and Richmond Counties to "protect the state from the marauding parties of the... tories..." On March 10th one observer wrote that "Parties of Men are dispersed all over the Colony, apprehending all suspected persons, and disarming all Highlanders and Regulators that were put to rout in the last battle."[4]

General Sir Henry Clinton

Still other units guarded the Cape Fear, setting up camps across the area at Swan's Point, Captains Mills, Brunswick Town, Orton Mill, and Lockwoods Folly. These troops patrolled "up and down the Cape Fear river" to prevent the British from landing.[5]

That same month North Carolina began recruiting and organizing its next three Continental Regiments, the 3rd, 4th, and 5th. All were organized in Wilmington. Men of the 3rd North Carolina were recruited in Wilmington, Halifax, Edenton, and Hillsboro. The 4th North Carolina had men from Wilmington, with some recruits coming from Salisbury and Edenton. The 5th Regiment consisted of soldiers from New Hanover County, New Bern, Edenton, and Hillsboro. The town was busy with officers enlisting the men, supplies being stockpiled, and troops drilling.[6]

Officers gathered material like oznaburg, checked cloth, and coarse linen for their men's uniforms. Three tons of gunpowder arrived, and so did chests of medicine.[7]

The men built barracks to house the several thousand troops now arriving, and one stood on modern Front Street, between Orange and Ann Streets. They also constructed a magazine for storing ammunition, protecting several tons of powder, as well as lead musket balls, cannon balls, and cartridge paper. Barrels of pork and beef, as well as corn and flour, arrived for rations. Nine pounder and six pounder cannons bolstered the city's earthen defenses.[8]

Despite the buildup, efforts to supply all the men adequately fell short. One officer noted that the soldiers were "badly Armed and many of the soldiers without Arms."[9]

Also on March 10th a British force of one officer and eleven men from the *Cruzier* tried to land and destroy what was left of Fort Johnston. The remains of the fort were used by the militia to harass and fire on the British warships. American troops in the fort easily drove them off.

More British ships arrived on the 12th, and a few days later Sir Henry Clinton arrived, but he still had to wait for the bulk of the flotilla and its overall commander, Sir Peter Parker. Clinton wrote, "There I continued for above a Month, sometimes on Board, sometimes on shore, casting an anxious Eye every day towards the Cape..." Clinton passed the time by noting the plants of the area and its wildlife, like hawks and eagles. He observed that, "Of all the countries for climate I ever visited, nothing can equal this. As the seasons advance, it must be intolerable."[10]

Some Loyalists refugees, survivors of the rout at Moores Creek, did manage to make their way to the river, evading American patrols, and joining the fleet. Others who were not at Moores Creek, coming from Cross Creek and other interior settlements, came too.

A large number of local slaves escaped from plantations to join them. Local slaves took advantage of the fleet's arrival to take their chances with the British. Throughout the war British commanders actively recruited slaves and

Wilmington slave Thomas Peters (right), opted to join Clinton's Black Pioneer Brigade (left) to earn his freedom with the British. He eventually went on to help found the African nation of Sierra Leone.

encouraged them to run away. Knowing they would probably see no
improvement if the Americans won, many slaves served with the British,
although some served with the Americans as well.

With them General Clinton formed a "Black Pioneer Brigade" under the
command of Lieutenant George Martin of the Royal Marines. The pioneers
performed manual labor like building roads and bridges, unloading supplies,
laying out campsites, gathering firewood, and building fortifications. Offered
their freedom, this tactic was used throughout the war, quite successfully, by
British commanders. More than once local slaves provided intelligence,
supplies, and labor to British forces during the war. Many, like John Porey, fled
to the British on the Cape Fear in 1776 and served with them through the rest of
the war, seeing action in New York, New Jersey, and Southern battles.

Clinton's orders stipulated that the men were to be "decently clothed"
and emphasized that the officers were to "treat these people with tenderness &
humanity." The volunteers were to take an oath to "cheerfully obey all such
directions" in their service to His Majesty.

Among the most famous to join was Thomas Peters, owned by William
Campbell of Wilmington's Committee of Safety. Tall, strong, and dark skinned,
Peters had been kidnapped from West Africa in his youth. The thirty-eight year
old slave made his escape and joined the Black Pioneer Brigade when the British
arrived on the Cape Fear. He served through the rest of the war, rising to the
rank of sergeant, and was wounded twice. Eventually his wife Sally and his
children were able to join him.

After the war he and his family fled with the British to Nova Scotia.
There he assumed leadership of a community of former slaves. In Canada they
received poor quality land, so he traveled to England to argue their case for
better land. Peters met with British leaders, who agreed to allow him to take
more than one thousand followers to Sierra Leone, where they established a
colony.

The Black Pioneers moved with the British forces after they departed the
Cape Fear, and traveled to New York that summer. There they were joined by
runaway slaves from New York and New Jersey. The Pioneers were later
stationed in other places occupied by the British, like Providence, Rhode Island
and Philadelphia. The unit returned to the South with British forces in 1780, and
would again enter the Cape Fear region in 1781.[11]

In the meantime, Governor Martin, still onboard a warship in the river,
was getting anxious. His attempted uprising had failed, the British who arrived
seemed unable to gain a foothold on the shore, and it seemed as if he would
never set foot on dry land again. On March 21st, while on board the *Peggy*, he
wrote of his condition, "Consider the wretched state of a Man not of Neptunes

element in the tenth month of his confinement on Board Ship." Since J
had not stood on solid ground.[12]

The effects of Moores Creek were having widespread consequences. On April 4th the Fourth Provincial Congress met in Halifax, the temporary capital of the colony. After debating issues of importance for several days, the assembly passed the Halifax Resolves on the 12th, the most tangible result of Moores Creek.

The Resolves instructed North Carolina's delegates in the Continental Congress, then meeting in Philadelphia, to vote for independence. It was the first colony to do so. The exact wording read: "Resolved, That the delegates for this Colony in the Continental Congress be impowered to concur with the delegates of the other Colonies in declaring Independency."

In the aftermath of Moores Creek, the North Carolinians realized the extent of the planned uprising and the consequences it held. Blood had been shed, and an uprising barely avoided. The time for negotiation was past, the Americans felt they had no choice now but full independence, a final break with England. It is easy to lose sight of the seriousness of this decision.

The Assembly wrote that their "sincere desire to be reconciled to the mother country on constitutional principles, have procured no mitigation of the aforesaid wrongs" and that they now felt that "no hopes remain of obtaining redress."[13]

Furthermore, the King and Parliament, "disregarding their humble petitions for peace, liberty, and safety," were supporting those who were "daily employed in destroying the people and committing the most horrid devastations on the country." Reports at the time referred to the Loyalists as "insurgents" and they were viewed with every imaginable amount of suspicion, fear, and hatred.[14]

The date of the Halifax Resolves, April 12, 1776, is one of the dates on the current state flag of North Carolina. The other, May 20th, 1775, records the Mecklenburg Declaration. Thus while more famous for its Civil War history, the state's official flag recalls its role in the start of the Revolution.

Back along the banks of the Cape Fear, Alexander Lillington, one of the commanders at Moores Creek, was promoted to colonel of the 6th North Carolina Regiment on the 17th. A few days later John Baptista Ashe was appointed brigadier general of the Wilmington District's militia. Efforts were also made to procure more weapons for the growing number of troops.[15]

The Committee of Safety ordered gunsmith Timothy Bloodworth to continue producing weapons, and paid him for work already completed. As with other skilled people like mill owners and ferry operators, his talents exempted him from militia service. He was a prominent politician from upper New Hanover (now Pender) County. Bloodworth served in the colony's General Assembly and on the Wilmington Committee of Safety. He was also treasurer for the Wilmington District and served in the Continental Congress. After the

The Halifax Resolves

The Select Committee taking into Consideration the usurpations and violences attempted and committed by the King and Parlia- ment of Britain against America, and the further Measures to be taken for frustrating the same, and for the better defence of this province reported as follows, to wit,

It appears to your Committee that pursuant to the Plan concerted by the British Ministry for subjugating America, the King and Parliament of Great Britain have usurped a Power over the Persons and Properties of the People unlimited and uncontrouled and disregarding their humble Petitions for Peace, Liberty and safety, have made divers Legislative Acts, denouncing War Famine and every Species of Calamity daily employed in destroying the People and committing the most horrid devastations on the Country. That Governors in different Colonies have declared Protection to Slaves who should imbrue their Hands in the Blood of their Masters. That the Ships belonging to America are declared prizes of War and many of them have been violently seized and confiscated in consequence of which multitudes of the people have been destroyed or from easy Circumstances reduced to the most Lamentable distress.

And whereas the moderation hitherto manifested by the United Colonies and their sincere desire to be reconciled to the motherCountry on Constitutional Principles, have procured no mitigation of the aforesaid Wrongs and usurpations and no hopes remain of obtaining redress by those Means alone which have been hitherto tried, Your Committee are of Opinion that the house should enter into the following Resolve, to wit

Resolved that the delegates for this Colony in the Continental Congress be impowered to concur with the other delegates of the other Colonies in declaring Independency, and forming foreign Alliances, resolving to this Colony the Sole, and Exclusive right of forming a Constitution and Laws for this Colony, and of appointing delegates from time to time (under the direction of a general Representation thereof to meet the delegates of the other Colonies for such purposes as shall be hereafter pointed out.

war Bloodworth served as commissioner of Confiscated Property in 1783, and was also a senator, as well as collector of customs for the port of Wilmington.[16]

At same time, the first of the long-expected British ships arrived in the Cape Fear. Others continued to drift in over the next few days and weeks. They began searching the shore for signs of the Loyalists who were supposed to meet them. Although the Americans had won at Moores Creek, they now faced British warships and thousands of well armed and well trained British troops. This would be the largest military force in the Cape Fear region until the Civil War, ninety years later.

Both sides prepared for a battle that never came. Two British deserters told Colonel James Moore of the English strength. Governor Martin still hoped to use the Loyalists in an attack on the area. By now nearly 2,000 Continental troops and militia were in Wilmington.[17]

On April 29th news of the British fleet's arrival off Cape Fear reached Wilmington. The flotilla consisted of over forty ships, carrying nine regiments of infantry. An observer wrote that, "The Militia, who have been here but a few days discharged, are coming in fast, and who, with the Continental forces already here, will be able to make a good stand."[18]

North Carolinians from across the eastern part of the state responded. On May 3rd, the Provincial Congress ordered 1,500 men drafted from Edenton, New Bern, Halifax, and the Wilmington Districts, to march to Wilmington to meet the invasion. Militia from all across coastal North Carolina was coming to the port city's rescue.[19]

The British did send some parties ashore to skirmish with the Americans. William Ward, a soldier guarding the river, wrote that "a galley, laden with the enemy, was decoyed ashore, & a few of them killed, besides one badly wounded who died next day." Between mid April and the end of May there were ship-to-shore exchanges of fire almost every day up and down the Cape Fear.[20]

That spring slaves continued to flee their plantations and made their way to the ships floating in the river. One ship took thirty-six on board, of which half were women. On another day over twenty fled to the British. While some men served in the Black Pioneer Corps, others joined the Royal Navy. When the British burned Robert Howe's plantation, his slaves helped, although not all fled with the enemy, yet.[21]

On May 3rd Clinton wrote that his army had little chance of success in North Carolina, and that Charleston looked like a better target. The banks of the Cape Fear were lined with American troops watching every move the fleet made. Clinton learned that the earthworks on Sullivan's Island were unfinished and began to consider moving there to attack Charleston. Sir Peter Parker finally arrived that day, after contrary winds had prevented the fleet from entering sooner, with Lord Cornwallis, bringing their total to seventy ships. American observers saw a forest of masts and canvas sail in the river.[22]

On board one of the British warships in the river was a special prisoner, Ethan Allen of Vermont. Allen had helped capture Fort Ticonderoga, New York the year before, leading a group of militia known as the Green Mountain Boys. He was captured in the ill-fated American attack at Montreal in December 1775 and taken to England. The British sent him back with the invasion fleet to be released.[23]

Allen, suffering from poor health, was taken to Halifax, Nova Scotia (an

General Sir Charles Lord Cornwallis

important British naval base, where he was to be hung but was spared) and eventually sent to British-occupied New York. In 1778 he was exchanged and finally rejoined the Americans.[24]

On May 7th, the 15th and 28th British regiments landed, in the words of a British report, "on a Peninsula at the Mouth of the River, but the Enemy not chusing to shew themselves, the General, after reconnoitering the Country, reimbarked them."[25]

A few days later on the 11th British forces raided Brunswick County. Rowing over with muffled oars, they landed at Robert Howe's plantation, Kendal, around two or three in the morning. The force, 900 men of the 33rd, 37th, and 44th Regiments under Lord Charles Cornwallis (who would later return to the Cape Fear), marched on the house. The guards only had time to mount horses and let the cattle out before the British closed in. Some of the Americans skirmished with the British as they came up to the home. "A few Women, who lived in the House, were treated with great Barbarity; one of which was Shot through the Hips, another stabbed with a Bayonet, and a third knocked down with the Butt of a musket." Nothing in the historical records indicates why the British troops acted in this manner towards the women. Clinton and Cornwallis later sent money to the injured females.[26]

The British lost two killed and several wounded, and a sergeant of the 33rd Regiment was captured. They then proceeded on to Orton Mill to attack a force of ninety men of the 1st North Carolina stationed there under Major William Davis. The Americans were alerted, abandoned their camp, and retreated. The British burned the mill and returned to their ships. The Americans lost five captured in this encounter.[27]

On May 15th troops from the 15th, 28th, 33rd, 37th, and 54th regiments landed and "encamped near a demolished post opposite to our shipping," according to one soldier, occupying Fort Johnston. The 46th Regiment was still on board ship. The Americans were camped just two miles away.[28]

In the meantime another British regiment landed on Bald Head Island (then named Smith Island), at the mouth of the Cape Fear River, and constructed an earthen fort on the island that they named Fort George. This was an important location as it commanded the entrance to the river.[29]

On the 16th American snipers hidden onshore fired on the sloop *Falcon*, which returned the favor with cannon fire, to no effect. Throughout the next few days, militia on shore exchanged fire with British warships on the river. Neither side gained much from these encounters, except aggravating each other.[30]

The next day Cornwallis led 900 men of the 27th and 33rd up

Small skirmishes between British troops and militia happened frequently after Moores Creek.

the Cape Fear to Brunswick Town, a base camp for the Americans. The British surprised the camp, but the Americans pulled back quickly. The redcoats lost one man killed, but took twenty cattle and six horses. They also burned the town, forever sealing its fate, as Brunswick was not rebuilt.[31]

Skirmishing took place often between patrols from the British and American camps in Brunswick County. John Peterson, a militiaman from Duplin County, noted that his company went to Brunswick Town and sent scouts out to stop the British from stealing cattle. They often took a few prisoners in these raids. Another soldier, musician Jesse Swinson, recalled encountering British troops at Old Town Creek.[32]

British troops camped at Fort Johnson ate local rice and other foodstuffs plundered from nearby farms. At night they lit the "cabbage trees" (as they called the palmetto trees), to illuminate the perimeters of their camps and keep American snipers at bay. On May 20th the Americans sent fire rafts down the river to damage the British fleet. These were wooden rafts loaded with combustibles that would hopefully strike a ship and become entangled with it, catching it on fire before the crew could extricate the ship. Alert sentries managed to stop the fire rafts and send them harmlessly towards shore, where they burned out.

General Charles Lee

A few days later both sides experienced a terrible storm. British Doctor Thomas Forster noted in his journal that *"A Thunder Storm by such the most dreadful one I ever saw in my Life, it terminated in a most violent storm of Rain and Wind, several Tents were thrown down, and others blown some distance from the spot where they were pitched and many of the highest Trees shiver'd by threads by Lightening - and others torn up by the Roots by the violence of the Wind, it was a most shocking night to pass in Camp."*[33]

During the storm three Americans crept up to the distracted British camp and fired at a sentry. The soldier, Private James Wilcox of the 33rd, was wounded in the hand, but fired back and killed one of the Americans; the rest fled.

British ships continued to arrive and by May 23rd the last of them entered the river. Feeling unable to mount an attack in the area, they decided to move against another target: Charleston, South Carolina. Between May 29th and 31st the ships departed for Charleston. Only three warships, and a small garrison at Fort George on Bald Head Island, remained on the Cape Fear. Upon re-occupying Fort Johnston, a militia soldier reported that, "They left behind them some blankets, with an intention, it is thought, of spreading some infectious disorder among us."[34]

Parker and Clinton felt that they could not gain a good foothold on land, and realized that earthworks protected Wilmington from attack. With a fleet and large force of troops, they did not want to leave the region without attempting something, so they decided to move on Charleston.

Just as the British were leaving, the Americans were building up their forces for a confrontation. The day after they began departing, on June 1st, General Charles Lee arrived in Wilmington with 1,900 Virginia Continental troops. Now almost 4,000 American troops occupied the city (more than tripling its pre-war population). Sensing Parker's next move, they moved on to Charleston, and participated in the defense of that city in late June.[35]

In Wilmington those with Loyalist sympathies felt pressure to join the cause or leave. Some had no choice. On June 15th the Committee of Safety ordered "Mrs. Jean DuBois and Mrs. McNeill and their Families remove from the Town of Wilmington" and remain at least twelve miles from it. Colonel Moore sent troops to oversee the order. Isaac DuBois was a wealthy businessman who owned a store on Market Street, as well as mills, wharves, and a large bakehouse. The home, now known as the DuBois-Boatwright House, still stands next to the Burgwin-Wright House. All of his property was confiscated, and put to use by the rebelling Americans. [36]

Although the immediate threat to the city had passed, Wilmington's leaders were still wary of attack. On June 24th the Committee of Safety wrote to North Carolina's delegates in the Continental Congress, urging them to find weapons for the state. They needed muskets to defend Wilmington, writing that they were in a defenseless state and were fearful of Loyalists who were "only waiting a more favorable opportunity to wreak their vengeance upon us."[37]

British forces assault Ft. Sullivan in Charleston harbor.

On June 28th, four regiments of North Carolina Continental troops, including men under the command of Moore and Howe, assisted in the successful defense of Charleston. British warships blasted Fort Sullivan, but could not weaken it, and a landing party failed to gain a foothold on the island. Sailing away in defeat, the British abandoned active efforts in the two Carolinas for several years.

Sick men of the 1st, 2nd, 3rd, and 4th North Carolina regiments who had been left behind were treated in Wilmington by Dr. John Fergus. Another physician, Dr S. Cooley, wrote "The sickly season is now coming on fast, and unless I'm speedily supplied I shall be destitute of such medicines as I find of most service here." One of the biggest fears at this time of the year was malaria, which not only was deadly in and of itself, but also so weakened its victims that they were susceptible to other diseases and infections.[38]

On August 1st in Halifax the Committee of Safety publicly read the Halifax Resolves, calling for independence, for the first time. At noon the militia gathered with drums beating and flags flying and escorted the Council and Cornelius Harnett to a platform, which they ascended. Harnett then read the bold declaration. Afterwards, "The soldiers seized Mr. Harnett and bore him on their shoulders through the streets of the town, applauding him as their champion, and swearing allegiance to the instrument he had read."[39]

Celebration soon gave way to serious concerns. By September salt was in short supply, as meat curing season was approaching. The Committee of Safety tried to procure more, sending ships to the West Indies. Throughout the region citizens were becoming desperate for this staple. The Committee reported to the state Provincial Congress that "...a certain James Love, of Duplin County, aided with a party of armed men, came to the House of Samuel Portevent, of New Hanover County, and violently broke open an outhouse, and took from thence a Quantity of Salt."[40]

Back on the Cape Fear, British warships still roamed up and down the river. The continued presence of even the small British force was a source of concern for American commanders in the region.

During the night of September 6th-7th the Americans attacked the British fort on Bald Head Island. Knowing that most of the British forces had left the area and supposing those left behind were weak, Col. Thomas Polk led a raid on Fort George.

Polk took 150 men of the 4th North Carolina across from Fort Johnston and they landed on the island at night. They arrived at Buzzards Bay on the north side of the island. On their way to the fort they encountered some sailors and captured them, but this encounter raised the alarm. The sailors in the fort opened fire, as did several warships anchored nearby. Polk pulled back and made it to the mainland, losing one killed and one wounded. Shallow draft

British ships pursued them back to the shore, but American fire kept them at a distance. It was one of the first amphibious operations in American military history.[41]

On October 8th British warships finally left the Cape Fear. Americans rejoiced that "We now have an open Port," yet this was not to last. American privateers (ships outfitted to raid and capture enemy vessels) continued to be captured offshore by the British.[42]

On November 13th the Provincial Congress appointed a committee to prepare a Bill of Rights and a Constitution for the government of the state. It was no easy task, as one delegate reported that they "can conclude on nothing." In the short space of less than a year North Carolinians had won an important victory, raised troops, subdued the Loyalist threat at home, and now had created a state government.[43]

A few days later, a newspaper reported that "the Sundry horses, and a chariot the property of the late Governor Martin, be sold for ready money." Martin journeyed with the British fleet to Charleston, where they were repulsed, and on to New York. He was North Carolina's last royal governor, and when he departed so did royal authority. He rejoined British forces in the South in 1780 and accompanied Cornwallis on his invasion of North Carolina, hoping to reclaim his colony. Several times during the campaign he issued zealous proclamations calling on Loyalists to join them. He left the army while in Wilmington in April of 1781 to rejoin his family in New York, thus avoiding capture at Yorktown. Martin died in England in 1786.[44]

In mid-December 1776, the Provincial Congress adopted the state's Bill of Rights and Constitution. Just a year earlier North Carolina was a royal colony still under British rule. Revolution and independence were far from most people's minds. Now independence had been declared, a new government formed, and troops were in the field to defend it.

Regulators persisted in being a threat in North Carolina long after the defeat at Moores Creek.

Chapter 6
The War Broadens: 1777-1780

In the aftermath of Moores Creek, Loyalists of the state's interior hid and were hunted down. Although largely dispersed, they were still a threat to American control of the region, especially in Anson and Cumberland counties. Here the Whig militia remained on alert for another Loyalist uprising. Rumors also circulated of an insurrection in Chatham and Orange Counties. In fact, tension was high everywhere as no one knew where violence might break out next. An enemy within is the most feared kind, and North Carolina had to not only contend with invasion from the coast, but also attack from the loyal population.[1]

In July 1776 David Jackson, a Loyalist captured at Moores Creek, escaped and along with Jacob Kragle, was harassing people. Apparently they "Shot & mortally wounded" a Wilmington Whig, and another "narrowly Escaped with his life." One person wrote to the Committee of Safety and recommended that the militia go "into their Settlements & put those Rascals to death on sight & that they lay waste the Country where the inhabitants refuse to deliver the Offenders...This may be thought Severe doctrine, but until something of this kind is adopted, you may rest assured no man there dare ever Say a word in favour of America."[2]

This shows how far things had come in a short time. Polarization came fast: it must have been disconcerting to the Americans to find enemies among their own people. This made the war more personal and more bitter, since the enemies were friends, neighbors, and business partners.

The rest of 1776 would be a year of disappointment for both American and British forces. That summer a large British and German force drove Washington's Continental Army from New York, and would hold the city for the rest of the war. Washington retreated across New Jersey, and put the Delaware River behind him to keep the British at bay.

Considering the campaign over, British and German forces went into winter quarters. Washington saw an opportunity and struck back at Trenton, followed by another strike at Princeton. He wintered at Morristown, not far from the British in New York City.

Both sides had fought and exchanged territory. Political negotiations got nowhere, and the Americans eventually refused to talk at all unless acceptance of independence was guaranteed. The year ended in a stalemate, with neither army feeling strong enough to attack the other.

In North Carolina tensions remained high despite the victory at Moores Creek and the departure of the British fleet. In July thirty Loyalists from the surrounding area attacked Tarboro but were defeated by the local militia. The prisoners taken were forced to take the oath of allegiance to the state. Rumors also circulated of uprisings being planned in Orange and Chatham counties.[3]

On July 14, 1776, the North Carolina Continental Regiments mutinied in their barracks at Wilmington. There had been growing unrest between the regular troops and the local militia, stemming from jealousies in the distribution of supplies. The men were also anxious, many suffering with poor supplies and having yet to see the enemy. Boredom, lack of adequate food and clothing, and frustration combined to produce a volatile situation.[4]

Militia under General John Ashe surrounded the Continentals and diffused the mutiny, and it ended without bloodshed. Ashe and other officers wrote that the Continental troops wanted to serve and do their duty, and that frustration and lack of good clothing and food were the root of the problem. About twenty mutineers were under guard when the week-old Declaration of Independence was read to the troops in Wilmington.[5]

The troops of many states mutinied at one point or other during the war, most often towards the latter part when pay and supplies were virtually non-existent. North Carolina's only Continental mutiny occurred early in the war and has not received much attention.

Reverberations of the Battle of Moores Creek were still felt months, and even years later. That fall of 1776 a group of nine wives from Guilford County petitioned the state government for the release of their husbands, who had been captured with the Loyalists in the wake of the battle. They noted that their husbands were needed to support them and that they posed no threat to the state. Such action was rare for women, but common suffering bound them together.[6]

In September 1776 North Carolina was ordered to send its Continental Regiments to join General Washington's army near New York. The men had returned from South Carolina and were now camped in Wilmington. Their orders changed while enroute and they turned around and returned to Wilmington.[7]

A new threat appeared further to the south, and in January 1777 the North Carolina Continentals marched instead for Charleston and eventually Savannah.[8]

Offshore, the British had returned to blockade the mouth of the Cape Fear. The journal of one ship reveals typical activities (original spelling and grammar has been preserved):

> *February 1777*
> *Thursday 6th*
> *Fresh breezes & Squaly*
> *At 1 pm fired 3 nine pounders to bring too the chace...a Sloop from Charlestown bd [bound] to Philadelphia loaden with rice & indigo, sent an officer & Men on bd [board] her*
> *Friday 7th*
> *At 1 PM saw 2 Sl [sloops] to the SW gave chase...fired 2 Guns for the Convoy to come under our stern...we could not come up with the Chace...*
> *Saturday 8th*
> *1/2 past 5 AM saw a strange Sl [sloop] gave Chace found her to be a Brig from St. Eustacia bd [bound] to Charlestown, 1/2 past 7 gave chace to another Sl to the Wt ward gave chace... fired a shot at her...* [9]

Meanwhile, North Carolina continued to bolster its war effort. At New Bern in January 1777 Richard Caswell took the oath of office as the state's first governor. The first General Assembly convened there in March. Both had their hands full. The state encouraged not only musket factories, but also lent support to iron foundries and furnaces in the piedmont. Another furnace on the Rocky River near Halifax made pots, kettles, and cannon shot. A paper mill began operation near Hillsboro to address the critical shortage of that article, and shoes were manufactured in Edenton.[10]

Another priority for the state was the completion of its small navy. With several important ports of entry for supplies that were now more critical than ever, the formation of a navy became paramount. Wilmington, New Bern, and Edenton were selected as ports for the construction of the state's three ships.[11]

In March 1777, naval officer John Forster, in charge of the *General Washington* on the Cape Fear River, wrote Governor Caswell that he was *"much afraid...she will be delayed much longer than I could wish for want of Hands, as from this Port being so long blocked up by the King of England's ships, most of the seamen have enlisted in the Land service...Those who did not enlist have gone to other ports, and the encouragement given in the Merchant Service and on board private vessels of war by our neighboring states, so far exceeds the Continental pay...there would be but very little probability of my shipping a sufficiency of men for the Washington, but as none are to be got here, I see no prospect of her being manned..."*[12]

In June Forster wrote Caswell that he was having financial trouble with the ship as well: *"I confess that I expected a considerable supply of money... or at least an immediate payment of the large sums I am already in advance for the public, but as neither has been done, (for want I believe of money in the Treasury) I have been debarred giving the assistance that my duty required in this affair . . It will at least require the sum of two thousand pounds for immediate and necessary supplies without which it will be needless to attempt anything further as to this ship."*[13]

These letters indicate the amount of work it took to fund, outfit, and get a ship ready. Naval officers were frustrated that after all that time, money, and effort, the ship never made a contribution to the war effort.

Matters progressed more smoothly for the state's land forces. Although North Carolina troops had already been on several operations outside the state, notably Great Bridge, Virginia, the Snow Campaign, and Charleston, South Carolina, they were about to embark for the main theater of the war. On April 7, 1777 the state's Continental Regiments left to join the army under Washington in Pennsylvania.[14]

They began their march from Wilmington, where many had been originally organized and trained. They marched north through New Bern and Halifax, and on to Richmond, Virginia.[15]

At home, North Carolina passed its first act of banishment in April 1777. Suspected Loyalists were told to take the oath of allegiance to the state in sixty days or leave. If their property was not sold before leaving the state would claim it. At the time one American militia officer estimated two-thirds of heavily Loyalist Cumberland County (which included Cross Creek) was ready to leave.[16]

There was more bad news that month when on the 15th General James Moore, one of the state's most prominent military officers, died of "a gout of the stomach," (a condition caused by too much uric acid in the blood). Moore had masterminded the victory at Moores Creek and overseen the defense of Wilmington in the spring and summer of 1776. He was forty years old. One observer wrote that "it is a pity he had not had an opportunity of showing his military talents in a more active scene." It is interesting to consider the possible result of Moore's involvement at the battles of Brandywine, Germantown, and at Valley Forge, had he been there.[17]

Unrest grew among the population of the Lower Cape Fear as the availability of supplies dwindled, and tensions mounted between Whigs and Loyalists. Loyalists became active in Craven County in September, and Governor Caswell told local militia to watch them and report on their activities.[18]

Another problem was counterfeiting, which was on the rise that summer. It undermined the efforts of Governor Caswell to stabilize the economy and became a widespread problem as currency and goods became scarce. Letters circulated warning officials to carefully inspect money to single out the counterfeited script.[19]

In the spring of 1777, two British warships began a blockade of the Cape Fear River, cutting off trade, and were soon joined by others. At one point they destroyed several ships anchored in the harbor at Brunswick. The brief period of having an open port now ended, and it would be a challenge for ships to enter the Cape Fear for the rest of the war. While the state began the formation of a navy,

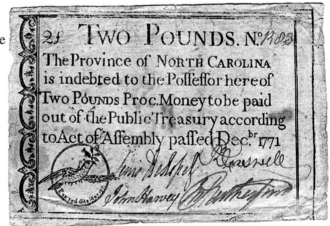

Colonial North Carolina currency

it never got off the ground. The brig *George Washington* was unable to leave the Cape Fear River since it was outnumbered by the presence of several British warships at the mouth of the river.[20]

American ships were also active, with several privateers taking British ships on the high seas that spring. In May 1777, the privateer *Coatesworth-Pinckney* made it into the Cape Fear, having "narrowly escaped" pursuit by British ships. Others ships were not so fortunate, being captured with their cargoes of tar, pitch, and turpentine.[21]

Cornelius Harnett was among those who chartered fast ships to the West Indies for supplies like weapons, gunpowder, salt, clothes, and shoes. Other goods made it through the blockade as well: salt, metals, food, dry goods, tea, pepper, gunpowder, saltpeter, iron, rum, coffee, furniture, slaves, horses, wine, spices, rum, sugar, molasses, linen, silk, leather, paint, lead, shoes, hats, earthenware pottery, glass, candles, wool, pewter, copper, and saddles. Nearly everything was in short supply, so any goods that made it through the blockade were welcome.[22]

That spring North Carolina organized two more regiments, the 8th and 9th, for the Continental Army at Halifax. The 8th Regiment consisted of men from the Wilmington, Halifax, and New Bern areas. By June they would be in Pennsylvania with the other North Carolina troops under Washington.[23]

By 1777 there were no active newspapers in Wilmington, making it difficult to find information on events and moods there at the time. It is clear from other sources that the lack of supplies was getting worse.

Lack of salt remained a pressing problem, and it became so acute that it nearly led to violence. In July Governor Richard Caswell learned that nearly one thousand people had assembled in Guilford, Orange, and Chatham Counties "who said they were going to Cross Creek to get the salt that was stored up." Other groups from Duplin, Johnston, and "back counties" marched to take "the salt by force."[24]

Cross Creek, at the head of navigation for the Cape Fear River, became an important supply station for the North Carolina military. Here the protestors were met by Colonel Robert Rowan's militia, and he noted that "Some made their escape on finding they were to be opposed, but we seemed the greater number, & upon their taking the oath to the State, and appearing very penitent, we allowed them what salt they wanted, at the market price, which is 5 dollars, and discharged them." Rowan also noted that the Scots of the area refused to take the oath of allegiance to the sate, "almost to a man." The Scottish settlers of the Cross Creek region would remain a source of concern, and be actively opposed to the war effort, for the rest of the conflict.[25]

In Wilmington merchant William Kenan wrote that tensions were caused "by the cursed Scottish race." He added that they were "sneering" and "threatening," and he blamed the Scots at Cross Creek for the recent problems. In the meantime, the Americans kept trying to get ships out to sea for salt, but the British blockade made it difficult.[26] Salt was a staple of life, and the lack of it prevented food preservation in an age that had no refrigeration. Not only people, but their farm animals required this valuable mineral, too.

While the mob marched on Cross Creek, Wilmington was also threatened. John Baptista Ashe reported that he suspected Loyalists would seize the ammunition magazine in that city. Many suspect persons were coming into the town, as he felt, under the pretext of getting salt. Ashe wrote to Governor Caswell that he was preparing to destroy area bridges and have the militia stop travel in the area if he had to. He strengthened the guards at the city's magazine. He called out the New Hanover County militia, and alerted militia in Bladen and Cumberland Counties as well. The measure must have worked, as nothing ever came of the plot. With the British gone from the Lower Cape Fear region, Ashe scolded people in June for becoming complacent and being unpatriotic.[27]

British ships blockading the Cape Fear made it hard to get supplies.

While many citizens supported the war effort, there were those who avoided military service or deserted. Ashe received orders to execute any soldier guilty of mutiny or desertion.[28]

Despite shortages, the threat of invasion or slave insurrection, and the absence of many leaders, Wilmington's residents tried to carry on. Court records indicate business as usual prevailed as much as possible. The court issued licenses to tavern owners, set rates for ferry operators, issued instructions to repair roads and bridges in New Hanover County, and oversaw legal cases regarding property disputes and estate settlements.[29]

Ships continued to try to enter and leave Wilmington and evade the British blockade offshore. In August two privateers, the *Resolution* and the *Polly*, arrived from Jamaica with badly needed cargo. The frigate *Randolph* managed to take four British ships at sea, and arrived with valuable rum and sugar from the Caribbean. Shortages continued, however, and Governor Caswell ordered that salt not be exported from North Carolina, hoping to keep whatever of that precious material that was on hand in the state. A newspaper also asked that citizens save rags, scraps of linen, and even donate handkerchiefs to use in making paper, a valuable and limited item.[30]

In August 1777 a large number of slaves on the Cape Fear River's plantations became ill and died. The cause remains unknown, possibly an outbreak of disease. No doubt the area's slave population watched events with great interest, many hoping the British would return, and wondering at the fate of their friends and family who had escaped the previous year when Sir Peter Parker's fleet was on the river.[31]

That same month a privateer arrived in Wilmington with a British ship captured in the Caribbean. Residents were anxious to learn what goods were on the ship, as supplies from the West Indies were valuable to the trade-starved city.[32]

When a British fleet moved into the Chesapeake Bay that summer, it caused great concern in Virginia and North Carolina. Its destination was unknown, and Governor Caswell ordered the militia of the state's eastern counties to be "in readiness to march at the shortest notice." Gunpowder and

North Carolina soldiers performed well at northern battles like Brandywine.

lead were removed from Wilmington to Kinston to keep it out of reach, should the British land there. In fact, their destination was Pennsylvania and the capital at Philadelphia.[33]

North Carolina's nine Continental Regiments fought at the battles of Brandywine and Germantown in Pennsylvania, some of the largest engagements of the war. They then wintered with the main Continental army at Valley Forge. The rigors of campaigning had worn down their numbers to half strength. Among the losses sustained by North Carolina on these distant fields was General Francis Nash of Orange County, killed at Germantown.[34]

Back on the Cape Fear, an incident in late November shows how crucial the supply situation had become in the state. The 4th Georgia Regiment, marching from Virginia to its home state, had stopped in Wilmington. The commanding officer wrote to Governor Caswell that his men were poorly supplied, and had been unable to obtain food and clothing since entering North Carolina. He was fearful of a mutiny, and even suggested he may have to disband the regiment, turning the men loose to forage on their own and make their way to Georgia in small groups. Caswell quickly replied that he would see they received supplies, and contacted local commanders to ensure it.[35]

In December 1777 the *George Washington* still had no crew, and was eventually sold for cash, "with her guns, stores, tackle, apparel, and furniture." The ship never left port or engaged the enemy, and spent its entire life waiting for a crew and being outfitted.[36]

Efforts to outfit the state navy and beef up coastal defenses continued to move too slowly, for which Wilmington would eventually pay. Cornelius Harnett wrote in early 1778 that, "I am distressed beyond measure to find Our Sea Coast so much neglected." He recommended fortifications at "Cape Look Out" as well as more defenses along the Cape Fear. Improvements were made on the Outer Banks, but slowly.[37]

Few records exist regarding daily life during these years, yet we can catch a glimpse of some events. The danger of fire remained constant, perhaps even more so, during wartime, with many refugees, soldiers, and officials crowding into the town. In January 1778 repairs were made to Wilmington's two fire engines, and two new ladders were ordered as well. Each home was also to have at least one leather bucket for fire fighting.[38]

City leaders ordered that hogs should not run at large in the streets, and citizens were responsible for removing rubbish and trash around their property. Fines were enacted for each of these transgressions. Speeding fines are not a modern phenomenon, as the city imposed laws regarding riding horses "immoderately fast" through the streets.[39]

In April 1778, British prisoners were kept on the unfinished *George Washington* and held there. Some were willing to serve on the ship, but apparently nothing came of the effort. It was not uncommon to offer prisoners the option of taking up arms against their countrymen. It eased the strain

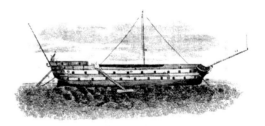

A British prison ship

on resources to feed, house, and guard prisoners, and supplied fighting men that were badly needed. Throughout the Revolution both sides used prison ships, especially later in the war, when neither side had the supplies or manpower to properly keep captives. Prisoners often chose to fight alongside their former enemies to avoid notoriously deadly prison ships.[40]

That summer workers continued to improve the city streets: adding fill to low ground and bricking up streams that ran through Wilmington. Records also mention public stocks, a pillory, a ducking stool, and a whipping post for those who broke laws. Among the more serious regulations passed were those for slaves. They were not to live separately from an owner and had a curfew of 9pm in summer and 10pm in winter. Fear and uncertainty during the war years led to increased security and regulation of slaves, but despite greater security and no British presence in the area, slaves continued to run away. Robert Howe's fourteen year old servant, Patty, fled in 1779, eventually reaching British forces.[41]

Repercussions of the Battle of Moores Creek still lingered two years after the event. In August 1778, Margret Cotton petitioned the state assembly to retrieve her husband James's property. He had been captured after Moores Creek and then fled to England. The assembly rejected her petition, but later her two sons got some of the estate back.[42]

In December 1778 the British captured Savannah, and in the process ruined the reputation of North Carolina General Robert Howe. He failed to stop their advance on the city and the British easily drove back his defenders. The sparsely populated colony of Georgia quickly fell under their control. This was the first move in a second campaign to conquer the South.

The breakdown in trade due to the war affected merchants and consumers throughout the Lower Cape Fear region. A visitor to Wilmington in 1779 wrote that "all goods had risen greatly, and could hardly be bought at any price. No ship could be expected this summer, and no vessel could sail because of the English privateers." Although the blockade was effective, some ships made it in and out until 1781, when the British captured the port city.

Fortunately, while Wilmington was blocked, Ocracoke Island and other coastal towns remained open to receive supplies, although the trade was not even a fraction of pre-war levels. Passage through the Outer Banks was precarious, and it entailed a long journey for supplies to reach the mainland and the interior. As stated earlier, Wilmington's advantage was that it was accessible directly from the ocean.

Other North Carolina towns felt the impact of war as well. In New Bern news of the French Alliance with the United States arrived in May 1778. Despite a celebration to announce the news, one observer wrote that it was "poor and trifling."

Just three days later a riot broke out when French sailors in the town attempted to organize a regiment for the Continental Army. An indentured servant tried to enlist, and his outraged master rounded up twenty armed men who went "running about the town" seeking to "put every Frenchman to death in town, or drive them out of it." The mob surrounded a schoolhouse in which the French were quartered, and "beat and abused" them with clubs. Needless to say, recruiting for a French regiment in New Bern did not get off the ground.[43]

During this time salt prices rose to "extravagant" levels in the Lower Cape Fear. Importers continued to try to get it from Bermuda, but shipments were few and far between. What was brought in was kept in storehouses in Cross Creek and Wilmington.[44]

Local entrepreneurs made salt on the coast using two methods: evaporation and boiling. Evaporation used wooden reservoirs with clay bottoms

A Civil War-era salt works. The valuable commodity would have been made much the same way during the Revolutionary War years.

to produce what was know as Sound Salt. Salt water was poured in, and salt eventually crystallized from the water.[45]

The second way was to boil sea water in iron pots. The Committee of Safety offered monetary assistance to anyone who built salt works. Many salt works were constructed north of Beaufort, as it was better protected from British raids.[46]

Despite the necessity of salt and the monetary incentives for it, manufacturers had difficulty getting materials. Other factors like nature affected its production as well. One manager wrote that "my Salt beds were promising something considerable of Salt in a day or two, there fell a heavy rain and blasted my hopes of this fall." Samuel Ashe had salt produced in the sounds of New Hanover County by boiling. Jonathan Dunbibin and Timothy Bloodworth also had salt works in the county.[47]

Despite all the efforts to produce salt, it fell far short of needs. By 1780 salt was selling for $625 a bushel, far out of reach for most people.

The blockade made obtaining supplies difficult, but it was the worthless currency that hurt consumers most. One observer wrote that the paper money issued by the states "had to be accepted, though each man passed it on as quickly as possible." Another stated more forcefully, "God Dam the Liberty money and them that made it for it was good for nothing." Prices skyrocketed, supplies dwindled, currency lost its value, and conditions worsened as each year passed.[48]

By 1779 the war was shifting. Several inconclusive campaigns had been fought in the north, and neither side held a decisive upper hand. The British began to reconsider another southern invasion, and set their sights on Georgia and Charleston as temping targets.

Their strategy was largely based on the assumption that great numbers of Loyalists were present in the South. Having been repressed for the last few years, it was assumed they were eager for revenge and only needed the presence of British troops to rise up and retake these colonies. Governor Martin and others who had fled the South still believed this to be true and made their arguments to policy makers convincingly.

While in 1776 there may indeed have been many Loyalists willing to fight, by 1779 that was not the case. Many had fled and joined British forces in the occupied areas of Florida or New York. Furthermore, those left behind were too intimidated to rise without total British occupation of the region. Nonetheless the British prepared their new strategy to reclaim the South on this mistaken assumption.[49]

The British launched a second southern invasion, first attacking the weakest colony: Georgia (and in the process ruining General Robert Howe's career). With the enemy poised to strike north, American forces began to concentrate again in the Carolinas. In November 1779, Brigadier General James Hogun left Pennsylvania with the nine North Carolina Continental Regiments, marching south for three months on their way to assist in the defense of Charleston, SC. While in Wilmington, the troops demanded pay before marching any further, a reflection of the serious inflation issues of the time. Another mutiny was avoided in the port city.[50]

In the meantime the witch-hunt continued as Loyalists were exposed and forced to change their persuasion or leave. Fifty-three of sixty-eight who were designated by name in the Confiscation Act of 1779 were merchants. Half who sought compensation after the war from Great Britain were merchants, and it seems that only six of Wilmington's merchants actively supported the Whigs during the war. These facts show how personal economics affected the side one chose to support.[51]

Also in 1779, the Loyalist officers captured in the wake of Moores Creek over three years earlier and then held in Philadelphia, Baltimore, and elsewhere, were finally released. Most were sent to British-held New York City. From there many joined the British forces, while others made their way back to North Carolina to rebuild their lives.

Wilmington merchant Alexander MacLean took seventy Loyalists to join British forces in occupied Philadelphia. Others made their way to Florida, a colony firmly in British hands, though a remote and sparsely settled outpost at the time. Still others traveled to join British forces wherever they could: Philadelphia, New York, or Georgia. These refugees endured countless hardships, crossing rivers, low on food, and passing hundreds of miles through what was a hostile country.[52]

The case of Thomas Wier reveals the trouble many Loyalists faced. A prisoner after Moores Creek, he was released and sent to British-held New York in late 1778. On his way, he was captured again and taken to Boston. After six months the Americans exchanged him and sent him to Savannah, but a French ship captured him at sea. Released again, he finally reached Savannah, Georgia, where he joined British forces. Wier accompanied the British army on its march through the Carolinas, but was captured again prior to the Battle of Guilford Courthouse. He was held as a prisoner in Virginia but managed to rejoin Cornwallis's army prior to Yorktown, where yet again he was taken prisoner. While attempting to join the fighting, Wier actually spent most of the war as a prisoner.[53]

The conflict returned to the Carolinas with a renewed British attempt to subdue the region. Charleston fell to the British in May 1780 and they quickly spread across South Carolina. Although suffering defeats at Kings Mountain and Cowpens, British commander Gen. Charles Lord Cornwallis pushed on, invading North Carolina in the winter of 1781 and pursuing the American army under General Nathanael Greene.

North Carolina's Continental troops had been captured at Charleston, and were now prisoners of war. Concern for the welfare of the troops led to an effort to supply them with provisions. The *Adventure* was outfitted at Beaufort with tobacco, clothing, and other supplies.[54] With permission from the British, the ship set sail for Charleston but was seized by a British warship. They took the cargo and imprisoned the crew. Through the Continental Congress, North Carolina protested, but the English government stalled on action.[55]

A premature Loyalist uprising in western North Carolina backfired with disastrous consequences. Although told to wait until military support was closer, Loyalists in modern day Lincoln County gathered at Ramsours' Mill in June 1780. Many did not have weapons, but their numbers swelled as word spread to Loyalists throughout the western region. Local Whig militia attacked and routed them, and only a few desperate remnants managed to reach Cornwallis. Thus when the main British army arrived later, few Loyalists were willing to openly come out and support them.

On September 10th American militia under Captain Herrick attacked a group of Loyalists at Mask's Ferry on the Pee Dee River in Anson County (north of modern Wadesboro). Several Loyalists were killed, and eleven taken prisoner.[56]

By now shortages were becoming severe for the state's militia forces. Col. James Kenan had his Duplin County militia manufacture cartridge boxes, bayonets, and other materials. He also wrote that they needed tents. Food was chronically short for the militia as well.[57]

Every year from 1776 to 1782 the State of North Carolina passed confiscation acts, seizing the property of Loyalists. Over time the laws got tougher, and more and more proof of support to the state was demanded of suspected Loyalists.[58]

Merchants tried to protest the tightening laws, but to no avail. In May 1780, the General Assembly rejected the "Memorial of the Merchants, Traders and Others Residing at Cape Fear" who argued that the Confiscation Act of 1777 was unfair. Over 330 men had signed this petition, showing the strong presence of Loyalist sentiment in the region.[59]

Men who had not taken the oath of allegiance to the state were required to after Moores Creek. The first oath, created in 1776, read:

> *I do sincerely promise and swear, that I will be faithful and bear true allegiance to the State of North Carolina, and to the Powers and Authorities which are or may be established for the Government thereof, and that I will to the utmost of my Power, maintain and defend the same against all Attempts whatsoever; and I do swear, that I will do no act willingly, whereby the Independence of the said State may be destroyed or injured. SO HELP ME GOD.*

The newer oath, established in April 1777, left little room for doubt:

> *I will bear faithful and true allegiance to the State of North Carolina, and will to the utmost of my Power, support and maintain, and defend the independent Government thereof, against George the Third, the King of Great Britain, and his Successors, and the Attempts of any other Persons, Prince, Power, State, or Potentate, who by secret Arts, Treason, Conspiracies, or by open Force, shall attempt to subvert the same, and will in every Respect conduct myself a peaceful, orderly Subject, and that I will disclose and make known to the Governor, some Member of the Council of State, or some Justice of the Peace, all Treasons, Conspiracies, and Attempts, committed or intended against the State, which shall come to my Knowledge.[60]*

The reality was that in managing a Revolutionary effort, the Americans found it was necessary to force unity. They could not tolerate division or dissension. Disagreement questioned the legitimacy of their cause and increased the potential for resistance on the home front, which had led to the dangerous Moores Creek uprising four years earlier in 1776.

In the meantime, events unfolding in the piedmont would soon affect the residents of the Lower Cape Fear River. The largest battle to be fought in the state was about to occur, and armies would once again converge on Wilmington.

British troops landed below Wilmington and took the city in 1781.

Chapter 7
The British Return

The war returned with a vengeance to Wilmington and the Lower Cape Fear region in 1781. By then Lord Cornwallis had moved his army from South Carolina into the western part of North Carolina near Charlotte, and part of the plan all along was to occupy Wilmington. British commanders felt that taking the port city was a critical part of subduing the state.[1]

Cornwallis had first agreed to it in November, while at Charlotte, when reinforcements were on the way to the Carolinas. He intended for the fresh British troops to land at Wilmington, but by December felt they were need more in South Carolina, so the plan was scrapped. The British defeat at Kings Mountain forced Cornwallis to pull back and delay his invasion of the northern state until the start of the new year.[2]

Cornwallis re-entered North Carolina after the stinging defeat at Cowpens in upper South Carolina, and again saw the need to occupy the Cape Fear for two reasons. First was for a supply base when he arrived in the state. Second was to encourage Loyalists to rise and join his forces.[3]

Through February and March Cornwallis moved across North Carolina from Charlotte to Guilford County, pursuing General Nathanael Greene's American army. The British moved on to occupy the capital at Hillsboro and declare the colony reconquered. Cornwallis then turned his attention back to Greene's army. The two forces met in a four hour battle at Guilford Courthouse

Greene's Continentals make a stand at Guilford Courthouse.

in mid-March, which the British won but at terrible cost. In the meantime a British expedition to the Cape Fear had been underway.

Wilmington was the largest city in the state with a population of 1,200, and roughly 200 homes. Knowing that Wilmington was linked by river to Cross Creek, and that from there roads stretched into the west, the British saw the advantage of occupying the city. From the coast, supplies and troops could move inland to Cornwallis' army.[4]

Since the start of the war in 1776, Wilmington had also been a major supply depot for the Continental army. The garrison included barracks for troops, and a magazine that held several tons of gunpowder, lead, and cannon shot. Mountains of stores included barrels of pork, beef, clothing, and ammunition, as well as artillery pieces and wagons. General Greene relied on the city to help supply his army in 1780, when it was one of his main sources of material.[5]

The commander of the British expedition to Wilmington was Major James Henry Craig, a thirty-two year old combat veteran. Craig had served with the army since the age of fifteen in 1763, first as an ensign with 30th Regiment at Gibraltar. He rose to the rank of Captain in the 47th Regiment, and fought at Bunker Hill in 1775 where he was wounded. Later that winter he helped repulse the American attack on Quebec. In 1777 he saw action at Freeman's Farm at Saratoga, and was promoted to major of the 82nd Regiment of Foot.[6]

An observer described Craig, "In person he was very short, broad and muscular, a pocket Hercules, but with sharp, neat features, as if chiseled in ivory. Not popular, he was hot, preemptory, and pompous, yet extremely beloved by those whom he allowed to live in intimacy with him; clever, generous to a fault, and a warm and unflinching friend to those whom he liked."[7]

The British force left Charleston, SC on January 21st, and arrived on the Cape Fear on the 25th. Accompanying them to provide assistance and knowledge of the area was refugee Isaac DuBois, whose family had been banished from Wilmington at the start of the war. The invasion force consisted of six companies of the 82nd Regiment, two brass 3 pound cannons, and two iron 6 pounders. It was a small force for such an ambitions operation.[8]

Major (later General)
James Henry Craig

The 82nd Regiment had been raised in the Scottish Lowlands, and was initially sent to Nova Scotia in August 1778. From there they were sent to the relatively quiet garrison at Charleston, SC. Thus it was a fairly new regiment and the men had seen no combat. The troops wore red coats with black trim on the collars and cuffs.[9]

On the 29th Craig's 300 men went ashore at Ellis Plantation, nine miles below the city. While Craig's infantry advanced overland, the British fleet under Capt. Andrew Barkley sailed up the Cape Fear River. This flotilla consisted of three warships and three galleys.[10]

Local militia under Col. Henry Young and Col. James Kenan felt they were too weak to resist, and began a retreat to Heron's Bridge on the Northeast Cape Fear River. A meeting of prominent citizens decided the best course was to meet the British and formally surrender the town. The American ships retreated up the Northeast River, following the troops. Those vessels were loaded with supplies and arms. As the British arrived from the south, 200 townspeople surrendered the city.[11]

The militia did not put up a fight because they were short on weapons and ammunition. Col. Young wrote "we are in great confusion here

Col. James Kenan

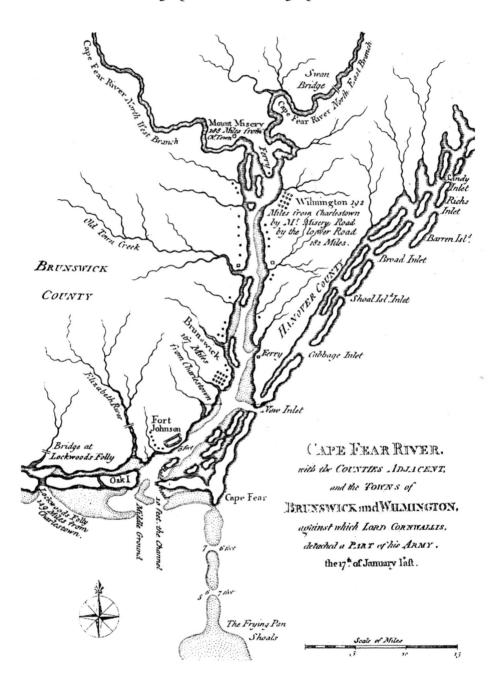

Map of the Cape Fear region used by the British in 1781.

and very much in Want of Arms." There were two batteries at the town, and their armaments included ten 9 and 12 pound guns, most spiked in the retreat (made inoperable by driving a nail into the touch hole where flame would be applied to fire the gun). They also destroyed the bridge behind them over Smith Creek, north of the town, as one last obstacle between them and the advancing British.[12]

Militia had been fortifying Wilmington for four years, since 1776, but the garrison was small and supplies were low. One soldier wrote that he had been "to an old fort and repaired it for use" a half mile below town just a few days before the British arrived. (This is likely a fort that stood at the end of Northern Boulevard, along the river. Nothing remains today.)[13]

For a city that had been fortified and preparing for defense for six years, it was an extraordinarily quick surrender. No doubt many civilians marveled at how quickly the militia retreated from their town without putting up any fight. What they may not have known was that the militia were asked by town leaders to withdraw, to prevent the town from being shelled.

The British strike was sudden and unexpected, interrupting everyday life for the garrison and civilians. It was only a few days after Lucy Bradley and Thomas Brown were married at her father's house that the British arrived. Lucy, her father and family, including sister Elizabeth, were force to flee from Wilmington to

Finian, William Hooper's Masonboro home.

their home in Bladen County for protection, where they stayed until the British evacuated months later. Thomas left to rejoin his militia unit.[14]

Cornelius Harnett left with the town's money for safe keeping. He kept going farther to the north, even though his gout was getting worse. He made it as far as his friend James Spicer's home (on Spicers Bay in southern Onslow County) before being bedridden there.[15]

William Hooper and Alexander Maclain fled as well. Hooper was especially fearful since he was a signer of the Declaration of Independence. He also suspected that his salt works and other property would be targeted. He wrote to fellow politician James Iredell "In the Agony of my Soul, I inform you that I am severed from my family - perhaps for ever!...I removed my family to Wilmington. Had I attempted to have carried them further I apprehended that they must still have been subject to parties of the enemy who would have been

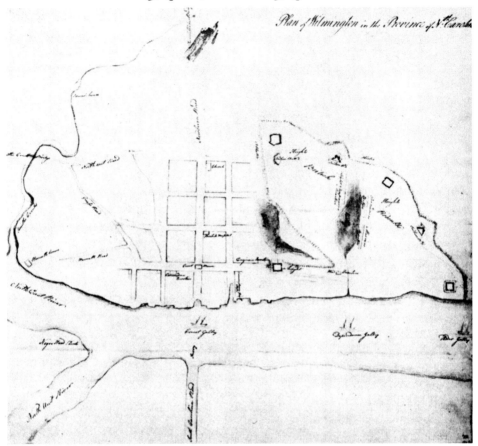

A British map of Wilmington depicting the town and British positions in it.

engaged in plundering without the restraint of any officers to check their depredations." Both Hooper and Maclaine went to Halifax, where the North Carolina General Assembly were meeting. Fearing for his wife's safety at their country home, Finian, at Masonboro, Hooper sent her into the British-occupied city, where she would be under official military protection.[16]

Tax collector Thomas Bloodworth sent the city's tax records and other documents upriver to keep them out of Craig's hands, but the British managed to capture and burn them.[17]

William Sharpless' slaves moved public stores before the British arrived, and at the same time some of his slaves escaped, hoping to join the British. Panic and confusion was everywhere, the streets were crowded with civilians packing to flee and soldiers gathering supplies.[18]

On the evening of January 27th, a committee of citizens met with Craig to discuss surrendering the town. The group included James Walker and John Dawson. They proposed:

Article 1: The Inhabitants and others remaining there to be Prisoners of War until regularly exchanged.

Article 2: The Inhabitants to remain in town and to have their Property's of every denomination secured to them and their Persons protected.

Craig refused these terms, and instead insisted that they "submit to be prisoners of war at discretion or take the Consequences of resistance, in the former case every exertion will be used to prevent Plunder or Personal ill usage to any Person." They were terms that the Americans had to accept.[19]

John Burgwin

Craig's troops occupied the town at noon the following day, and Wilmington was now securely in British hands. In January 1776 the British effort to take the city failed. Now in January 1781, they marched in unopposed. Upon taking control, Craig's men moved into the abandoned American barracks and took over their earthen defenses. The major apparently used John Burgwin's impressive home at Third and Market Streets for his headquarters.[20]

The American militia fled northeast to a position at Heron's Bridge on the Northeast Cape Fear River. Craig followed his bloodless victory with a quick strike three days later at Heron's' Bridge on January 30th.[21]

Heron's Bridge, one of only two drawbridges in America at the time of the Revolutionary War. It was located roughly where I-40 crosses the Northeast Cape Fear River between New Hanover and modern Pender Counties.

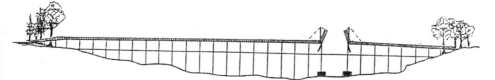

The I-40 bridge crossing the Northeast Cape Fear River, near the Heron's Bridge site.

Craig's report contains the best account of the battle. Upon learning that Col. Young was stationed at the bridge with a force of militia, he decided to strike quickly. The British did not know the Americans' strength, and Craig admitted "I was at a loss to form any judgment of them." However, knowing that following up the capture of the city with another victory would crush them, Craig moved his forces out to attack.[22]

The site was well chosen for defense. The Northeast Cape Fear River is about four hundred feet wide there. The drawbridge not only provided a narrow and exposed crossing point, but on the other side was a narrow causeway that ran "through a very deep marsh a quarter of a mile in breadth which terminated in a hill on which they were encamped." It was not unlike the defensive position at Moores Creek, only on a larger scale.[23]

Craig's forces left the town at four o'clock in the afternoon and marched the ten miles along the Great Duplin Road to the bridge. Daylight was fading fast, and Craig hurried his men along. He had 250 men and two 3 pounders, leaving Major Daniel Manson with the remainder of his force to hold the town.[24]

Craig continues: "A little after dark one of the light infantry with great spirit made himself master of one of the rebel light horse [lightly armed cavalry] who was on the lookout, and from him we got such intelligence as determined us to attempt surprising them. We accordingly moved on within about a mile of the bridge and there lay on our arms, meaning to attack them between three and four in the morning. Volunteers immediately turned out for the dangerous service of seizing the necessary sentinels, every precaution taken for securing any patrol which might come near us, and I have not the smallest doubt of our having succeeded had not an unlucky accident put and end to all our hopes."[25]

Conditions change rapidly in battle, and can be either opportunities or challenges. Such was the case here for the British. Craig continues, "A sergeant and a private man found themselves so closely beset by six horsemen before they were aware of it that they had not time to throw themselves into the wood but were obliged to fire. As all idea of surprising them was now over, we pushed forward directly and followed the patrol so closely that they had neither time to take up the bridge or use any other precaution. The light infantry...and grenadiers formed within 50 yards of the rebel party on this side the bridge who challenged us and fired. They were immediately charged and run over the bridge."[26]

   With momentum on his side, Craig made the most of the opportunity. "As I found they had not taken the bridge up and seemed in a great panic I determined to push them, and not withstanding the strength of the ground thought circumstances bid fair for succeeding in an attack on their post itself..." Here Craig made the critical decision to push on over the bridge. With the Americans confused and retreating, he did not hesitate to drive home his advantage. The Americans "gave way," retreating in confusion over the bridge.[27]

Craig's redcoats skirmish with Lillington's militia at Heron's Bridge.

Troops under Captains Colebrooke Nesbit and Thomas Pitcairne rushed over the four hundred foot long bridge while the two artillery pieces were set up to cover their advance. For the redcoats charging across the long, narrow bridge over the river, it must have taken forever to reach the north shore. Hearts pounding with adrenaline, the British were relieved when the Americans did not contest their crossing.

As they raced onto the bridge, they were several feet above the wide river, and exposed on the wooden structure. Some may have looked down to see the water flowing below them, then glanced back up to the opposite shore, where the high ground held enemy troops. They quickly crossed and gained the north shore. The long, narrow bridge, the most dangerous part of the attack, was now behind them. Young's men retreated hastily, and the British occupied their camp. It was certainly no Moores Creek.

Here Craig's men found "a number of arms, canteens, some provisions, etc." After waiting for a counterattack that never came, the British recrossed the bridge and set up camp to rest on the south shore. Craig "wished the men to rest in security after the fatigue of 2 days march and lying 5 nights either on their arms or on the decks of sloops and boats without covering."[28]

Craig reported finding only three American dead and taking eight men prisoner, though more dead may have been carried off. The British lost six wounded, including Captain Nesbit. He had been hit twice in the leg on the first fire of the Americans, but he exerted himself so much that Craig did not realize he was wounded until the action ended.[29]

The British burned the bridge but only partially destroyed it, and it remained important for future operations. They also threw a captured 3 pound iron cannon into the river, after breaking off the trunions (parts that hold the gun into a carriage).[30]

The next day Craig's forces captured five of seven American supply ships nearby, while two others were run aground and burned. The brig *Rose* had two 3 pound guns, as well as rice, tobacco, and bale goods. The schooner *Betsy* held six 9 pound guns, along with rice, flour, rum, and ammunition. The schooner *Flying Fish* held rice, flour, turpentine, rum; and the schooner *Ceres* contained rice, flour, and ammunition. It was an impressive victory, not only routing the American troops and capturing the bridge, but also taking their entire fleet and all supplies as well.[31]

Craig's forces did not rest long. The next day they marched five miles further and destroyed supplies of rum and other stores to deny them to the Americans, before returning to Wilmington.[32]

Craig wrote that "In justice to the troops and marines under my command I cannot help mention that the town of Wilmington was taken possession of and an extent of country upwards of 45 miles marched over with only one single instance of any article being touched or inhabitant injured in his property..."[33]

The British were also desperately short on horses for their cavalry, having only thirteen good mounts by this time. On February 9th Captain Pitcarine and the Light Infantry surprised a group of Americans while out foraging. The Whigs only fired one volley and fled.[34]

On February 10th, Craig wrote to Cornwallis, his first letter from Wilmington. He noted that area Loyalists were reluctant to join him for fear the small British force could not protect them. As time would tell, they were right.

Craig also wrote that he agreed that his force was small for its intended mission, but noted that they were fortifying the town. At times British sailors from the *Delight* and *Otter* had to man the city's defenses when the troops went out on expeditions. The American defenses had been built well south of the city, and Craig, with a small force, had to build earthworks directly around the town. He also noted that the Northeast Cape Fear River was an effective barrier, keeping the American militia at a distance.[35]

Curving above the city and stretching nearly all the way across the peninsula, the Northeast Cape Fear River had few crossing points and did, in fact, influence all troop movements in the area. It acted as a barrier to movement and allowed the British free reign on the peninsula below the river, so long as American raiders were kept above the river. It also served to keep the British contained and made it difficult for

General Nathaniel Greene

them to venture into the interior of the state.

With only 289 men fit for duty, Craig's force was barely enough to hold on to Wilmington. At one point he suggested going up to attack General Nathanael Greene's force, trapping the Americans between Cornwallis and his own troops, yet abandoned the idea since his force was too small.[36]

Craig's letters illustrate an important point: the British view from Wilmington. They had occupied the town and controlled the river, but were in a hostile area and could not venture into the countryside. They had good troops but too few of them.

A few days later Craig wrote that his troops had nearly completed an abatis (obstacles of sharpened stakes) around the earthworks surrounding the town. He also noted they were "occupying an extent of ground beyond proportion to our numbers." The abatis would be an effective barrier to an attack. The defenses stretched along a ridge of high ground that ran from Second to Fourth Streets in Wilmington. The sturdy brick St. James church was incorporated into the defenses, and they also knocked holes in the walls to allow for ease of firing through them. In some places the British added two rows of abatis in front of the earthworks. Across the river on Eagles Island, a brick house overlooking the ferry was fortified and barricaded, with abatis surrounding it. The countryside around the town would have been cleared of foliage: wood was needed for fuel, but when cleared it also it provided a clear field of fire, so no one could approach the town unseen. A hospital was set up at the corner of Market and Second Streets. By the summer of 1781 a bleak and desolate landscape surrounded Wilmington.[37]

Craig also reported that he sent three messengers inland to try and link up with General Cornwallis. One returned unsuccessfully, but Craig hoped the others would find him. Moving through enemy territory with no guides, it is no wonder his couriers had trouble accomplishing their mission.[38]

In a letter dated April 6th, Craig wrote to Cornwallis that he was concerned the marines were leaving with the warships, which would reduce his already small garrison. He also passed along some news that the general would not have learned of in the interior. Holland and England were now at war, adding the Dutch to the list including France and Spain that were fighting the British around the world. The struggle had widened into a world war, and England was being spread thin by fighting around the globe. Craig also noted that General William Phillips had landed in Virginia with a sizable force of troops. This last news would have important ramifications for Cornwallis's future planning.[39]

In coming to Wilmington, Craig wrote that he hoped to create a "State of Disorder" in North Carolina. His presence did exactly that, interrupting trade from overseas and occupying the state's largest town and only major port. Soon he would launch raids into the interior to extend his disruption of the state's military effort.[40]

How citizens in Wilmington fared during the occupation is hard to tell, though it largely depended on loyalty. There are no records on how the British ran the town or what regulations they imposed. It is difficult to assess how citizens fared, but no doubt it was challenging for all. Some were glad to see the British come and made the most of the chance to proclaim loyalty and receive protection from them. Elizabeth Parker, for example, furnished horses, room and board for the British. Others paid for their support of the Whigs. Mary Boyd, wife of publisher Adam, "was in a constant state of alarm" and depended on her slaves for "help and comfort."[41]

Eventually Mary fled to The Oaks, a plantation on the Northeast Cape Fear near the mouth of Turkey Creek. There she joined several refugees, who hid in a cellar until dark. At that point British gunboats came up the river. One of the men, John Brown, "with a flag of truce went out to hold a parlay, as soon as they saw him they fired at him but he escaped & got back safe to the house." The British shelled the home for a short time, then fell back down the river.[42]

Captain Thomas Rutherford, a Loyalist who was captured following the battle at Moores Creek, was later paroled and assisted the wife of William Hooper. Craig had ordered her to leave the area, and Rutherford helped her obtain horses and carriages for her valuables.[43]

South Carolina Governor John Rutledge sarcastically noted that "6 of the Town's people left it, the rest receive the Enemy with 3 huzzahs," commenting on the number of Loyalists in the town. With Craig's British troops in the area, many Loyalists who had fought at Moores Creek felt confident enough to openly support the British. Some came forward to act as scouts and spies for Craig's forces.[44]

John Rutledge

Many Loyalists from the interior flocked to Wilmington for either protection or to actively join the British forces. A number of slaves from plantations along the rivers ran away to join them as well. Major Craig appointed Isaac DuBois as Commissary, and instructed him to oversee the distribution of cattle and other supplies seized from the hostile inhabitants.[45]

The British required citizens to sign an agreement "to be admitted to a dependence on Great Britain" - in other words, taking the oath of allegiance to the Crown. Only two Wilmington men refused: Thomas Maclaine and John Huske. William Hooper wrote that they held out, despite "all the powers of persuasion, insult and menace" that Craig could muster. Both were harassed and forced to leave the city.[46]

Civilians in the town suffered as there was no trade or access to the surrounding countryside. The British were bottled up in Wilmington, being unable to move beyond the Northeast Cape Fear River, which served to cut off the area from the rest of the state. Civilians were thus denied the freedom of movement that allowed them to purchase or sell supplies from outlying areas. One observer noted that prices for goods tripled.

There were also no courts held in New Hanover County (which included modern Pender County) for an entire year, from January 1781 until January

1782. It caused headaches for those who had legal matters to pursue and business to conduct.[47]

The British needed shallow draft vessels that did not draw over three feet for operations on the inland waterways, and began to build some at Wilmington. In the meantime the Americans reoccupied Heron's Bridge.

The half-moon gorget worn by Lillington's men.

Alexander Lillington set up a base camp there from which he could strike at the British, and at the same time prevent them from crossing and raiding the interior of the state. Craig noted that "The Rebels have continued at the Bridge the whole time, their numbers fluctuating between four and eight hundred..."[48]

On February 18th Barkley and his marines and sailors left, leaving a small number of warships, galleys, and gunboats at Craig's disposal. The relationship between the army and navy commander had been poor, possibly due to the divided nature of the command. While Craig lamented the loss of the men, he was not sorry to see Barkley go.[49]

Craig said of Barkley when writing to his superior, *"May I beg if you can ever turn the scale relative to his returning here, that it may be in the negative—he & I differ so much in our sentiments that I much fear we can never carry on service together with that cordiality requisite to do it effectually... Pardon me if for your private information I warn you to receive it with caution every thing he tells you – [his] interest will be his chief inducement. I had once thoughts of returning him his marines that he might have no reason for coming back but I could not part with six and twenty fine fellows."*[50]

In the meantime North Carolina Governor Abner Nash arrived at Heron's Bridge to review the troops, meet with Lillington, and bring reinforcements. As long as the Americans held the bridge, the river was an effective barrier, keeping the British bottled up to the south.[51]

Lillington was criticized by some in the state government for his inaction, since he outnumbered Craig's garrison. On the other hand, his militia had few supplies, and they were inexperienced compared to the British regulars.[52]

On February 22nd the British ship *Delight* sent a seven man shore party to bury a sailor who had died on board. American troops hidden on shore fired on them as they landed, killing one and capturing three. Quickly the ship returned fire, and the militia fled, having to leave their prisoners, who the British then rescued.[53]

One of Craig's primary goals was to hunt down the local rebel leadership, and one of his biggest targets was Cornelius Harnett. Craig said of him "he was employed to the most traitorous purpose; it determined me to turn any risk to seize him."[54]

Craig learned that he had fled to the north, and immediately set out after him. Harnett had stopped at the home of Col. John Spicer in Onslow County, about thirty miles north of Wilmington. Harnett's health had been poor for some time, and the stress of the war only worsened it. Bedridden and unable to proceed any further, there the British found him.[55]

Cornelius Harnett's grave

Harnett was bound and taken back to Wilmington. One witness who saw them returning with the prisoner noted that he was "thrown across a horse like a sack of meal." Harnett was held in roofless pen exposed to weather, then later paroled to the Wilmington city limits.[56]

Fearing for his health, townspeople asked Craig to let Harnett go, but it was too late. Weakened by the rigors of his flight and capture, he died on April 28th and was buried in the St. James cemetery with "utmost frugality," as his will specified, he wanted a simple funeral. Harnett was fifty-eight years old.[57]

Harnett dedicated his time and treasure to the cause of independence, and paid the ultimate price for it. His grave today stands in the corner of St. James Church's cemetery in downtown Wilmington, and nearby stands a marker to him, on Market Street.

General John Ashe had also fled when the British arrived, hiding in a swamp. A slave betrayed his location, and he was shot in the leg while running. He was captured and imprisoned in town. There he contracted one of the most feared diseases of the day: smallpox. Paroled to the city (he had freedom of movement within city limits, but could not leave), it was too late for him as well. Thus the British gained a reputation for being ruthless while in Wilmington, as two important men died while prisoners in their custody.[58]

On March 1st the first letter to Craig from Lord Cornwallis, written on February 21st, arrived asking for supplies to be sent up the Cape Fear River.

British troops with cannon set out for Heron's Bridge.

Specifically Cornwallis needed shoes, boots, and saddles. Craig's reply explained that the bluffs of the river were occupied by the Whigs, and he could not move upriver. Any attempt would be met by hostile fire.[59]

With the Americans reoccupying Heron's Bridge the British in Wilmington were hemmed in, and could not forage for food or supplies. Not only did the militia keep the British within their Wilmington defenses, but they also occasionally harassed the British there. Mounted militia often rode up to the edge of town as far as the church, hoping to draw the British out. If they gave chase, the Americans would retreat and draw them into pre-arranged ambushes along the road.[60]

The source of the problem clearly was Heron's Bridge. Forage for Craig's horses was nearly gone and the Americans at the bridge made it "dangerous to proceed a great distance" beyond the town. In early March Craig decided to strike again, taking 200 men (including thirty sailors), and his two 3 pound guns. The British arrived and set up their two guns facing the bridge to prevent an attack.[61]

Lillington learned of their approach and prepared an ambush. He had about four hundred militia and six cannons above the river. According to soldier Joseph Humphrey, General Lillington ordered a company to march down from their camp and cross the river, while another crossed the bridge and circled around. Thus they would attack the British from front and rear. From his campsite on the north side of the river, he sent Col. Henry Young with sixty cavalry and Col. Thomas Brown with seventy infantry around to hit the British rear.[62]

Unfortunately Maj. Dennis, with a force of cavalry, disobeyed orders, causing the entire plan to go awry. He was to take twelve horsemen down the road on the south bank and watch for the British. Instead they stayed in camp, and there the British surprised them. His detachment suffered one man bayoneted, and one drowned while running across the dismantled bridge and falling into the river. With the element of surprise lost, Lillington ordered Brown and Young to attack. Thus began the second Battle of Heron's Bridge, fought on March 9, 1781.[63]

Craig wrote that, "Our Advanced Guard surprised a piquet [guards] of Light Horse most of which was bayoneted or rushed into the River and drowned, and by the Prisoners taken I learnt that a party under a Colonel Brown consisting of 150 Horse and Foot, were then on the sound." Craig then posted his men on a hill, and had his artillery take position.[64]

The main action began at four o'clock when Lillington ordered his cannons to begin firing on the British position below the river. Young and Brown then began their attack. They were repulsed because, according to Lillington, "the infantry being badly placed, did not do that execution they ought to have done." It seems that the Americans, in forming for the attack quickly, were not as prepared as they should have been. The two British artillery pieces provided support to their infantry, and helped beat back the attack. James Malpass recalled that General Lillington was on the other side of the Bridge, and he tried to direct the battle from there.[65]

Col. Thomas Brown was severely wounded at the battle. His arm was broken, and he lost full use of it afterwards. Private Bezzant Brock saw him receive his wound during the action. Another solider, John Edge, was wounded and never fully recovered, suffering the effects until his death in the 1840s.[66]

About twenty Whigs were killed and about eleven taken prisoner. The British pursuit stopped due to the thickness of the swamps and nightfall. Craig's men lost two wounded and one cavalryman captured. They remained at the bridge four days, gathering forage and then marched back to Wilmington. For

Craig's men make a second attempt against the Amricans at Heron's Bridge.

the second time the British had won an engagement at Heron's Bridge. Lillington sent his cavalry over to pursue and harass the British on their march, but in another example of failing to follow orders, they did not press Craig with vigor.[67]

John Fowler, a militiaman in the battle, recalled that "a detachment of British then under the command of Major Craig at Wilmington came out to attack the American force stationed at Holly Shelter. From inferiority of force, Captain Dann ordered a retreat and they were so closely pursued by the British as to be obliged to throw their ammunition into the River. The men...were ordered to disperse and return home."[68]

The second battle at Heron's Bridge was a confused affair, with each commander claiming the other side lost more heavily, and both accounts of it differ wildly. No doubt it was even more confusing for the men who fought in isolated detachments, slashing through the woods and swamps. The common soldier had no concept of the larger picture, only knowing what they were seeing around them. Lillington wrote that the British had "taken great pains to conceal their Dead," and accused several blacks serving with them of cutting the throats of Americans wounded on the battlefield. Lillington's enraged men asked permission to burn Mount Black, Craig's headquarters during the battle, in revenge. Lillington refused, but his men did it anyway.[69]

On April 9th Lillington's militia retreated from Heron's Bridge to Rutherford's Mill, sixteen miles to the north, near modern Burgaw. Here they established a new base from which to guard the interior and keep an eye on the British. Lillington wrote that "the Militia is not to be depended upon."[70]

Although the British had won the battle, the Americans remained on the north bank of the river. Hoping to trick his opponent, Craig sent a flag of truce to Lillington, requesting that he surrender: "Sir—as the people under your Command are all militia, whom we always rather...pity than wish to destroy – I will now acquaint you that I have taken Post here, to cut you off from all possibility of escape. In a few hours Lieut. Colonel [Banastre] Tarleton will be upon you with a detachment superior to yours even in Numbers—to spare your People therefore and to Preserve their farms (every one of which whose owners is absent will be Destroyed) I am to propose to you to deliver up your Arms to me, on which Condition your People shall have full Liberty to return home unmolested, & I will take effectual measures to secure their Property from the resentment of Lieut. Colo. Tarleton's Party." Tarleton was, of course, nowhere near the area at the time, and Craig was merely using the cavalry commander's reputation to his advantage.[71]

Lillington was not fooled, and answered, "Were it reasonable to suppose that you were well acquainted with the strength of my Army, & be sure of Lieut. Colo. Tarleton's success in an engagement with us, I should feel the full force of the humane Terms offered my men. But while we have Arms in our hands, and are appraised of your intentions, my prospects of success are very fair. I shall not yield up this post until compelled to it by superior force when my Army shall have an opportunity of signalizing their valour."[72]

Frustrated, Craig tried again, saying "my coming here is the effect of a preconcerted scheme & I beg you to be assured I should not have given you notice of your situation, had my so doing, been in the smallest Degree likely to have Afford you the means of extricating yourself." Again Lillington responded in the negative, for his forces were ready to attack.[73]

Lillington posted men on the outskirts of Wilmington to watch the British, and from his camp he wrote Governor Caswell, his co-commander at Moores Creek, "there was a Most Glorious Opportunity offered when they were at the Bridge, if we that day had the Troops that Major Dennis Carried off we Positively Should have killed & taken Craig & All his little Army – I cannot put it out of my mind." To General Greene he said, "we are not in a situation to drive [Craig's] Troops out of Wilmington & I am afraid we shall not be able to hold this part of the State long, unless we have a timely reinforcement: The militia is not to be depended on"[74]

Heron's Bridge probably *was* a lost opportunity for Lillington's force. If they had been able to soundly defeat Craig, they would have crippled the bulk of his force. With no reinforcements on the way, the tiny British force would not have been able to hold Wilmington, and would probably have been forced to evacuate the city.

It would have changed the whole course of the war in North Carolina, for with Wilmington in American hands Cornwallis would have had no secure supply base and no safe harbor to march to. It is not worth speculating further, yet the destruction of Craig's army and recapture of the city would have certainly altered the war.

Combat is chaos: action becomes fluid and events happen quickly, sometimes too quickly to react. While Lillington may have had a plan in mind, his troops could not execute it, and as he noted, his "glorious opportunity" was not to be. He probably reflected on this lost chance through the rest of the war, replaying it in his mind and only wishing for another opportunity.

In the meantime, a court martial of Maj. Dennis, in which he denied that he was irresponsible, found him guilty and dismissed him. Lillington wrote that he had "shamefully neglected his duty." He was declared "incapable of holding any Office of our trust." The trial was held at Mulberry Plantation near Beufort's Bridge in late March.[75]

Lillington has remained a somewhat forgotten Revolutionary leader. He fought at Moores Creek, yet never again had the chance to fully prove himself. During 1781 he had too few men and resources to block Cornwallis's march, Craig's raids, or deal with the Loyalist population. We many never fully measure the abilities, and shortcomings, of Lillington due to these circumstances.

A few days later on April 11th the British hung William Cain, a blacksmith from Brunswick Town accused of spying. He had been a member of the Brunswick Committee of Safety before the war. Cain had previously been captured and signed a parole, agreeing not to fight again.

He continued to aid the Whig militia, however, and was caught "holding a correspondence and giving intelligence" to the enemy. He was "instrumental" in the ambush of a British naval crew from the *Delight* that had come ashore at Brunswick in late February 1781.

Cain was captured and accused of "violating his parole for aiding the Rebels." On board the *Delight* the sailors hung him from the yardarm of the ship. They then threw his body overboard into the Cape Fear River.[76]

While the British occupied Wilmington, the American militia patrolled the countryside surrounding the city. Statements by militiamen indicate they were "constantly in active service in protecting the country from the enemy." They were "never permitted to stay at home but for a few days at a time" before returning to the field.[77]

It was often tedious and tense work, with very little contact with the enemy, but the constant threat of attack. Some militiamen wrote years later that the only action they saw was guarding Heron's Bridge or marching around the area and watching the coast for signs of British ships.[78]

Thomas Brown, a soldier who had fought at Moores Creek, was taken prisoner at one point in June and held in Wilmington. His wife Lucy was allowed to "approach the Court House in which he was confined and to peep at him through the side of the house."[79]

Despite holding the city, the British were unable to raise widespread Loyalist support. A Quaker of central North Carolina noted that "they had so often deceived in promise of support, and the British had so often relinquished posts, that the people were now afraid to join the British army, lest they should leave the province, in which case the resentment of the revolutionaries would be exercised with more cruelty; that although the men might escape, or go with the army, yet such was the diabolical conduct of these people, that they would inflict the severest punishment upon their families."[80]

British efforts suffered another setback known as Pyle's Defeat, fought in February near the Alamance battlefield of the Regulator War (near modern Burlington). Dr. John Pyle, who led former Regulators from Chatham and Alamance Counties to join the Loyalist army in 1776, again recruited forces for

The road where Loyalists under Pyle were destroyed by Whigs in a case of mistaken identity.

the British in 1781. His militia were on their way to join Tarleton's British cavalry when they encountered horsemen wearing green coats.

During the war each side wore a variety of uniforms and it so happened that Tarelton's British Legion and Col. Henry Lee's American cavalry both wore green jackets. Mistaking Lee's men for the British, Pyle's troops marched up along side them and began conversing with them.

Lee apparently knew from the start what was happening, and hoped to guide the Loyalists to the American army and capture them. At the rear of the column, however, men began talking and realized they were on the opposite side. Quickly swords were drawn and the Americans began hacking at the Loyalists, many of whom had their muskets slung over their shoulders. It was a complete rout, and within minutes about 250 Loyalists were dead or wounded, while others scattered into the woods. It could not have come at a worse time for Cornwallis's army, as he desperately needed help from the local population.[81]

Back in Wilmington, the British established prison ships in the Cape Fear as they had at New York and Charleston. They were an easy answer to a growing problem: how to deal with prisoners when they had neither men to spare as guards or space to house them. Prisoners suffered terribly in often crowded and unhealthy conditions. The *Forby* (also spelled *Torbay* or *Forbay*) was anchored in the river as a prison ship that spring and summer. Among those held there was Captain Daniel Buie, a militia commander from the central part of the state. Over 130 prisoners, many captured at Camden a year earlier, languished aboard the ship.[82]

In June the American cavalry received orders to protect the salt works on Topsail Sound, Masonboro Sound, and others near Wilmington and in Onslow County. Fortunately, the British never tried to destroy them.[83]

In Wilmington the British had created an outdoor prison known as the Bull Pen, "in the depression on the north side of Market street between Second and Third" (where a bank stood in 2007). It was "made of rails" and its occupants were exposed to the elements.[84]

At some point that summer Craig sent troops to permanently occupy Heron's Bridge. This was a critical position as it not only ensured access to the interior, but also kept the American militia at a distance from the city. Heron's Bridge was, and would remain, the front line for the rest of the British occupation.[85]

A war of words began between Major Craig and Governor Thomas Burke. Recently in Kinston the local militia had captured five Loyalists and executed them. On June 21st Craig wrote to Burke that, "Had I listened to the first emotions excited by...deliberately murdering five men at Kingstown and...inhuman treatment of the King's friends, Mr. Samuel Ashe and his comrades in irons would have become the immediate victims of Caswell's unwarrantable cruelty." In other words, in reprisal for the killing of Loyalists, Craig threatened to execute prisoners he was holding. The Caswell referred to here was the son of Richard Caswell the former Governor, an officer with the militia.[86]

Craig also wrote that he called on Burke to "use your efforts to put a stop to a proceeding which promises such additional misery to the people over whom you now preside." He went on to state that, "After allowing a reasonable time for the interposition of your authority I shall think myself called on by Justice, Duty, & I may add ultimately by every consideration of humanity, to give the people who from the most laudable principles of loyalty take up arms in the King's favor, ample revenge & satisfaction for every instance of murder committed by any party of Militia on one of them..."[87]

The governor responded by observing, "In several parts of the country, the war has, unhappily kindled the most fierce and vindictive animosity between the People who adhere to the Government of Great Britain and those who resolved at all hazards to oppose what they deemed an unconstitutional exercise of power..." He went on to note that early in the war the state made efforts to encourage Loyalists to leave, thus hopefully preventing this type of violence.[88]

Burke also admitted, "it is certain that many people have been killed by those whom you are pleased to call the King's friends where nothing could be assigned as provocation or excuse." In addition, he promised to use "Efforts for checking and, if possible, entirely preventing those practices..." He ended by stating that, "I cannot see the Justice of your present Treatment of Mrs. Samuel Ashe..." The discussions went nowhere, as the situation had deteriorated to the point of mistrust.[89]

While in Wilmington Craig's officers held balls and invited local civilians to attend. At one such party was a woman named Ann Fergus, a well educated and wealthy lady, who was extremely tall at 5' 10" (taller than the average man's height of 5'8"), and was close to 6" in heels. A short British officer stepped up to her and asked for a kiss. She said yes, if he could take it without standing on a stool. Undeterred, the officer stretched up on his tiptoes, but she did likewise, and remained beyond his reach. The crowd laughed and he retreated. This story, although romanticized, sheds light on one way civilians snubbed the British who occupied their town.[90]

Although Craig's force was small it would not be alone for long. While it was never intended, General Cornwallis' army was soon heading for Wilmington as well. The city's population was about to double with the arrival of these additional enemy soldiers.

British and American cavalry clash at Guilford Courthouse.

Chapter 8
British Occupation

While Craig's forces occupied Wilmington, other events were in motion that would bring even more British troops to the Lower Cape Fear. The year 1781 saw violence return to the region as civil war erupted with the arrival of these British forces. Among those traveling with Cornwallis's army was Governor Josiah Martin, who brought a printing press and assisted with putting out announcements to garner support from the Loyalists of the state.[1]

Martin was ineffective, however. Lt. Col. Banaster Tarleton wrote that "The length of time that had elapsed since Governor Martin quitted the province, and the variety of calamities which had attended the exertions of the loyalists, had not only reduced their numbers and weakened their attachment, but had confirmed the power and superiority of the adverse party, and had occasioned a general depression in the King's friends, which would not easily have been shaken off in the most prosperous times, and therefore was not likely to be warmed into action with the present appearance of public affairs."[2]

Having fought the Battle of Guilford Courthouse at modern Greensboro, General Cornwallis needed to rest and resupply his battered army. Although they won the battle, it came at the cost of one fourth of their men killed or wounded. The troops were in terrible shape, shoes were worn out, clothing threadbare, tents were scarce, and food was not to be had.

News of the victory at Battle of Guilford Courthouse reached London on June 5th, where it was apparent that while force of arms had won a hard fought engagement, the army had gained very little. Charles Fox said in Parliament that, "Another such victory would ruin the British army."[3]

In the aftermath of the battle Cornwallis took stock of his army and what it had achieved. The British captured all of the American artillery at Guilford Courthouse (four 6 pounders), along with two ammunition wagons, over two hundred shot (cannon balls), and gunpowder. The army took these needed supplies with them.[4]

The British also captured 1,300 small arms (rifles and muskets), which they distributed to their Loyalist militia. The leftover were destroyed to prevent the Americans from recapturing them. They also paroled the American prisoners, as they could not be taken with them and could not be properly fed or cared for.[5]

Cornwallis decided to move his army to Cross Creek to resupply. With Wilmington in British hands, he felt that Major Craig could move provisions up the Cape Fear to Cross Creek. The British army marched from Guilford Courthouse on March 18th. The Earl was unaware of the troubles Craig was having in carrying out his resupply mission. They left sixty-four of the most seriously wounded at New Garden Meeting House under the care of a surgeon. A small cemetery at the Meeting House today in Greensboro holds the remains of several British soldiers.[6]

That same day Cornwallis issued a proclamation, claiming that he had defeated Greene (which he had) and that Royal control was now re-established in North Carolina (which anyone who looked at the small, ragged British army could see, was not the case). Few local residents came out to support the King's army.[7] His proclamation read,

Whereas by the blessings of Almighty God, His Majesty's Arms have been crowned with signal success, by the complete victory obtained over the Rebel forces on the 15 Instant, I have thought proper to issue this Proclamation to call upon all loyal Subjects to stand forth and take an Active part in restoring good Order & Government. And whereas it has been represented to me that many Persons in this Province who have taken a share in this unnatural Rebellion, but having experienced the oppression and injustice of the Rebel Government, and having seen the errors into which they have been deluded by falsehoods and misrepresentations, are sincerely desirous of returning to their duty and Allegiance, I do hereby notify and promise to all such Persons (Murderers excepted) that if they will surrender themselves with their Arms & Ammunition, at Head Quarters, or to the Officer Commanding in the district contiguous to their respective places of residence, on or before the 20th day of

April next, they shall be permitted to return to their homes, upon giving a Military Parole, and shall be protected in their persons and properties from all sort of violence from the British Troops, and will be restored as soon as possible to all the Privileges of legal and Constitutional Government.[8]

Cornwallis' numbers had been declining since January. That month he had 3,224 men under his command. By March, prior to the battle of Guilford Courthouse, he was down to 2,213. By the time the army left Wilmington on its march north to Virginia, the general led only 1,723, half the number he had just three months earlier.[9]

Battle loss (principally at Cowpens and Guilford Courthouse), along with disease, desertion, and the strain of the campaign took a hard toll on his own army. Unlike the Americans, who could replace men easily, British numbers would only go down. While the Americans may not have been as well trained, the veteran British troops faced the prospect of no reinforcement while moving through a hostile area where they only enjoyed temporary rests in friendly regions. It was a rigorous campaign that tested the endurance of all in Cornwallis's army.

As Cornwallis moved southeast, Greene cautiously followed with his army. This part of the Southern Campaign is often overlooked yet it was of primary importance. General Nathanael Greene broke off his pursuit of Cornwallis and turned instead to the British forts spread across South Carolina. The British moved on to Cross Creek, and later Wilmington. As events will prove, the seed was planted for the army's later move into Virginia.

Thus the two main armies of the South would never meet again in combat. Their movement in opposite directions laid the groundwork for all that followed. Through the summer and fall of 1781 General Greene and other American leaders like Thomas Sumter and Francis Marion attacked British posts across South Carolina. This led to another round of violent battles at Hobkirk's Hill, Ninety-Six, Fort Motte, and Eutaw Springs

Francis Marion (left) and Thomas Sumter (right).

Intent on ending the war in Virginia, Cornwallis moved toward that goal, and ultimately met defeat at Yorktown. Events in southeastern North Carolina in March and April 1781 led to these later, better known events.

At Barbecue Church in late March (near modern Sanford), Tarleton's cavalry rode ahead of the main army, only to be ambushed by American militia. The troopers rode in amongst the soldiers, scattering them. Militiaman Duncan Buie had his head split open in the melee, but recovered and lived a long life afterwards. Most of the militia were captured, but some escaped. The prisoners taken, including Daniel Buie, were marched under guard with the British forces, eventually ending up on a prison ship in the Cape Fear River (there were many Buies living in the area, and most were closely related).[10]

Barbecue Church as it looks today

As the British crossed the center of the state and entered the coastal region, General Nathanael Greene ordered Lillington to harass and slow their march. With fewer men, most of whom were militia, and no artillery, Lillington could do little to delay Cornwallis' march.

In a letter to his superiors in London, Cornwallis noted the state of his battered army, "With a third of my Army Sick & Wounded which I was obliged to carry in Waggons or on horseback, the remainder without shoes & worn down with fatigue, I thought it was time to look for some place of rest & refreshment."[11]

At the same time he praised his tattered army: "I cannot sufficiently commend the behaviour of both Officers & Men under my Command. They not only shewed the most persevering intrepidity in Action, but underwent with cheerfulness such fatigues & hardships as have seldom been experienced by a British Army..."[12]

On March 30th the British army entered Cross Creek, where "500 rebels had taken their position, but who withdrew on our approach, having partly burnt their stores and partly carried them off. The remaining stores of provisions were collected together and distributed amongst the troops." Yet the captured material would not go very far.[13]

Upon arrival at Cross Creek, he sadly learned that Craig could not forward supplies to them there. The disappointed general noted, "On my Arrival there, I found to my great Mortification & contrary to all former accounts that it was impossible to procure any considerable quantity of provisions..."[14]

Cornwallis wrote that "Provisions were scarce, not four days' forage within twenty miles - and to use the navigation of the Cape Fear River to Wilmington impracticable, for the distance by water is upward of an hundred miles, the breadth seldom above one hundred yards, the banks high, and the inhabitants on each side generally hostile."[15]

Cornwallis vented his frustration in a letter to his superior in British-occupied New York, Sir Henry Clinton, overall British commander in North America. Cornwallis wrote that, "the Inhabitants rode into Camp, shook me by the hand, said they were glad to see us and to hear that we had beat Greene, and then rode home again. For I could not get 100 Men in all the Regulator Country to stay with us..." He also noted that, "Their numbers are not so great as had been represented and their friendship was only passive."[16]

Already Cornwallis was thinking ahead to his next move. He wrote Clinton that "I cannot help expressing my Wish that the Chesapeak may become the seat of War, even (if necessary) at the expense of abandoning New York. Until Virginia is in a manner subdued, our hold of the Carolinas must be Difficult if not precarious."[17]

At the British camp in Cross Creek, many loyal citizens showed "great zeal for the interest of the royal army" and brought out food and supplies and treated the army's sick and wounded. It was probably the warmest reception the British army had received in North Carolina. Inspired Loyalists also took revenge for years of oppression by damaging the mills and property of Whigs.[18]

British officer Charles Stedman said they were "disappointed" on arriving in Cross Creek, for "provisions were scarce, four days forage not to be

The Fayettevile Arsenal as it looked in the Civil War. It was once Haymount Plantation.

procured within twenty miles, and the communication expected to be opened between Cross Creek and Wilmington, by means of the river, was found to be impracticable."[19]

While the British were in Cross Creek, they camped one day and one night at Haymount Plantation on the west end of town, now site of the arsenal. Some men went to plunder a bakery owned by Lewis Bowell, the only baker in town. Bowell hid in an empty barrel as the British went upstairs. During their looting they picked up a heavy barrel, threw it onto its side, and kicked it down the stairs. Upon bouncing down and hitting the wall, the barrel burst, and a dazed Bowell jumped out. So startled were the British soldiers that they left without taking any supplies.[20]

With few supplies in Cross Creek, Cornwallis felt he had no choice but to move on to Wilmington, which was securely in British hands. The army left, marching down the river road that MacDonald had intended to use five years earlier. For the next few days the army averaged between fourteen and sixteen miles a day.[21]

Supplies had been low since the army entered North Carolina in January. To assist the army Stedman organized the runaway slaves who flocked to the army into foraging parties. They gathered food for the troops, and were to be marked for identification. Like the soldiers, they were subject to military discipline.

The former slaves were difficult to control, and Cornwallis received complaints of "Negroes Straggling from the Line of March, Plunder'g and Using Violence to the Inhabitants." Any caught were ordered to be whipped or shot.

The army was no doubt in low spirits, having endured battle, cold, rain, and low provisions. Another blow came on Monday, April 2nd when Col. James Webster of the 33rd Regiment died of his wounds from Guilford Courthouse. Webster was a popular and respected commander. Where the British buried Webster is a mystery. In the 1850s a local resident found an old black man who was a guide for the British sixty years earlier and enlisted his help. They found the spot, and began to dig up the grave. The body was found, but upon exposure, the corpse crumbled, and they filled the grave back in. Its location was not recorded.[22]

The army lost other officers on the march, Captain William Shultz and Captain Maynard of the Brigade of Guards and Ensign de Trooss of the Von Bose Regiment among them. A trail of graves followed the British on their slow and steady march down to the coast.[23]

On the 3rd the army reached Brown's Creek, two miles south of Elizabethtown. Along the way the British encountered broken bridges that forced the army to halt while troops repaired them. Three days later another officer, Captain von Wilmosky died at Alston's Plantation along the Cape Fear.[24]

On Saturday, April 7th the army marched fourteen miles and camped at Macleans Bluff or Machaines' Bluff on the Cape Fear River. The site was probably near modern Navassa. A Hessian officer wrote that the army remained here from the 7th through the 10th. On the 9th Cornwallis' severely wounded were rowed into Wilmington, followed by the less seriously injured on the 10th. The army moved into Wilmington in stages, arriving piecemeal from the 11th through the 13th. Although the army had reached safety at Wilmington, another officer, Lieutenant von Trott, died of wounds on the 19th.[25]

Cornwallis's army of roughly 1,500 British and German troops occupied the town from the 13th through the 24th of April. Since Guilford Courthouse they had marched over two hundred miles, often on poor roads, and through territory that if not hostile, was not openly friendly.

Upon entering Wilmington, one German officer noted that he observed "row-galleys and provision ships were moored in the Cape Fear River not far from the town. The great transports, etc., however, on account of the shallowness of the water, lay 16 miles further down the river, and most requirements and necessities had to be brought up to the town in sloops." Here he was referring to The Flats at Brunswick, which prevented large ships from coming all the way up to Wilmington.[26]

General Cornwallis used the Burgwin house at the corner of Third and Market Streets as his

The Burgwin-Wright House served as Cornwallis' headquarters.

headquarters, allowing the family to reside in part of the home. Five years after he was forced from power, Governor Josiah Martin finally entered Wilmington with this weak but conquering army. Also returning to the region was the Black Pioneer Brigade, first organized from the area's runaway slaves in 1776. Former runaway slaves and former royal governor now walked the streets of the town.[27]

St. James Church (located on Fourth Street at the time) was used as a stable by Tarleton's cavalry, the wooden pews being removed. Later during the summer it was also used as a hospital. The brick building, standing on the edge of town, was also incorporated into the city's defense, with earthworks and abatis (obstacles of wood) built around it.[28]

St. James Church in Wilmington was taken over by the Britsh.

One American who had been sent to spy on the British reported that they camped "on the heights back of town." The troops spread out over the area now bounded by Water, Dock, Third, and Nun Streets.[29]

Their fortifications stretched in an arc of high ground that is still visible in Wilmington's historic district today, beginning on Front Street at the intersection with Church, and running over towards St. Mary's Catholic Church. In the schoolyard near the church stands the Boundary Oak, an ancient tree that has seen armies come and go from Wilmington for more than two hundred years.

A report made on April 15th showed the army's strength:

Officers, chaplains, and surgeons	*127*
Sergeants, drummers, and privates	*2059*
Total	*2186 (rank and file: 1829)*

Not all the troops were present with the army. Some were detached, sick, or wounded:

On command:	*544*
Prisoner of War	*694*
Sick	*436*
Wounded	*397*
Detached	*214*[30]

Cornwallis wrote to Lord Germain, Secretary of State for America, that he approved of Craig's operations. "Major Craig now took possession of the place in the latter end of January, has conducted himself with great zeal and capacity, having with a very small force not only secured the Post from all insults, but made himself respectable in this part of the Country by several successful excursions."[31]

On April 21st prominent Loyalist citizens of the town petitioned Governor Martin that they wished to be recognized as British subjects again, and asked for British protection. Now that the British were in control, Loyalists could openly support them. Some of the petitioners were no doubt only trying to protect their property, switching sides as the fortunes of war changed.[32]

Martin, seeing that his colony remained largely unconquered, left for England, thus avoiding the march north with Cornwallis that ended at Yorktown. He died in London in 1786.[33]

The Boundary Oak

While in Wilmington a series of important exchanges between Cornwallis and various people took place. Cornwallis corresponded with his adversary General Greene regarding a prisoner exchange. The issue of prisoners was an ongoing one, as neither side had the resources to properly take care of them, and each army badly needed the fighting men. Discussions with Greene had begun in December 1780, but it was not until the spring of 1781 that an agreement was hammered out. A prisoner exchange was arranged at the home of Claudius Pegee along the Pee Dee River of South Carolina.[34]

Cornwallis also discussed his next move, a subject that would lead to considerable controversy after the war. His army could not remain in Wilmington. It served no purpose staying there with the countryside in the hands of the American militia. Cornwallis became convinced that the key to winning the war was to invade Virginia. As long as reinforcements and supplies could flow from that state, the Carolinas could not be held.[35]

While the British army could have returned to South Carolina to face General Greene, it was not a desirable option. The country between Cross Creek and Camden was "barren, and intersected with creeks and rivers," the roads were poor, and in moving back south it would appear that the British were retreating.[36]

Lord Cornwallis wrote to Maj. Gen. Phillips in Virginia, "Now my dear friend, what is our plan? Without one we cannot succeed, and I assure you that I am quite tired of marching about the country in quest of adventures. If we mean an offensive war in America, we must abandon New York and bring our whole force into Virginia: we then have a stake to fight for, and a successful battle may give us America. If our plan is defensive, mixed with desultory expeditions, let us quit the Carolinas (which cannot be held defensively while Virginia can be so easily armed against us) and stick to our salt pork at New York, wending now and then a detachment to steal tobacco etc."[37]

On April 23rd Cornwallis considered his options and decided on a move north into Virginia, rather than south to follow Greene's army into South Carolina. He noted the difficulty of marching south towards Camden, and that they would be delayed too long if they waited in Wilmington for transport by sea. He also called it "Disgraceful to Britain" for the army to return to the southern province after having just marched across North Carolina. He hoped to "take advantage of Gen'l Greene having left that part of Virginia open and march immediately into that province to attempt a junction with General Phillips."[38]

Despite having been in Wilmington for two weeks, his army was still low on supplies. Shoes, uniforms, other clothing, and rifles were received by the German and British troops. Units who received new weapons in turn gave their old arms to the local Loyalist militia.[39]

One officer wrote that many in the army were barefoot when they arrived, and some had made shoes from cowhide. In Wilmington each man received two pairs of shoes. Linen was made into trousers for men who needed them.[40]

A German soldier in the Von Bose Regiment recalled that they received double rations of rum each day and plenty of provisions of meat and ship's bread (hard bread, like hardtack). Shoes, shirts, and breeches were replaced, welcome changes for the men in worn out clothing.[41]

For many British and German troops in Cornwallis' army, Wilmington must have been an oasis. For the first time in months the troops were in a secure place, relatively free from attack behind the city's defenses. They were also in an area with an openly Loyalist, and supportive, civilian population. Supplies from the sea also eased the suffering of long marches, cold nights without shelter, and poor rations. Warmer spring days also served to raise their spirits.

Cornwallis wrote that "Neither my Cavalry nor Infantry are in readiness to move. The former are in want of every thing, the latter of every necessary but Shoes, of which we have received an Ample Supply; I must however begin my

March tomorrow. It is very disagreeable to me to decide upon measures so very important & of such consequence to the general conduct of the War..."[42]

The general also noted a fact that would only worsen and that contributed immensely to his army becoming trapped at Yorktown: "...the delay & difficulty of conveying Letters, & the impossibility of waiting for Answer..." Communication between Cornwallis in the field and Clinton in New York was erratic. It took weeks to relay messages, receive instructions, or get answers to questions. By the time a letter arrived the information was often out of date or circumstances had changed, and the issues were no longer relevant.[43]

On April 25th the British army left Wilmington, marching to the site of Heron's Bridge and then north on the Duplin Road. A detachment of Jaegers (German riflemen) and the Royal North Carolina Regiment (Loyalists), were left to bolster the small Wilmington garrison. At Heron's Bridge, the troops were ferried across, as the bridge was in disrepair. Lt. Col. Banastre Tarelton's cavalry had been sent out to seize all available boats and use them to ferry the troops. Craig's gunships sailed upriver to protect the army during the crossing. That night they camped at Swan's Plantation.[44]

The bridge was rebuilt by the 1790s, and rebuilt again in 1810. It was used until replaced in 1847. In the late 1980s Interstate 40 arrived at

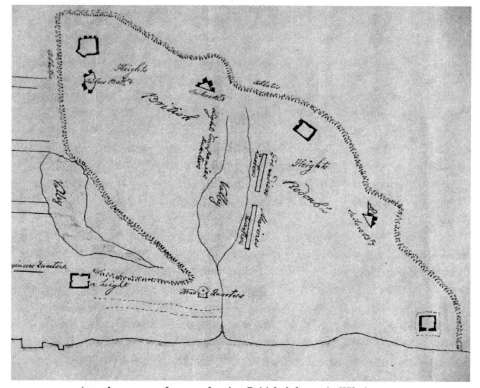

An enlargement of a map showing British defenses in Wilmington.

German Jaegers were among the troops left behind in Wilmington by Cornwallis.

Wilmington, and the northbound lanes cross the river just 250 feet west of the old bridge site. Heron's Bridge was one of the most significant historic sites in the region. Besides its importance as a unique drawbridge before the war, it was also the site of numerous river crossings and campsites, and the scene of two battles.[45]

Later it was known as Blossom's Ferry, and figured prominently in the Civil War. As Union forces captured Wilmington in early 1865, Confederate forces retreated across the river there, and skirmished with the advancing Federals. Thousands of motorists travel past the site daily with no inkling of the location's importance.

That April Cornwallis' force numbered 1,435 men fit for duty. By now many sick and wounded officers and men had rejoined their units. Along with them the British brought two small boats mounted on carriages to assist with crossing the numerous creeks and rivers that flowed across their path. While he intended to march straight north and invade Virginia, Cornwallis was also ready to backtrack to Wilmington if needed. He anxiously awaited news from Col. Francis Rawdon, who commanded British forces in South Carolina. If Rawdon needed help, Cornwallis could return to Wilmington and board transports for Charleston. In Halifax on May 12th Cornwallis learned of the British victory at

Hobkirk's Hill, near Camden, and felt Rawdon was secur⸍ continue on to Virginia.[46]

On April 30th Clinton wrote to Cornwallis from New ⸝ "sorry to find your Lordship continue in the opinion that our hola ⸝ Carolinas must be difficult, if not precarious, until Virginia is in a man. Subdued..." Clinton felt that such a move would take a long time and that ⸝ too late in the season to launch an invasion of Virginia. Rather than suggesting an alternative or firmly denying Cornwallis this move, however, he left it up to his subordinate to decide: "This...will greatly depend on Circumstances of which our Lordship and General Phillips may probably be better judges hereafter." Thus Clinton left the door open for Cornwallis to move north in pursuit of his Virginia plan.[47]

American forces were too small to interfere much with Cornwallis's march north through the eastern part of the state. Robert Sloan, commander of the militia at Heron's Bridge, had his troops and artillery pull back as the British approached. They retreated to Limestone Bridge, then on to Kingston.[48]

The Americans abandoned their trenches dug at Rutherford's Mill across Holly Shelter Creek. The site had been defended by two artillery guns under William Ward, but they knew they were no match for Cornwallis's larger force.[49]

Soon the militia and civilians of Duplin County felt the impact of the British army. Along their march the British managed to

Colonel Francis Lord Rawdon

capture several militiamen, including Captain Joseph Wade, John Bradshaw, and two others. At their home near the old Duplin Courthouse, Barnet Buck's wife May Ann was forced to feed the British troops who occupied their farm.[50]

The British army entered modern Wayne County (then still part of Duplin) on May 1st at Thunder Swamp Bridge, after crossing the Goshen Swamp on the road from Duplin Courthouse. On the 3rd they camped at William Reeve's Plantation on Brooks Swamp, just above modern Mount Olive. The weather was hot and dry, and due to the heat they began marching at night.[51]

Next the army moved to Gray's Ford on the Neuse River, then across Nahunta Creek to Cobb's Mill. Tarleton ordered local people to bring meal to

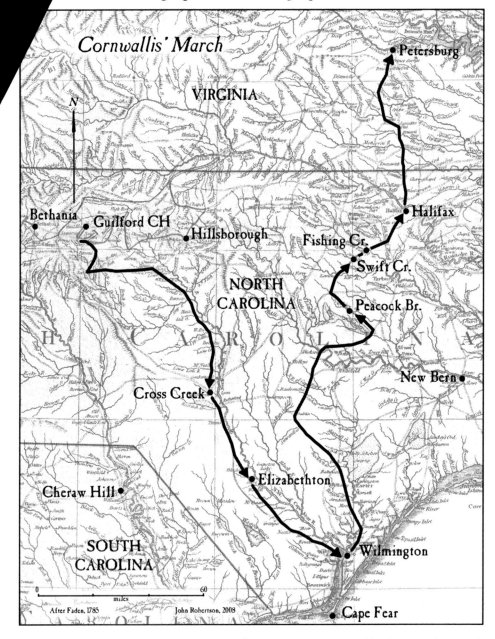

Cornwallis' March

VIRGINIA

N

Bethania
Guilford CH
Hillsborough
Fishing Cr.
Swift Cr.
Halifax
Petersburg

NORTH
CAROLINA

Peacock Br.

New Bern

Cross Creek

Elizabethton

Cheraw Hill

SOUTH
CAROLINA

Wilmington

Cape Fear

0   60
miles

After Faden, 1785   John Robertson, 2008

their camp at Nahunta Creek on May 5th, about two and a half miles southeast of present Fremont. The British used Cobb's mill to grind meal.[52]

As the army proceeded, Tarletons' cavalry remained in front ahead of the main army. The British looted homes while in Wayne County, but Loyalist refugees and camp followers were the worst. One North Carolina militiaman wrote, "The outrages were committed mostly by a train of loyal refugees."

Banastre Tarleton's dragoons scouted ahead of Cornwallis' main force.

Civilians who had come out to support the British were forced to flee with them when Cornwallis left the vicinity; otherwise they faced revenge from their neighbors. More specifically, he said that the women camp followers were "a swarm of beings (not better than harpies). These were women who followed the army in the character of officer's and soldiers' wives. They were generally mounted on the best horses and side saddles, dressed in the finest and best clothes that could be taken from the inhabitants."[53]

William Dickson, who resided in the area where Cornwallis' army passed through, wrote that, "The whole country was struck with terror, almost every man quit his habitation and fled, leaving his family and property to the mercy of merciless enemies. Horses, cattle, and sheep and every kind of stock were driven off from every plantation, corn and forage taken for the supply of the army and no compensation given, houses plundered and robbed, chests, trunks, etc. broke, women's and children's clothes, as well as men's wearing apparel and every kind of household furniture taken away." Dickson's and the homes of his brothers were all visited by British foragers.[54]

As Clerk of Court, Dickson felt it was his duty to save Duplin County's records. He hid them in an iron pot and buried it in Goshen Swamp. Upon going back to retrieve them, they could not be found.[55]

Tarleton's cavalry continued to move ahead of the infantry as the British army moved north. At one point they rode up to the Slocumb farm in modern Wayne County, near the current site of Dudley. Mary (Polly) Slocumb encountered Tarleton and his men, who demanded to know the whereabouts of her husband Ezekiel.[56]

She replied he was serving his country, which led to a heated discussion of the war and the fact that her husband was out with his militia fighting the British. In the meantime Tarleton had ordered his men to set up a camp around the home. They began to pitch tents in an orchard that was hidden from the road leading up to the home. A local Loyalist, a neighbor that Mary recognized, was sent out with some troopers to scout the area.[57]

Tarleton ordered Mary to prepare food for them, which she did. As she was serving the officers, they heard gunfire in the distance, and it became closer. They all rushed out to the front of the home.

Sure enough, the Loyalists who went out earlier were racing back, pursued by Whig cavalry being led by Mary's husband Ezekiel. Mary had sent a slave, Big George, to warn him to stay away from the home, but he had not gotten off the property yet. George was taking shelter in hedges along the road leading up to the house when he managed to stop Ezekiel.[58]

From the road they could not see the British camp, and Big George warned him that a large force was camped at the house. Quickly Ezekiel led his men back, avoiding riding into a trap.[59]

The story of Mary and Ezekiel Slocumb has no doubt been embellished over time, but certainly has a basis in truth. Mary is also associated with another legend that she rode to find her husband after the Battle of Moores Creek. Evidence does not seem to support her midnight ride to Moores Creek, however.[60]

The British continued their march north, taking them through a sparsely populated area that includes modern Wayne, Wilson, Nash, and Edgecombe Counties. Tarleton noted that it was "barren" and that supplies could not be "taken or bought" from the inhabitants.[61]

American militia tried to delay the British but could not stop them. On May 6th Col. James Graham with 400 militia from Pitt County made a stand at Peacock's Bridge over Contentea Creek in Wilson County. Tarleton's cavalry easily pushed them back. The next day they fought again at Swift Creek, above Rocky Mount. The battle was fought near where Interstate 95 crosses Swift Creek. Tarleton again pushed the militia back. Next at Fishing Creek, the militia made a third stand, and Tarleton again broke through.[62]

The next British objective was the town of Halifax, where North Carolina's government had met at the start of the Revolution. Tarleton came into Halifax from the north, hitting the militia and forcing them out of town. The Americans retreated to a redoubt (fort) across river. Eventually they abandoned this and retreated again.[63]

Behind Tarleton the main British army arrived and camped in the town. Here they had the good fortune to capture supplies that the Americans had failed to move or destroy. Among the goods: rum, whiskey, bacon, tobacco and corn.[64]

While in Halifax, local citizens requested that Cornwallis bring to justice men who had committed rape and robbery one evening. The general quickly had his troops formed up and the civilians pointed out a sergeant and one cavalryman who were immediately executed. This swift justice served to give a better impression of the British among the local residents.[65]

Moving north from Halifax, the army crossed the Roanoke River. In Northampton County the British burned warehouses full of supplies and private property.[66]

In early May Cornwallis's army left North Carolina for good, heading north to link up with General Phillips in Petersburg, Virginia. Their march would take them across eastern Virginia, during which time they largely moved at will, with American forces too weak to stop them.

That changed when Washington's Continental Army and a French force led by General Rochambeau arrived in September. They managed to trap Cornwallis at the small port of Yorktown. The army surrendered just twenty miles from Jamestown, where Englishmen had first landed to plant a colony in 1607. Yet that was all in the future. For North Carolina, the most painful part of the war was just beginning in that summer of 1781.

Loyalist leader David Fanning terrorized North Carolina despite several narrow escapes.

Chapter 9
Civil War

Two factors combined to escalate the violence in Southeastern North Carolina in the summer of 1781. The first was the arrival of Cornwallis's army. While Cornwallis was in the region, Craig felt that his small garrison could venture into the countryside from Wilmington. Although Craig was under Cornwallis' command, he virtually had an independent army while in Wilmington, as he was too isolated to receive frequent orders.

The second event was the arrival of David Fanning in the state. Fanning, who resided in North Carolina prior to the war, had been living near Ninety-Six, South Carolina when the war broke out. He was an ardent Loyalist and fought the Whigs in that area. With British failure to control the backcountry, he returned to central North Carolina. He was a charismatic and successful leader who would have been regarded as equal to Thomas Sumter or Francis Marion had he fought for the Americans. In truth, Fanning was no more brutal than any of the American partisans, but stories of his exploits became more exaggerated and embellished over time.[1]

Both of these events allowed for increased Loyalist activity. Many had been persecuted ever since Moores Creek in early 1776. With British troops and a charismatic leader like Fanning in the region, Loyalists turned out to exact revenge for years of harassment and oppression. In fact, by the summer of 1781 Americans effectively lost control over large areas of eastern North Carolina. One officer wrote that Bladen County had disintegrated into a "Frontier County."

David Fanning's background provides evidence of his resiliency and stamina. While living in central North Carolina, Fanning was orphaned as a young man and found employment with various families. He suffered from a scalp infection that left him scarred and bald, and eventually found a cure with one woman who helped treat him. It also provided good fodder that his enemies used to ridicule him, calling him "Scaldhead Dave." Fanning soon settled in South Carolina and became involved in trade with the Cherokee.[2]

Fanning was a fervent Loyalist when the war broke out in the South Carolina backcountry in 1775, and fought at the siege of Ninety-Six that year. He led Loyalist militia forces against Whig militias in many small battles across upper South Carolina for several years. By 1781 he saw the futility of fighting there, and moved back to central North Carolina.

Although well known to the South Carolina backcountry combatants, he seems to have been relatively unknown to North Carolinians when he first arrived in the state. It was not long before Major Craig commissioned him colonel of the Chatham County Loyalist Militia upon recognizing his zeal, prowess, and knowledge of the Deep River country. It was then that Fanning solidified his fearsome and charismatic reputation in the Cape Fear region.

Fanning established a base at Cox's Mill, at the mouth of Mill Creek on the west side of the Deep River, in Randolph County near modern Ramsour. From here Fanning, a flamboyant and compelling leader, recruited men to accompany him on raids against Whig militia. Initially he could only arm fifty men, and his numbers fluctuated depending on the season and the local situation. For the next two years Cox's Mill remained his base of operations.[3]

Back at Wilmington things had reached a stalemate. On April 9th General Alexander Lillington's force arrived at Rutherford's Mill from Heron's Bridge. He sent his cavalry to run off cattle near Wilmington and keep them out of British hands. His cavalry managed to bring in 150, but lost ten men in a skirmish with the British. Lillington had between four and five hundred men, who he could not keep due to low supplies. It was certainly a low point for the American militia: first the loss of Wilmington, now forced back from Heron's Bridge. An American observer called them "confused rabble."[4]

Craig left a small force at Heron's Bridge to control the river crossing, but he was not yet ready to venture into the interior that spring. In the meantime, encouraged by the British presence in Wilmington, Loyalists became more active in the surrounding counties.

With Cornwallis's army coming through Duplin County in May, local Loyalists were inspired to organize. An uprising led to days of violence and uncertainty in modern Duplin and Sampson Counties. A group of Loyalists gathered at Coharie Swamp near modern Clinton. They were a loosely knit group with no leader or plan yet. They began to harass and take prisoners from the Whigs and Col. James Kenan realized he needed to stop them.[5]

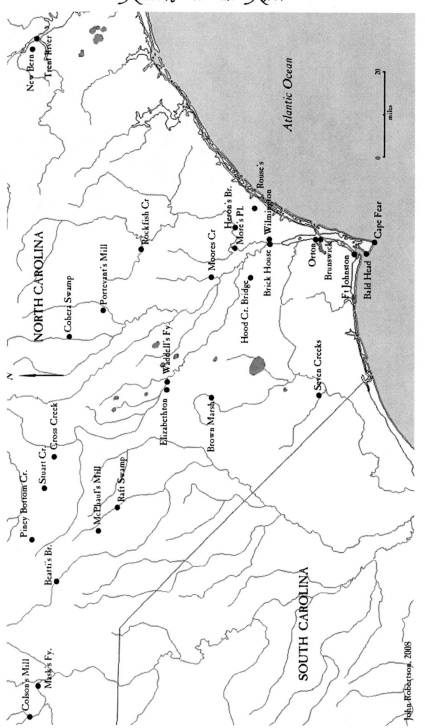

Locations in southeastern North Carolina where significant clashes occured.

The swampy terrain of the Coharie made maneuver a nightmare.

Kenan led a force of about fifteen to their campsite in the swamp to attack them. While scouting the camp, they were surprised by a hidden guard. In the ensuing firing, Owen Kenan, the colonel's brother, was killed. Private David Tucker was shot in the thigh. Unable to accomplish much in the swamps, both sides soon retreated. The skirmish emboldened more Loyalists to gather, and they chose Middleton Mobley as their leader. Now numbering about 120, they left their camp since it had been discovered, and headed down the Black River. They formed a new camp on the west side of the Coharie. In the meantime Kenan gathered about sixty men to pursue them.[6]

An American scout reported that he found the Loyalists at Isaac Portivents's Mill. Quickly Colonel John "Shea" Williams moved there with his men. Williams formed a makeshift militia unit from various men, including farmers, loggers, and runaway sailors. As they reached the mill, the cavalry rode in, firing pistols and wielding swords made from saws. From inside the mill house the Loyalists fired back.[7]

One Loyalist, while trying to rally his men, was hit and fell, with his horse falling on top of him, pinning him. Mobley's Loyalists were able to push William's cavalry back until Williams led a counterattack. The sudden charge broke their spirit and the Loyalists began to flee. Many scattered into the nearby swamps and creeks, hearts pounding as they scrambled through brush and thickets. The advantage of being mounted was now a hindrance for the Americans, as horses could not penetrate the swamps where the Loyalists had fled. While they had gotten away, some of the fleeing Loyalists encountered another group of militia approaching on foot.

Here the Whigs fired, wounding many, and the Loyalists fired back. The Loyalists were pursued to what is modern Clinton. Williams again caught up with them, and fighting became hand to hand, with swords and knives. Loyalists began to surrender or scatter and get away as best they could. Adrenaline sustained the men but could not support them long. Fatigue and stress grew among the men of both sides.

Kenan's mounted force caught up with the weary Loyalists about three miles from the old campsite. Rushing in on them, the American cavalry fired their pistols and muskets, but had to fall back and reload. Few had sabers, thus they could not move in close and fight hand to hand, as cavalry preferred to do. The Loyalists took cover behind trees, and knowing the Americans had emptied their weapons, fired back. Mobley's men then broke and took off through the swamps, which horses could not enter.[8]

Next Kenan drew Mobley out of a fortified camp to attack him by sending some men forward to lure them out. While crossing Mayhand's Bridge, the Americans ambushed them, firing on them from both sides. The bridge crossing, now gone, stood near the Sampson County airport, west of the town of Clinton.

Militia under James Kenan ambnushed Mobley's Loyalists as they crossed Mayhand's Bridge, west of modern Clinton.

The Loyalists fled down the Little Coharie, leaving several dead and wounded. The Americans took about ten prisoners. The pursuit did not go as well, with the rough terrain impeding the movement of Kenan's force. At one point a snake from a tree struck at one man, biting him in the face repeatedly. Back in the abandoned camp, some of the Americans found rum and became drunk.

Mobley's men made it to Boykin's Plantation, where they killed two cattle for food and rested. The next day the Loyalists continued to move south towards Wilmington.

Col. Kenan and Col. Williams had lost Mobley and spent some time trying to find their route. Many of the militia were intoxicated, others tired and hungry, and many felt they had done enough and wanted to return home. Mobley's Loyalists were worn out as well, and small groups and individuals began to break away. Some of them tried to get back home, others surrendered to the pursuing Americans. Sometimes the Loyalists would fire on the American militia, causing uneasiness among the pursuers. When they encountered a Loyalist straggler they did not know if he would fight or surrender.

The Americans began to fire at anyone who approached them, and one soldier wounded his own brother, who was a messenger. Friendly fire became a serious concern, adding to the heightened tension of both sides. It became a matter of shoot first, ask questions later.

One group of Whig militia stumbled on a camp of about twelve Loyalists, whom they immediately killed. The firing attracted more militia, and when they came into contact they opened fire on each other, not knowing who the other side was. Fortunately this friendly fire resulted in no casualties.

Biggars Mobley, brother of Middleton, led a small group of survivors away and made it to Wilmington. Middleton remained in Duplin County, where he organized other small groups of Loyalists. He was later captured in Martin County trying to raise Loyalists troops, taken to Wilmington, and executed. Biggars signed a parole and lived in peace in Sampson County for a decade after the war.[9]

All of this fighting resulted in three Americans killed and several wounded, along with the loss of several horses. Mobely lost twelve killed, four wounded, and twelve captured. It had been an exhausting few days, fighting and maneuvering through swamps, over creeks and rivers in the oppressive heat. The bloody and desperate march down the Coharie through Sampson County tested the nerves and will of both sides.[10]

There were many small raids and skirmishes across Duplin and Sampson Counties that summer. Joseph Williams, a private from Duplin County, recalled another skirmish in which his militia group fought a party of Loyalists under an officer named Scarborough on the South River. Here they "found the Tories too much for them," and they retreated to Widow DeVane's on the Black River, where they expected to surrender.

Upon reaching the home, they changed their minds, deciding to fight instead. When Scarborough's Loyalists arrived, they "jumped them and captured all eleven without firing a gun." They took these prisoners to the Duplin jail, known as the "bull pen," where all ten soldiers switched sides, but Scarborough refused.[11]

In June Major Craig set up a post at Rutherford's Mill on Ashe's Creek, seven miles east of Burgaw. There the British built a small fort so they would have a presence in the interior. Lillington tried to gather more militia but men were reluctant to turn out.[12]

That summer Colonels Hector McNeil of the Bladen Loyal Militia, Duncan Ray of the Anson Loyal Militia, and Archibald McDougald of the Cumberland Loyal Militia attempted to hammer out a truce with Col. Thomas Robeson of the Bladen Militia. Much of their desire for a respite stemmed from the ruthless and brutal treatment of Loyalists at the hands of Captain Peter Robeson, Thomas' brother. Efforts came to nothing, however, and bitter partisan warfare resumed.[13]

Violence was everywhere, but the worst was yet to come. At Piney Bottom in June (a branch of Rockfish Creek; the battle site is now in the northwest corner of Fort Bragg Military Reservation) a force of Loyalists routed a group of American militia, leading to days of bloodshed and terror. While the exact date of the attack remains unknown, it was after General Greene moved his army into South Carolina, and Cornwallis took his to Virginia, in the summer of 1781. With the British army gone, Whig militia commanders Col. Thomas Wade and Captain Culp felt it was safe to return to the area, having sought refuge along the Neuse River. The militia force crossed the Cape Fear River at McNeill's Ferry and camped for the night at Piney Bottom. They had several wagons loaded with salt and supplies. That evening some of the men stole a coarse piece of wool or linen cloth from Merren McDaniel, a poor servant girl who lived nearby.

A girl of about thirteen indentured to a farmer named John McDaniel, Merren had been ashamed to wear her shabby everyday work clothes to church on Sunday (sources say she attended Barbecue Church). She determined to gather the flax or wool fibers herself, process it, and spin it into thread, then have it woven into a cloth from which she would make her own gown. Upon doing so over time, she took the thread to the local weaver, whose name does not survive. The weaver agreed, as was customary, to weave it into cloth for 10% of the final product, which he could sell for profit. After the specified time Merren returned to the weaver to get the cloth, but the weaver refused to give it to her stating that the thread, and subsequently the cloth, was so poor in quality that he could in no way make a profit from 10% of it, or any percent for that matter. He would either have to keep the entire quantity for his trouble, or she would have to pay the full price.

She had no money, and so was very grieved at hearing this after going through so much trouble, not to mention being denied the opportunity to make suitable church attire. She pleaded with the weaver, but to no avail. As she cried and begged a kindly old gentleman by the name of Daniel Monroe happened along and heard her pleas. Taking pity on her he agreed to pay the weaver the full price so the poor girl could have her wish. He did so and Merren returned to the McDaniel farm with her prized cloth. This was the piece that was stolen by the Whigs.

Wade, Culp, and company could probably have passed through the area without incident had it not been for their vengeful attitude toward the locals, whom they knew to be mostly Highland Scots and Loyalists. The McDaniel farm was said to be just one of the farms they ravaged and abused. That is what set off violent response from the local Loyalists.[14]

John McNeill, who owned the ferry, sent word of the militia's presence to the local Loyalists. They agreed to gather at Longstreet Church and march on the unsuspecting militia (the church is now within the southern sector of Fort Bragg Military Reservation). About 200-300 met and marched on Wade's slumbering force.

On the day prior, John McNeil crossed the Cape Fear and visited the home of Col. Ebenezer Folsome of the Cumberland (Whig) Militia. They sat and pleasantly chatted the day away until sundown when John bade his farewells and mounted for home. He left the Folsome place at a leisurely pace, but once out of eyesight spurred his horse to the river, crossed it, then rode hard to Longstreet Church to rendezvous with the Loyalist force.

Just before dawn the Loyalists approached the sleeping camp. A guard called out to the approaching men, who didn't answer him. He called a second time and again got no response. He fired his weapon, upon which the Loyalists

When his challenge went unanswered, a sentry's shot sprang the Loyalist attack on Wade's militia at Folsome's home.

opened fire on him. One soldier, Duncan McCallum, fired at the flash, it still being dark, and hit the sentry, breaking his arm. The Loyalists then charged into the camp, just as the Americans were being aroused. The Americans broke and ran, not even attempting to make a stand. Five or six were killed in the brief attack.

Left behind in one of the wagons was an orphaned boy who had been traveling with the troops. As the Loyalists closed in he stood and begged for his life. One Loyalist, Duncan Ferguson, reined his horse toward the boy and told him he would spare him if the boy would dismount the wagon. The boy did so, but then apparently panicked as Ferguson rode up brandishing his broadsword. He bolted down the road with Ferguson in pursuit. As Ferguson took off after the boy another Loyalist, one Col. McDougal shouted at Ferguson warning not to harm the boy or else he would cut him down, to no avail. Ferguson caught the boy and using his broadsword, split his head, one half falling on each shoulder. One account described Ferguson as a "renegade deserter from the American Army." Constant violence had hardened men of both sides to thinking nothing of taking a life so quickly.[15]

The Loyalists plundered the wagons, taking as much as they could carry. The wagons and any excess supplies were put to the torch. They hastily buried the dead and went home, but a few days later the shallow graves were exposed by wolves. In the meantime the Loyalists scattered, returning home. When Wade's men returned to the scene, one of the American corpses was found with the piece of stolen cloth, and it was returned to Marron. One historian called this "The only good which resulted from that tragic affair."[16]

A few weeks afterwards Culp and Wade collected about 100 men from Montgomery and Richmond Counties to hunt down Loyalists who had attacked them. These vigilantes were out for revenge, and delivered the message they intended to send to the Loyalists. Several days of bloodshed followed, with militia under Wade and Culp raiding and plundering homes of suspected Loyalists. At the home of Daniel Patterson on the west shore of Drowning Creek they whipped Patterson until he gave the names of all the men he knew who were at Piney Bottom. Next they arrived at the home of Kenneth Black and his wife on the Little River. Two of Flora MacDonald's daughters had the misfortune to arrive while the Whigs were looting the home. The Americans harassed them, taking their rings and tearing their clothing. They also tortured several other Loyalist families, trying to obtain information on the whereabouts of the Loyalist militia. Wade and Culp were not finished by a long shot, and although they left the region they were determined to return.[17]

At one point that summer a command controversy surfaced in David Fanning's camp. Another officer spread rumors about Fanning and aspired to take command of the group from him. Fanning confronted the situation by asking his men who they would prefer to serve under, and he won the vote.

To clear up the matter, Fanning went to Wilmington to request an official commission as a militia colonel. He arrived on July 5th and met with Major Craig, who gave him a sword, pistol, and an officer's red coat. While there he told Craig he would "establish certain regulations for the conduct of the militia." Fanning lived up to his pledge and did impose rules on his men, which somewhat contradicts his later reputation as a violent and lawless partisan. At this point in the war both sides looted, murdered, and executed prisoners, and many could have been accurately described as violent and lawless partisans.[18]

Fanning's rules required each man to take an oath and be personally responsible for his actions. The men were prohibited from leaving camp, disobeying orders, plundering, and "all irregularities and disorder."[19]

Gov. Benjamin Smith

While visiting Craig in Wilmington, Fanning's militia camped with British troops at Belvedere Plantation (near modern Leland). Benjamin Smith owned Belvedere, served as an aide to Gen. George Washington, and was later elected governor. At the Smith plantation both groups shared use of the home's spring, and at some point an argument broke out between the British and Loyalist troops. Three of Fanning's men were arrested and held by the British.

When Fanning got word of the incident he took three of the British soldiers as prisoners and informed the unit's commander that he would hold them until his three men were released. Angry at having his men arrested by a Loyalist officer, the British commander went over to Fanning's tent and entered with his sword drawn. British officers often looked down on the Loyalists who accompanied them in the war, as many lacked military experience. The officer took a swing at Fanning with his sword.

Fanning ducked to avoid the blow and drew his own recently acquired blade. Instantly Fanning had the British officer pinned and demanded he cease resisting. Now in a position of authority, Fanning again demanded the release of his men, which was immediately done. Fanning's militia soon left, and were back along the Deep River by mid July.[20]

Fanning scored an impressive victory on the morning of July 16th at the Chatham County Courthouse (modern Pittsboro). Moving about forty miles

Craig's redcoats surprised James Love's men at Rouse's Tavern (also known as Eight Mile House), in modern Ogden.

from their base at Cox's Mill in present day Randolph County, they closed in on the building. Knowing that the court was to meet that day, he sent his troops out on all the roads leading into the town at 7 a.m. They were to capture anyone who came past them. Within two hours the Loyalists had taken fifty-three men, including nearly all the county's officers. Fanning paroled most, taking some of the prisoners to Craig in Wilmington.[21]

Havinng only about forty men and capturing more than their own number in prisoners, it was one of the most successful Loyalist operations in North Carolina to that time, and would only be surpassed by Fanning again later. Three of the prisoners, Gen. Ambrose Ramsey, John Williams, and Col. Griffiths were allowed to ride horses, giving their word they would not escape.[22]

That summer one of the most infamous actions of the war occurred about eight miles from downtown Wilmington, along what is modern US 17, at Rouse's Tavern. The story could not be more astonishing and would likely be called fictional were it not for a unique eye witness.

Local militia commander Captain James Love and ten other soldiers stopped for drinks at Alexander Rouse's tavern, along the road running out from Wilmington. At about 9 a.m., Love's brother Thomas arrived and joined them, although he did not get drunk with them. After a few drinks the still sober Thomas left and walked outside, where he climbed a nearby mulberry tree, and found a comfortable spot between two limbs. There he fell asleep. It was an unusual place to rest but one that would prove to be fortunate.[23]

British soldiers end Capt. Love's break for freedom at Rouse's Tavern.

Late in the evening, having their fill of spirits, the men went to sleep. Outside in his perch, Thomas awoke to the rattling of sabers and the thundering of horse's hooves. Looking down, he saw about sixty or seventy British troopers with torches surround the house. Some were infantry soldiers but most were cavalrymen. They were led by a Loyalist guide, and a small detachment of men were left near the road to guard the horses. With his heart beating rapidly, and trying not to stir, Thomas watched as a British captain whispered orders to his men.[24]

A group of redcoats stood ready at the door, when it flung open and Captain Love jumped out, apparently having heard their approach. Using his saddle on his left arm as a shield, he held his sword in his right hand, and made a dash through the rapidly encircling British. The redcoats stabbed and hacked at him, thrusting bayonets and swords at Love. Within thirty yards he fell lifeless.[25]

Meanwhile most of the men inside were not yet awakened by the commotion. Upon entering the tavern the British troops killed some in their sleep, while others put up some resistance. Of the eleven Americans at the tavern, eight were killed. Two survived with severe wounds. Lillington wrote that these men had disobeyed orders, as they were to be out guarding cattle and keeping the British from their beef supply.[26]

One man named Wilson, a soldier from Duplin County, escaped the attack by hiding in a garret, or loft. Forced out of hiding, he was questioned by the British soldiers. They promised to spare his life if he told where other Americans were located. He did so, upon which the British then killed him.

Another disaster was in store for the Americans as the British learned from this man that a second group of militia were at a home five miles up the road to the west. There, at the Widow Collier's house, the British surprised yet another group of Americans, capturing six.[27]

After the British departed Rouse's Tavern, Thomas Love waited in his tree until dawn. At daylight a Continental officer arrived and dismounted, looking over the scene. He cried out, "My God it is just as I expected!" Thomas called down to him, and told him what he witnessed the night before. Thomas then climbed down and together they walked up to the tavern, passing several bodies on the way including his brother James, covered with wounds, an empty carbine in his hands. Inside, the "floor was covered with dead bodies and almost swimming in blood, and battered brains smoking on the walls." A woman stood at the fireplace, several young children clinging to her in terror. The woman seemed in shock, unable to speak. The officer commented that Love was "brave, generous, and noble."[28]

The mulberry tree where he hid was pointed out by Thomas Love to a newspaper writer nearly forty years later in 1819. Today nothing marks the site and thousands of vehicles drive by it daily, unaware of what transpired there. In 1934 a local chapter of the Daughters of the American Revolution placed a marker at the site, but over time as the highway was widened, the marker was taken down and not replaced. Rouses' Tavern stood along what is today US 17, near the Ogden area of Wilmington, about eight miles from downtown.[29]

Captains Love and Young had been harassing the British often that spring and summer. They sometimes rushed up to the edge of town, shot at the British guard, and lured them out of the town's defenses. With their carbines slung over their shoulders they raced back with the British in hot pursuit, leading them into an ambush where their men waited. Although poorly armed with swords manufactured by backwoods blacksmiths, they persevered nonetheless in fighting the British.[30]

Love had also planned to capture Craig himself. One day he and his militia waited for Craig and his escort to ride over Walkers Bridge, about a mile from town. Today this is where Market Street crosses Burnt Mill Creek, near the National Cemetery. The British rode up in single file, and would be easy to pick off. As the British approached, some of the militia began to have second thoughts, and began to panic and break away. Love was determined to go through with his plan, and stayed to shoot Craig. At his side, Young realized it was foolish to carry it out with only the two of them now against so many British. Young eventually managed to talk him out of it, and the two silently fled. It would have been quite an accomplishment to kill or capture the British commander.[31]

On July 8[32] American militia fought a small skirmish near New Bern, the old capital. Men under Caswell beat back a force of Loyalists, killing one and wounding several more.[32]

That July Col. Thomas Bloodworth (also spelled Bludworth), a skilled gunsmith, apparently found a way to harass the British garrison in Wilmington. While fox hunting on Negro Head Point (also known as Point Peter) opposite the city, his dogs disappeared, but he could still hear them. Following the sound, he realized they were under an ancient cypress tree seven feet in diameter. The tree was rotted and hollow in the base, under which a large chamber existed. The tree appeared solid, with no visible entrance.

About fifty feet away he found a tunnel, and crawled on hands knees to the chamber under the tree. He immediately realized that from here he could harass the British across the river, a distance of nearly 500 yards. Bloodworth had lost a friend at Rouse's Tavern and wanted revenge.[33]

Directly across from the tree was Rock Spring, at the northern limit of town (site of the 1970s parking deck above Water Street). Bloodworth returned home to make an extremely long rifle and experimented with it (500 yards was an extreme range for weapons of the day). Having perfected his rifle, "Old Bess," he brought his son Tim and an employee named Jim Paget back to the tree.[34]

They took supplies and set up quarters in the underground chamber. The men bored holes in the tree for the rifle and for light and air. They also built a scaffold inside for standing up to the firing hole. On July 4th, Bloodworth tried his luck on targets across the river. He shot first at a British solider on the wharf (near the modern Coast Guard, or Government, Landing). Confusion resulted as the nearby soldiers ran for cover. They could not see or hear the shot, and did not know where it came from.

For about a week Bloodworth kept the British guessing as he fired at them. Soon a Loyalist neighbor informed the British that Bloodworth was missing from home, and rumors began to circulate that he was the one causing the mayhem. Craig sent a detachment across the river to search for him.

From their tree Bloodworth and his companions saw the boats coming. They closed the hole, and waited inside the tree, confident that they could not be found. Twenty British soldiers landed and searched the area. They noted the large tree and even considered cutting it down. As night descended, ten returned to Wilmington and ten stayed to set up a camp and continue looking in the morning.

When all was quiet the Americans snuck out and headed for their hidden canoe. They passed the British camp, and saw a sentry sleeping, snoring with his mouth wide open. It was a moonlit night and they had no trouble avoiding the British as they made their escape. The English never apprehended Bloodworth and never did solve the mystery of the sniper that harassed them.[35]

If true, Bloodworth had pulled off an incredible feat, terrifying the British garrison from his hidden lair. Unfortunately the site of his sniping has been altered by industrial activity, and is no longer accessible. The story also lacks adequate proof. No British accounts mention the incident, while other events like the attack at Rouse's are clearly documented by Craig. In addition, Bloodworth, later a Senator in Congress and Collector of Customs for Wilmington, never wrote about this event. The story originates from a series of incidents collected after the Revolution by the son of a veteran.

Later that month a battle was fought at Colson's Mill, near modern Norwood, overlooking the Pee Dee River at the lower corner of Stanley County. Loyalist forces under Col. Samuel Bryan had been using the mill and its surrounding buildings as a base of operations. Militia led by Col. William Lee Davidson and Major Joseph Graham rode to attack them.

On July 21st the militia arrived and surrounded the mill and farm buildings. Loyalist sentries saw them coming and opened fire. The Americans fired back and launched a determined charge. Davidson suffered a painful wound in the stomach.

The Loyalists fled, leaving three killed, five wounded, and losing ten captured. Graham wrote that, "Being in their own neighborhood and where they knew the country, most of them escaped. Their numbers exceeded that of their assailants, which was about two hundred fifty. Among the Whigs no person was injured save Col. Davidson and one other." The site of the mill was at the junction of the Pee Dee and Rocky Rivers, and today is inaccessible. It is shown on the Collet Map.[36]

Other Loyalist groups were becoming more active to the west of Wilmington as well. Col. Thomas Robeson, militia commander from Bladen County, wrote to the Governor that his forces were in a "Distressed Situation" and that the Loyalists had become powerful enough to control an area 100 miles by 50 miles wide (including most of modern Richmond, Scotland, Robeson, and Bladen Counties).[37]

He also wrote that the swampy terrain of the region would prevent his forces from being effective in fighting the Loyalists. The nature of the many creeks and swamps made it ideal for partisan (guerilla) warfare, raids, and small ambushes. "Without help," wrote Robeson, people will "leave their Homes" or face "immediate Destruction."[38]

Another skirmish occurred at Stuart's Creek in Cumberland County near the intersection of Robeson, Hoke, and Cumberland Counties, and about two miles north of Davis' Bridge. Davis' Bridge crosses Rockfish Creek along what was once the Camden Road. Stuart's Creek is a tributary that crosses the old Camden Road and empties into Rockfish Creek a mile or more downstream from Davis' Bridge.

Here on July 26th Col. Peter Robeson with 300 Bladen County militia stopped at the creek, a branch of Big Rockfish, and began preparing breakfast. They had taken two Loyalist prisoners, Ralph Barlow and another whose name was not recorded, and were going to execute them. A firing squad assembled and the prisoners were placed in front.[39]

Barlow requested time to pray, and it was granted. Thinking he would be short, his captors became annoyed when he continued to pray, delaying the execution. Barlow's prayers were about to be answered.

Suddenly Col. Hector McNeil rode up at the head of a group of Loyalists, and one of the Americans cried "Red Caps!" and "Tories!" One man shot at the prisoners but had a flash in the pan (his weapon misfired), and they scattered, escaping in the confusion. Barlow broke the rope binding his hands and swam across a mill pond to get away. A brief fight ensued, and the Americans retreated with the Loyalists in close pursuit.

Private Elijah Wilkins wrote, "we reserved our fire until they charged on us, when a few of us fired, and then tried to make our escape. Some undertook to cross the creek below the mill, but the banks being very steep, they were thrown from their horses. It was rather a running fight from there to a fork on Rock Fish, near the junction of the two steams. On crossing Rock Fish our scattered party was pursued by some of the Tories. Two or three of us concealed ourselves in the bushes near to each other, and immediately a mulatto approached us who held some office. When within a few paces of us, he fired at some one who was at a distance, on which one of our party rose and presented his gun. He cried for quarters, but as he uttered the words, I saw a streak of fire pass beyond his body, as the charge passed through, and he fell dead." In the brief fight McNeil lost three men killed. American losses are not known.[40]

Some of McNeil's men had arrived in boats coming up from Rockfish Creek. They quickly withdrew to the water and left. For the two condemned men it was a stroke of good fortune, rescued in the nick of time. As both sides departed quickly from the area, local women were left with the grim task of burying the battle's dead.[41]

In early August one of the most famous battles of the Revolution in North Carolina occurred at the Alston house near Sanford. Philip Alston was a local militia commander who was out patrolling with a small group. They encountered Kenneth Black, a friend of David Fanning. Black was a staunch Loyalist, and had previously given shelter to Flora MacDonald when her property was seized in the aftermath of Moores Creek.[42]

Black had in fact just left Fanning a short time earlier. Fanning was on his way to Wilmington to deliver prisoners and resupply, and Black was guiding him through the myriad longleaf pine forests, known then as the "pine barrens." The two friends were riding and had switched horses, Fanning taking the better animal and Black, being close to home, taking the weaker horse.

Philip Alston's home, also known as the House in the Horseshoe.

When Alston and his men came across Black, the Loyalist turned and fled, but was unable to get away on his tired mount. He was shot from his horse and fell on the ground. Then "they smashed his head with the butt of his own gun, and when begging for his life." The militia left his body in the mud. The next day Alston stopped by Black's farm to inform his wife that her husband was dead. He "expressed much regret" for the incident.

Upon returning from Wilmington and learning the news, Fanning was determined to get revenge. He led his men, only twenty-five at the time, to attack Alston. He wrote that, "I was determined for to make Example of them." They found Alston's party at his home, and quietly surrounded the house early on the morning of July 29th. The home stood at a bend in the Deep River, thus giving it the name, "House in the Horseshoe."

One group of sentries were captured by the Loyalists, but another set of guards caught them approaching and fired, alerting all of the Whigs. Fanning's men took shelter behind fence rails around the home. The defenders fired from windows while Fanning's men returned fire from behind the fence. A British officer who had accompanied them, a Lieutenant McKay of the 71st Highland Regiment, tried to organize a charge on the house. He leaped the fence but was met with a hail of gunfire, killing him instantly. The survivors fled back to the safety of the fence.

After several hours Fanning saw a cart and had it loaded with hay and set on fire. The defenders had been able to keep the Loyalists at bay with

Temperance Alston bargains with David Fanning for her husband's surrender. (Karen Smith)

musket and rifle fire, but a cart with burning hay was another matter, and they knew it would engulf the wood framed home. The Loyalists were about to push it up to the home and burn the defenders out when Alston's wife intervened. Temperance Alston had been hiding upstairs with her children during the fighting. She insisted that she call for a truce but her husband said it was too dangerous. When the cart was brought forward, he consented and she stepped outside.

Temperance met Fanning on the front porch and negotiated a surrender. Impressed by her bravery, Fanning agreed to spare their lives and the engagement ended. In this battle, known as the Battle of the House in the Horseshoe, Fanning lost two killed and four wounded. Alston's force of about thirty lost four killed and many more wounded.[43]

Also in early August, militia under Colonels Wade and Culp launched another raid against Loyalists in revenge for Piney Bottom. They encountered some Loyalists at Beatti's Bridge on Drowning Creek (at present-day Camp Mackall, near Pine Bluff, near where US 1 crosses Drowning Creek, and where the old Yadkin Road crossed). On August 3rd the two sides exchanged fire until dark and both withdrew. Here Wade lost four men wounded, Col. McNeil's Loyalists lost twelve killed and fifteen wounded. Years later, musket balls were found in the old timbers when workers replaced the bridge.[44]

Next at Kenneth Clarke's house they rounded up locals suspected of being involved and tied them up at the home. They beat their prisoners with swords, put one man's thumb in a gun lock and screwed it down on his thumb, and otherwise tormented them until they told all they knew. Most had no information on the attack.

Wade and Culp decided to kill their prisoners as the innocent boy had been slain, with a sword blow to the head. The first prisoner taken out began to block the sword blows with his arms, and the others broke and ran. Many were shot in fleeing.

The militia raided and burned other homes in the aftermath of the attack at Piney Bottom. One British deserter from Cornwallis's army had the misfortune to be picked up by this group, and was immediately executed. These incidents illustrate how violent and ruthless the war had become in southeastern North Carolina. Piney Bottom was a low point for both sides, as each resorted to new levels of brutality.

Piney Bottom continued to haunt Wade (for whom the town of Wadesboro is named) for years. After the war he took John McNeill to court, accusing him of being responsible for murdering his men there. Col. Folsome testified that McNeill had, in fact, paid him a long visit that day and that the visit had been cordial and pleasant. The jury, seeing inconsistency with the visit and later massacre, acquitted McNeill of the charges. The locals, who knew the truth, thereafter always referred to McNeill as "Cunning John." Tension remained high after the war as these former enemies lived as neighbors in an uneasy truce, and only among the next generation did hostility begin to ease.[45]

Also that August of 1781 Major Craig launched a raid into the interior from Wilmington. He hoped to drive off the American militia, enlist Loyalists, and seize supplies. Craig moved north from Heron's Bridge on the Duplin Road. On August 2nd he defeated Americans under Col. Kenan at the battle of Rockfish Creek, two miles east of modern Wallace. Although the Americans outnumbered the British by a margin of 500 to less than 200, Craig's men had the advantage of being regular combat troops, and were well supplied. Kenan's militia were very short on ammunition.[46]

Kenan's force had thrown up earthworks overlooking the bridge, and he readied his men. His force consisted of militia from Duplin County with a smaller contingent from Halifax. No doubt the steep banks of the creek added to their confidence as they crouched behind their defenses. The British moved forward to attack, and artillery opened up to assist their advance.

Craig's main effort was a strike at the Americans' rear, and the frontal assault was merely to draw their attention. The impact of cannonballs must have been intimidating to the militia overlooking the bridge. Yet before they had a chance to repel the British infantry, word came that British cavalry was behind them. Panic set in, and spread rapidly despite Kenan's best efforts to stop it.[47]

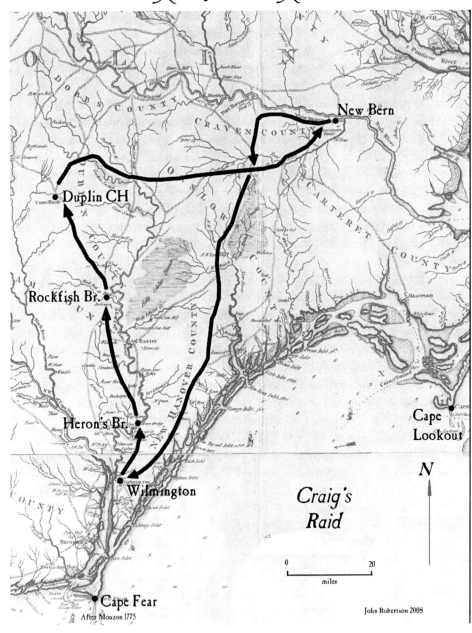

American private Arthur Mattis recalled that the British infantry attacked the bridge head on, while cavalry under Captain John Gordon circled around to hit them from behind. Gordon was a Wilmington merchant serving with the British as their cavalry commander. Rather than falling back to inform Kenan that they were being attacked, the American pickets fled, opening the way for the British.[48]

The Americans lost no men at first, but broke and ran after only a few shots were fired. In the retreat they suffered many casualties. Soldier John Knowles wrote that he was struck by a British horseman's sword, which nearly severed his left arm, and disabled him for life.[49]

Another militiaman wrote that the army was "defeated and scattered hither and thither." William Dickson recalled that "I narrowly escaped being taken or cut down by the dragoons." He also described how the army was engulfed by "confusion and dismay," with "our Ammunition, Baggage, Provisions, etc." falling into British hands. Soldier John Holley said there was "no regular order in the retreat and the regiment was placed in a scattered condition." Kenan himself wrote that it was "out of my power and all of my officers to rally them." Private Joseph Williams recalled that in the retreat they "subsisted on pork and bread and some days with nothing but cowpeas boiled in bog pond water without salt." The conditions were so poor that twenty deserted in one night.[50]

Despite holding what should have been a secure position with earthworks and the physical barrier of the creek, panic spread rapidly among the militia once the British attacked from the rear. It was devastating, since the rear was the place of safety, and the soldiers quickly grasped that they were now caught between two enemy forces. Morale continued to plummet after the

Rockfish Creek, where Craig smashed American forces under James Kenan.

retreat, and Kenan's militia was no longer a viable force for the immediate future.

The Americans lost sixty killed and thirty prisoners out of about 300 engaged, an incredibly high number of killed for such a short fight. It was especially telling since the casualties were taken by Kenan's force after the initial British attack: in other words, most of the men were shot while retreating. Craig lost none of his 250 men, a good thing since he could not get any more. As the Americans retreated to Island Creek, Jacob Wells was captured. The battle of Rockfish Creek is not well known but it was an impressive British victory and a good start to Craig's campaign.[51]

The battle was fought where Route 117 crosses Rockfish Creek, near Wallace. Traces of the earthworks were still visible until the early 1900s. A historic marker stands near the site today.[52]

Governor Thomas Burke was not pleased that his orders had been disobeyed, writing that Kenan's defeat "was owing to the want of due precaution and imprudence of attempting a stand under the several disadvantages of inferior numbers, want of cavalry and uncovered flanks, not to mention the want of discipline." The Governor continued, "In consequence of this indiscreet officer, the country is now uncovered." He had instructed the militia to not risk a major battle, but pull back in the face of a British attack. The interior now lay open to Craig's force.[53]

Gov. Thomas Burke

Reiterating his orders, Burke sent word to the militia to "retreat and avoid all action, except with parties greatly inferior to them, and nowhere will it be of any use to make a stand against them in force." He wrote to General Greene that it was an "unlucky affair." Local militia had been instructed to "watch the motions of the Enemy...and to Check their ravaging parties" but not to engage them directly. "The trifling affair would not have been worth troubling you with," wrote Burke, but it did "Shew how very deficient we are..." Supplies of food, clothing, weapons, and ammunition were critically short for the militia of Eastern North Carolina.[54]

Civilians in the path of the British march in Duplin County suffered. Resident Nathan Bryan recalled that "The British army...called on me and took off all my negroes and horses and robbed my house of our clothing. Their mallace was principally against my family as we were the principal sufferers."[55]

Craig's little army stayed in Duplin County for ten days, whe
were joined by 300 Loyalist militia. The addition of the Loyalists, anu later
escaped slaves, more than doubled the number of Craig's raiding force. It must
have been an intimidating force that moved across Duplin, Jones, and Craven
Counties. From Duplin they went on towards New Bern, with Col. Alexander
Lillington's militia trying to stay ahead of them. Lillington arranged for militia
to meet at Rich Lands Chapel in Onslow County. He wrote that "The people
there may have to give up in order to save their property if help does not come,
but that will be the last step."[56]

On August 16th near Kingstown (now Kinston), John Gordon's British
cavalry dispersed Caswell's militia. The next day at Webber's Bridge,
Lillington's militia again made a stand.[57] Here they only delayed Craig's march
on New Bern. At Webber's Bridge Lillington's men removed the planks and
took up a defensive position on the other side, not unlike what they had done at
Moores Creek. A British scouting party approached and the Americans fired on
them, killing three and wounding five. Not wanting to get drawn into a major
battle (and repeat the disaster at Rockfish Bridge), Lillington's force withdrew.[58]

The Americans remained a step ahead of the British, staying just out of
striking distance by falling back on the town of New Bern. Once the colonial
capital (the state then used Hillsboro as its capital), the village was fortified with
cannon, and militia guarded all the entrances into the town. Yet realizing they
did not have enough troops or ammunition to properly defend the town, the
Americans pulled out before Craig arrived. Governor Burke felt that the loss of
the old colonial capital was "not fatal" as it would not impact the course of the
war.[59]

Soldiers had removed the lead gutters from Tryon's Palace, the former
royal governor's home, "without hurting the building," in order to deny the lead
to the British as ammunition. Despite frantic efforts, there were still supplies in
the town when the militia pulled out.[60]

Three days after the skirmish at Webber's Bridge, Craig bypassed
Lillington's force and took New Bern on the 19th without a fight. Some militia
stayed in the town, however, and shots from one of the buildings killed Captain
Gordon, Craig's cavalry commander. Gordon had been a Wilmington merchant,
a partner of Joseph Titley.[61]

The British stayed two days, during which they destroyed 3,000 bushels
of salt, burned several ships docked there, and looted the town's shops. They
also destroyed supplies of rum and naval stores. Next they left for Kingstown,
and picked up forage along the way.[62]

They moved seventeen miles up the Neuse River, where on August 21st
near William Bryant's Mill, Craig's force skirmished with militia under Col.
James Gorham, who had assembled 150 men. Gorham sent his cavalry to guard

General "Mad" Anthony Wayne

his right flank, but along the way the troops found some liquor and got drunk. The British were thus able to send their cavalry around to cut off the American's retreat while they assaulted the main position.[63]

The American militia would have been caught in a trap had not Bryant, owner of the property, shown them a way through the swamp to escape. That night the British camped at Bryant's mill, and burned several homes, including Bryant's. They were about to march on Kingstown when they learned that American Continental troops under General Anthony Wayne were on their way from the north. Washington had detached these troops to assist the Southern Department. These veteran Continental troops, and their well known commander, were a formidable force. Craig's army turned back on September 2nd, and returned safely to Wilmington, having had a successful raid into the interior. It was the second time that a British army crossed Duplin County during the war.[64]

The raid painfully demonstrated American inability to prevent the British from invading the interior now that Craig's troops held Heron's Bridge. It also illustrated the poor state of the militia's supply system. During the march Craig lost about fifteen killed and fifteen wounded, yet doubled his force from Loyalists picked up on the way.[65]

About five hundred slaves had also joined the British on the march. This had a tremendous effect on everyone involved. Militarily, the loss of so much manpower was a serious blow to the American war effort, and also fed fears of a slave revolt. For the British it was a boost in laborers.

In human terms the implications were even more dramatic. For the slaves it meant freedom, but at a price. Many family members were separated, and those who were recovered later by the Americans suffered punishment. They also faced an uncertain future with the British. Craig's garrison already had trouble getting supplies before the raid, now there were more mouths to feed.[66]

After Craig's army passed, Bryant and his neighbors took revenge on local Loyalists for the loss of their property. They burned the homes of several Loyalists along the Neuse River.[67]

Duplin County's Loyalists rose up and began harassing Whig families and militia soon after Craig arrived. The county had experienced draft riots a few years earlier, and had a sizeable Loyalist population. After Craig's force departed Duplin County for New Bern, however, local Whigs attacked Loyalists in revenge. One soldier wrote that they were "determined to be revenged on the Loyalists, or neighbors or hazard all." He recalled that, "we collected about eighty light horsemen and equipped them as well as we could, marched straight into the neighborhood where the Tories were embodied, and surprised them, they fled, our men pursued them, cut many of them to pieces, took several of them and put them to instant death." The war had become a cycle of violence and revenge. Neighbors, friends, and even family members were now bitter enemies.[68]

Duplin County militia led by Col. James Kenan shadowed British forces who came up from Wilmington to occupy Rutherford's Mill while the main army marched to New Bern. From here the British launched raids to capture beef cattle. At one point American militia captured a British courier with a letter from Craig to Cornwallis, but it was in code and they could not read it.[69]

Craig's raid had been successful in raising Loyalist troops and seizing supplies, but it had little long term impact. On the return march to Wilmington, a British soldier hid in the top of an oak tree to spy on the Americans as

Many runaway slaves gambled on the British to secure their freedom. (Karen Dunkerly)

they came by. A militiaman noticed him and the soldier was ordered down, and executed by hanging from the tree. The Royal Oak, as it became known, was a local landmark along the Richlands-Comfort road at the Onslow-Jones County line until it died and the stump was eventually removed during road work in 1916.[70]

About a week later, Loyalist forces under Col. John Slingsby captured Cross Creek, which had been an important supply base for the Continental Army. The Loyalists, largely Highlanders, were most likely emboldened by the presence of Craig in Duplin County and Fanning to the west. Now they punished merchants and townspeople who supported the Americans, and seized supplies.[71]

The capture of Cross Creek was an important development in the area to the northwest of Wilmington. Now British and Loyalist forces controlled both Wilmington and Cross Creek, the arrival and dispersal points for supplies on the Cape Fear. The bold taking of Cross Creek also encouraged more Loyalists to rise and become active. At no other time since early 1776 were the Loyalists in such a commanding position in the Cape Fear. American forces had clearly lost control over much of the region.

Fanning stopped there with a force of militia on his way down the Cape Fear River. He was making another trip for ammunition resupply. Before leaving the Cross Creek area he crossed to the north side of the river and raided a Whig supply depot where he destroyed twenty-five valuable barrels of salt and took several prisoners. He re-crossed the river and proceeded downriver until he came across the Robeson plantations. The Loyalists burned the homes of Col. Thomas Robeson and Captain Peter Robeson, brothers who were commanders in the local Bladen Militia. Fanning's force continued down the river, raiding homes of Whigs and capturing militiamen, until they reached Wilmington.[72]

He arrived in the city on the 24th, making a triumphant entry into the town. For the city's Whigs, it must have been a humbling sight, seeing the Loyalist raiders arrive with their American prisoners.

The balance in the region shifted when local American militia scored an important victory on August 27th at Elizabethtown on the Cape Fear River. Col. John Slingsby set up camp there with a force of about 300 Loyalists. Elizabethtown was an important town along the road that linked Cross Creek to Wilmington. At the time the Loyalists felt relatively secure in the area, as the town sat on a rise of ground overlooking the river.

David Fanning barely missed the battle at Elizabethtown, having just left. Fanning departed Wilmington and was on his way back to the Deep River area, leading approximately 250 men. He had warned Col. Slingsby that he had too many American prisoners in his camp and that it represented a serious danger. Fanning wrote that he "disapproved of keeping them there, and told him I thought it imprudent and unsafe..." His warning did not move Slingsby to tighten his security. Slingsby was lenient towards the Whigs and did not advocate a heavy hand towards his enemies.[73]

There has been considerable debate among local historians about details surrounding the Battle of Elizabethtown. In fact, records are not clear on who commanded the American troops, but it seems to have been Peter Robeson (whose house had been burned by Fanning). The attack may have been an act of vengeance carried out by one or both of the Robesons, who recruited angry, determined local Bladen Militiamen. Clearly Fanning, not the congenial Slingsby, was the target.

One account notes that the militia subsisted on a little "jerked beef and bread," though it was written decades later. Another local tradition claims that before arriving opposite Elizabethtown, Robeson was aided by good intelligence obtained from thirty-nine year old Sallie Salter, a local woman who volunteered to enter the Loyalist camp. She went in that morning with a basket of eggs to sell, and carefully noted Loyalist positions and numbers. After selling her goods, she quickly returned to Robeson and told him what she saw.[74]

Now with a plan in mind the Americans moved out. Reaching the north bank of the river below the town, they could not find any boats. It is not known where the army crossed, but it may have been at Waddell's Ferry, a convenient and well known crossing point. Men struggled against the current of the wide Cape Fear River. Upon reaching the road on the south bank, they scrambled up from the riverbank through thick cane, prepared their weapons, and moved on. After crossing the river road (modern NC Hwy 87), they divided to attack from several directions. Again, some accounts, collected in the 1840s, emphasize the hardships of the river crossing. All that is known for sure is that they crossed at some point below the town. The moon was nearly full that night, aiding their movement.[75]

The Sallie Salter monument in Elizabethtown

The Americans quickly drove in the Loyalist sentries and rushed into the main group, who were mostly their neighbors from Bladen County. Here another local tradition adds color to the story: to add to their confusion, officers yelled orders to fictitious companies. Robeson and a group of officers moved rapidly along the line, firing and adding to the impression of having more men. At first the Loyalists held their ground, but soon retreated into the town, where many took shelter in the various homes and buildings from which they continued to resist. At this point both Slingsby and another officer, Godden, were hit. The loss of these two commanders resulted in a breakdown in command, as panic spread among the Loyalists. Eventually the bulk of the Loyalists retreated to the river where many were cut down at a site known as Tory Hole. Here the ground drops off sharply, forming a cliff overlooking low ground along the river.[76]

Thomas and Peter Robeson crossed the Cape Fear with Bladen militia to attack the Loyalists.

As confusion shot through their ranks, the Loyalists began to break for the rear. Unfortunately, they ran down the steep hillside to the Cape Fear River. Hearts pounding, terror and disorder took hold as they scrambled down the slope to get away. Those making it to the river slashed their way through thick briars and underbrush to reach the river. From the heights above, American militia could pick off easy targets.

The Whig attack was aided by the fact that several American prisoners in the Loyalist camp had concealed weapons and struck unexpectedly from within the secure area of Slingsby's camp. They quickly killed several Loyalist officers, and no doubt spread confusion and chaos in the rear of the Loyalist camp, where the Highlanders did not expect it. Unfortunately few accounts of the Battle of Elizabethtown have surfaced, and it remains an obscure event, one shrouded in myth and memory.[77]

Slingsby was an unfortunate casualty of the battle. He was an enemy of the Americans but was even tempered and lenient. It is unclear which American officer led the attack, but the command was likely shared by the brothers Thomas and Peter Robeson, whose houses had recently been burned by the Loyalists.

Col. Slingsby was a Quaker and a native of England. Before the war he was a wealthy merchant at Cross Creek, had served in the Provincial Congress, the Wilmington Committee of Safety, and the militia. In the winter of 1775 he switched sides, and fought at Moores Creek. He then served time in the Halifax jail, before being released. Mortally wounded at Elizabethtown, he was well treated but did not linger long until he died. In the meantime his property was confiscated. The Loyalists lost seventeen men, including five captains, while American losses were only four wounded. Following the battle the American militia recrossed the river, taking their wounded. Loyalists still controlled much of Bladen County and Robeson felt he could not stay long on the south bank of the river. The engagement was a morale booster for the Whigs, but Loyalists were still strong in the area.[78]

Unfortunately not much is known with certainty about the Battle of Elizabethtown. The facts are an American force surrounded and attacked Slingsby's men, and they retreated down to the river. Details such as the meager supplies of the Americans, their hardships in crossing the river, and their deception in attacking the Loyalsits, may be fact or embellishments, but it is difficult to establish.

Fanning and his force had missed the Battle of Elizabethtown, as they were moving north to McPhaul's Mill, which they reached on the 29th. Operated by John McPhaul, the mill was surrounded by a small settlement and was a

The Tory Hole gully was a steep slope down which the Loyalists retreated. The modern foliage is likely very different from that of 1781.

The site of McPhaul's Mill, north of Elizabethtown.

center of operations for local Loyalists. Here Fanning learned that Anson
County militia under Col. Thomas Wade were after Hector McNeil's Loyalists.
Fanning offered his assistance, and took his force to meet with McNeil. Together
the combined Loyalist force went to find Wade's position at Drowning Creek
(near modern Camp McCall), about eighteen miles from McPhaul's Mill.[79]

There the Loyalists arrived at sunrise, and sent scouts out to find the
Americans. Col. Thomas Wade's camp was located on a hill between Beatti's
Bridge and a swamp. His 400 men had prepared a defensive position facing the
swamp to the west, the direction they anticipated any attack coming from (some
accounts state he had 600 men).[80]

For clarification, this was not "Lumber River" but "Drowning Creek."
The lower section of Drowning Creek would not be renamed "Lumber River"
until the end of the century. The upper part, including that section in question,
would retain the name "Drowning Creek."

Fanning used deception to fool Wade. He had his men ride with "great
Vacancies in order to appear as numerous as possible and to prevent the turning
of my flank." McNeil's force went around Wade's campsite to the right to cut
off their retreat over Beatti's Bridge, while Fanning prepared to assault their
front.

At eleven o'clock Fanning was nearly in position when one of his men fell from his horse, causing his weapon to go off. Alerted, Wade's militia formed for battle and began firing. Caught while still mounted and not in position, Fanning's attackers lost several men in the first volley, but kept coming. They quickly dismounted and advanced, firing as they went uphill. It was a critical moment, as the stunning volley could have sent the Loyalists reeling back in retreat. Fanning, however, kept them moving up. Due to being on higher ground, many of Wade's defenders overshot. Troops have a natural tendency to shoot too high when firing downhill. The Americans were also silhouetted on the hilltop and made good targets for Fanning's troops.

Fanning's men were exposed but he urged them on with his usual charismatic leadership. "Dressed in his rich British uniform, he rode between the lines during all the fight, and gave his orders with the utmost coolness and presence of mind. It is strange that he had not been selected by some of Wade's men, as he was at the close of the fight not twenty yards distant from them."

The Loyalists came to within mere yards of the Americans when the Whigs began to retreat. At this point McNeil's force should have been in position to intercept the retreating militia at the bridge, but they were not. Only a few Loyalists were in place, and they were easily swept aside. Wade's forces retreated across the wide, murky waters of Drowning Creek over Beattie's Bridge.

The remains of McPhaul's Mill, and the marker remembering the nearby battle.

Fanning's militia engage Wade's Whigs at Drowning Creek.

Fanning pursued the Americans for seven miles, rounding up 250 valuable horses. Fanning reports having taken fifty-four prisoners, four of whom died that night. When he returned to Wade's campsite he found nineteen Whigs dead. The entire affair lasted about two hours. It has been suggested that Hector McNeil did not spring the trap since his cousin Alexander was a captain with Wade's force. It was not uncommon for families to straddle both sides in this bitter civil war.[81]

The fight at Little Raft Swamp on September 1st (also known as the battle of McPhaul's Mill or Drowning Creek) was one of Fanning's best victories, and could have been outright decisive if the Americans had all been caught as he intended. With only 155 men he had defeated a force of over 400 (again numbers are debatable, some Loyalist accounts mention that Fanning had 200 to 300 men - but McNeil's force was not fully engaged in the battle). Wade lost at least nineteen killed and over fifty taken as prisoners, while Fanning lost only four killed and about twenty wounded.[82]

Fanning wrote that "On our Return we found 19 Dead and the next day several came in and surrendered all of which were wounded, and we had reason to suppose several died in the Swamps by accounts Received from those who Came in afterwards."[83]

When the Loyalists took stock of their prisoners they found among them Col. Joseph Hayes, who was recognized by Capt. Elrod of Fanning's militia. Elrod claimed that Hayes had plundered his home and mistreated his family. Immediately Hayes was hung, and in fifteen minutes cut down. Sensing he was not dead, Fanning's surgeon resuscitated him, and Elrod allowed him to live. The prisoners taken that day were sent to British-held Wilmington.[84]

Thomas Robeson noted that the civil war was becoming more violent and bitter, writing that civilians were "obliged to leave their Habitation every Night to take their rest." American militia forces, both large groups and individual soldiers, avoided passing through the area if they could help it. Conversely, Loyalists felt that the American militia were no better than "Banditti ...traversing the Country."[85]

An American officer summed it up best when he wrote that "...we have by our own imprudencies & irregular proceedings made more Enemies than have become so from mere inclination..."[86]

Both sides used intimidation and coercion against those who opposed them. At one point Wade recruited Loyalists from among those he called "deluded peoples" and used them in his militia. He hoped to make them "useful members" of society, as it was "better than to Kill them."[87]

In the meantime, Governor Thomas Burke realized he could not contain Craig's forces in Wilmington, and the British were able to launch raids at will that summer. Nor could he control the growing civil war that was becoming more violent and bitter. General Nathanael Greene wrote to the governor that

"I perfectly agree with you in opinion that the best way of silencing the Tories is by routing the Enemy from Wilmington; for while they have a footing there the Tories will receive such encouragement as to keep their hopes and expectations alive; and their incursions will be continued. Nor will it be in your power to crush them with all the force you can raise as they act in small Parties, and appear in so many different shapes, and have so many hiding places and secret springs of intelligence that you may wear out an Army, and still be unable to subdue them. Strike at the root of the evil by removing the British...I have long had it in contemplation to attempt something against Wilmington; but my force and situation has put it out of my power. I shall be happy to aid you in advice or in any other way which may serve to give success to your plan."[88]

Later in September Colonel Leonard with thirty Whig militia set up a camp a few miles above Wilmington, where Hood's Creek empties into the Cape Fear north of modern Leland. Here they intended to disrupt the flow of supplies to the British in Wilmington. They halted, ate dinner, and rested, using their saddles for pillows. Their intention was to prevent British foraging and intercept slaves who were running away to join them. Their camp was above a bridge that crossed the creek.

Craig learned of their presence, and sent out a force to attack them. He knew that this location enabled the militia from Brunswick and Bladen Counties to communicate with those at Heron's Bridge and New Hanover Counties. Being ill at the time, Craig instead sent Major Daniel Manson at the head of eighty men. The British intended to surround Leonard's camp and strike at dawn. The English divided into two forces, hoping to strike the camp from both sides. As one group prepared to march around behind the Americans, they were told to take no prisoners. Upon learning this, the local guide, who had many friends in the American camp, took them on a long route and led them up to the camp in hopes that the guard would see them coming.[89]

British troops wait to ambush Whigs camped at Hoods Creek, above Wilmington.

Getting impatient, the British waiting for the attack near the bridge sounded a horn to let their comrades know that they were ready. The American camp heard the horn and thought it was a boatman. Four men, including two Smith brothers went down to the bridge to investigate. Upon riding up, the British, who were hidden on either side of the road, suddenly rose up. An officer shouted, "Give it to them!" and they opened fire. The Americans quickly wheeled their horses and raced back.

Their leader, Captain Basil Manly, had his hat shot off while one of the Smith brothers was wounded and fell from his horse. The group rode on to warn the camp. With the enemy right behind them there was no time to stop for the wounded man. The British raced up and bayoneted him to death. The Americans quickly abandoned their camp before the trap closed in. The Whigs lost one corporal killed, and one soldier wounded. Lieutenant Winter of the British navy, who was in charge of transporting the troops, was badly wounded.[90]

One of the most successful Loyalist raids, north or south, of the entire war occurred in North Carolina in September 1781. Col. David Fanning and

Loyalists under Fanning and McNeil herd captured Continental soldiers at Hillsboro.

Col. Hector McNeil led over 500 Loyalists from Bladen, Randolph, Chatham, and Cumberland Counties on a raid to Hillsboro, the state capital. On September 12th they rode into town, capturing not only Continental Soldiers but also Governor Thomas Burke (who had replaced Caswell). Many of the Loyalists were Highland Scots who had fought at Moores Creek five years earlier.[91]

    Burke and his aide, John Reid, defended themselves from inside a house, while Continental troops fought back from other homes in the town. Burke wrote that they were "armed with only our swords and pistols." The fighting was "close and hot" until an officer in a redcoat uniform approached. It was Fanning, who called on Burke to surrender. Upon considering his situation, and expecting good treatment, he agreed. The Whigs lost fifteen killed and twenty wounded in the attack.[92]

    The next day Fanning's army left at dawn. Some men had gotten drunk and were left behind. The following day they were ambushed at 10 a.m. at Lindley's Mill by Americans who had gathered to rescue the governor. The battle site is in lower Alamance County on Lindley Mill Road.[93]

    Lindley's Mill, or Cane Creek as it was also known, was a long and hard fought battle.

Gov. Burke surrenders

Lindley's Mill, where the fierce Battle of Cane Creek was fought in Alamance County.

As the Loyalists descended the road to cross Cane Creek the Americans struck. Col. Hector McNeil, a veteran of Moores Creek, was killed near the outset. He was an elder and held a position of authority and respect among the ethnic Scots. It was a tremendous loss for the Loyalists.[94]

As the battle raged, the Loyalists kept Governor Burke and other important prisoners in the Springs Meeting House under guard. Colonel Archibald McDougal took command of McNeil's men upon his death and made every exertion to prevent the Americans from freeing the prisoners. Gen. John Butler's forces simultaneously attacked both ends of the Loyalist line of march: the initial ambush at the creek, and an attempt on the prisoners in the rear.[95]

In the meantime Fanning took some of his men and circled around to lead a charge and push the Americans back. Fanning himself merely wrote that, "... after securing the prisoners, I made the necessary preparation to attack the enemy; and after engaging them for four hours they retreated."[96]

McDougal formed his men around the hill from where the Whigs had initially struck. He assaulted their position to draw their attention away from Fanning's attack to the north.[97]

Caught off guard by the counterattack, General Butler ordered a retreat. In the meantime Col. Robert Mebane exerted himself, inspiring his men to hold off the surge. When some men ran low on gunpowder, Mebane made his way along the line, handing out more.[98]

The Americans broke off the engagement and retreated, leaving the shaken Loyalists in control of the field. Towards the close of the fight Fanning was seriously wounded. He wrote that "... I received a shot in my left arm, which broke the bone in several pieces, my loss of blood was so great, that I was taken off my horse, and led to a secret place in the wood. I then sent Liet. Woleston to my little army, for Col'n Arch McDugald, and Major John Rains and Lt. Col'n Arch Mckay, to take command...I also desired that Mjor Rains return as soon as he could leave Col. McDugald, as I thought he might be able to save me from the hands of my enemies."[99]

His wound took Fanning out of action for several weeks. His charismatic presence was sorely missed by the region's Loyalists. By October he wrote that he was finally "able to set up." Fanning recuperated in western Chatham County on Brush Creek, at the home of one of his most faithful officers, John Raines (near modern Siler City).[100]

Lindley's Mill was one of the hardest fought battles of the war in North Carolina. It lasted for several hours, and raged over a large area of hills, woods, and streams. The Americans lost twenty-five killed, ninety wounded, and ten captured, while Fanning's Loyalists lost twenty-seven killed and ninety wounded.[101]

Eighty miles farther at McPhaul's Mill, McDougald's forces met up with Colonel Duncan Ray's men. Being fresh, Ray's men relieved the fatigued Loyalists who had captured Hillsboro and fought at Lindley's Mill, and took custody of the prisoners. McDougald accompanied this force as they continued the march to Wilmington, while Fanning stayed hidden to recover from his wounds.

On September 23rd, Butler's forces caught up with the Loyalists and fought a skirmish above Livingston Creek near the modern towns of Delco and Riegelwood, on US 74/76. Fanning missed the fight, still recovering from his wounds at Lindley's Mill.

Major Craig, learning of the successful raid on Hillsboro, marched with troops from the 82nd Regiment out to meet the returning Loyalist forces and their prisoners. They rendezvoused at Livingston Creek, from which they could march back to Wilmington. Just a few hours later, fifty American cavalrymen appeared briefly near their camp, then fell back. The British pursued them with cavalry and sixty mounted infantry until they reached an American defensive line three miles up the road. Here both sides briefly exchanged fire. The forces soon disengaged and fell back, each assuming the other had more troops coming up.[102]

Craig marched back to Wilmington with his forces and the prisoners in tow. It was a fortuitous meeting, as Craig's larger force rescued McDougald's and Ray's troops and their valuable prisoners. It was also lucky, as Craig wrote that he moved from Wilmington "without any previous communication with them, as I only guessed at their route from my knowledge of their usual mode of conducting themselves."[103]

All along Governor Burke had hoped that he would be rescued. Probably his best chance was during the battle at Lindley's Mill, but Fanning had fought so aggressively the Americans could not reach him. General John Butler had pursued them from Lindley's Mill, but was never able to overtake them. Butler's force had fought hard there and suffered many casualties in the repulse. They were also outnumbered by the Loyalists they were pursuing.[104]

After delivering their prisoners to Wilmington and resting and refitting for a few days, Colonels Ray and McDougald and Major Daniel Manson moved back up the Cape Fear. They came across Butler's forces camped at Brown Marsh in Bladen County.[105]

Here (near modern Clarkton) both sides fought an intense battle. Major Daniel Manson with 180 men from the Royal North Carolina Regiment (a unit of redcoated Loyalists) and the Anson County Loyalist Militia under Col. Ray split into three groups to attack General John Butler's 400 Whig militia. The American force included militia from Alamance, Orange, Bladen, and Sampson Counties. Butler was hoping to retaliate for the raid on Hillsboro and defeat the Loyalists who had embarrassed them in their strike on the capital.

After crossing Waddell's Ferry on the Cape Fear River (just south of Elizabethtown), General John Butler's force camped on the east side of Brown Marsh. Here, along modern Red Hill Road, they were attacked before dawn. Captain James Shipman wrote, "The back country men fled immediately. The Bladen Militia under Col. Owen & the Sampson Militia under Capt. Dodd, stood their ground until their ammunition was expended. A man by the name of Sigourres, a brave soldier belonging to the Bladen Militia was killed; a lad by the name of Stephens belonging to his company, was also killed, by my side. One or two of Capt. Dodd's men were killed and wounded. The backcountry Militia lost a great many of their horses."[106]

Night maneuvers were risky and full of uncertainty, but Manson's boldness paid off. The Americans were caught completely off guard and confusion rapidly engulfed their camp. Nothing is more terrifying than being attacked and overrun in the darkness.

Craig had dispatched troops from the Royal North Carolina Regiment to assist the local Loyalist militia in their attack on Butler. Manson divided his men into three wings. The first group got lost in the swamps, but the other two groups of Loyalists hit the Americans on both sides and overran them before dawn. Mistakenly assuming that the British had artillery, Butler quickly ordered a retreat. Col. John Mebane ignored this and rallied his men, inspiring them to put up effective resistance for some time before retreating. Manson wrote, "The Rebels were completely dispersed." It was an impressive victory, given the difficult terrain and the fact that one group of Loyalists missed the battle entirely. The Americans lost twenty killed and twenty-five prisoners, while Manson lost only two killed and five wounded. In addition the Loyalists took about forty horses, a valuable capture.[107]

One American wrote that "if it had not been for old Col. Mebane of the Orange [County] Regiment, we would have all been taken prisoner...and a brave officer he was." Another wrote of Mebane and Col. Thomas Owen, "The two Colonels made quite a manly resistance for a while, but were overpowered." At the battle site, about five miles southeast of Clarkton, musket balls were found in the 1800s on the property of J.M. Shipman, a descendant of Capt. James Shipman.[108]

Back in Wilmington, Governor Burke did not enjoy his confinement as a prisoner. The British put him in a home and debated how to treat him. If Burke was a prisoner of war he was subject to certain rights, and could hope to be exchanged like other POWs. If he was a political prisoner, his good treatment would not be guaranteed, as he would be considered a traitor (the British considered the Americans as rebels against the legal government). While Craig waited for instructions from his superiors, he kept the governor isolated with only a sergeant allowed to speak to him.[109]

Burke complained and eventually his secretary, John Reid, was allowed to make contact with him. Reid helped get Burke some furniture, a bed, and a servant. In the meantime Alexander Martin became the acting governor of the state.[110]

Gov. Alexander Martin

Martin wrote to Craig, asking for Burke's return, which he refused. Craig saw Burke as a valuable prisoner, one that could be used as a bargaining chip later. Craig also refused to parole the Continental soldiers captured at the same time.

Eventually the British sent Burke to Charleston, where Craig instructed the commander, Col. Balfour, not to exchange him. Burke was paroled to James Island, which he was not to leave. At least he had some freedom of movement, however.

Yet James Island was not a good place for the governor of a rebellious state, for many Loyalists resided there. They harassed Burke, and one even shot at him. Feeling that the terms of his parole (safe and secure treatment) were violated, Burke made his escape.[111]

Burke eventually returned to Hillsboro and reclaimed his position as governor. Ironically many Americans felt he had broken his parole, and the circumstances were irrelevant. In this day honor and procedure were taken seriously, and many looked down on his escape, no matter what the situation. Burke died in 1783, largely unredeemed by the public.[112]

During the civil war that raged across southeastern North Carolina, many local leaders emerged among the Whig militia. James Gillespie, born in Ireland, served as a major in the Duplin County militia. He was elected to the Provincial Congress in 1776, and fought at Elizabethtown in 1781. That summer his home was destroyed by Craig's raid. After the war he served in the state senate, was in the Constitutional Convention, and was also a United States Senator. He died in 1805 and is buried in Washington, DC.[113]

Richard Herring from Sampson County helped establish the county seat and jail for Duplin County. He led Duplin militia during the war. William King of Duplin County fought at Moores Creek and later served on the State Constitutional Convention.[114]

Alexander Outlaw fought at many of the important battles in the South, including Moores Creek, Kings Mountain, Eutaw Springs, Savannah, and Charleston. He later served in the state legislature. After moving west he served in the Tennessee Senate for sixteen years.[115]

Thomas Routledge served in the Wilmington Committee of Safety, on the Provincial Council, and was a justice of the peace for Duplin County. During the war he was captured with the American army at Charleston. He later fought with the militia in the guerilla war that broke out in 1781. During the raid in early August of that year Craig took over Routledge's home as his headquarter for three days, during which the British plundered it. They also burned the homes of other local leaders like Gillespie and Houston.[116]

John Sampson served in the Royal Governor's Council in the 1760s, in the North Carolina Committee of Safety, was a sheriff of New Hanover County, a justice in courts, and a lieutenant colonel of the New Hanover County militia. He helped repel the Spanish attack on Brunswick in 1748. Sampson County was named for him.[117]

One soldier, William Ward, recalled after the war that his mounted militia styled themselves the "Knockem Down Men." They carried pistols and white oak staffs for close quarters combat. The "Knockem Down Men" numbered about seventy troopers from Duplin County, led by Col. Thomas Routledge. At this point in the war, with the British in control of Wilmington and cut off from supplies, they probably had limited access to swords or carbines.[118]

Thomas Wade was a planter, tavern keeper, and justice of the peace in Anson County. He was appointed to the Provincial Congress in December 1776. He was appointed a colonel of militia the same year and served in that capacity throughout the war. He served as state senator in three sessions of the General Assembly – 1780, 1782, and 1783.

Thomas Robeson was a member of the Bladen County Committee of Safety in 1775, and appointed colonel of the Bladen militia the same year. He represented his county in the Provincial Congresses of 1775 and 1776, and served as state senator from Bladen County in 1777. In 1787, after his death, Robeson County was named for him.

Peter Robeson, Thomas' brother, was a member of the Bladen County Committee of Safety and served as a captain in the Bladen militia throughout the war. He served two terms in the House of Commons during the period 1784-1787, and was a major of militia for the Wilmington District in 1787.

With Cornwallis's army out of the state, North Carolina could now focus its attention on recapturing its most important city and port. Military and civilian leaders set the wheels in motion to organize an expedition to march on Wilmington that fall of 1781.

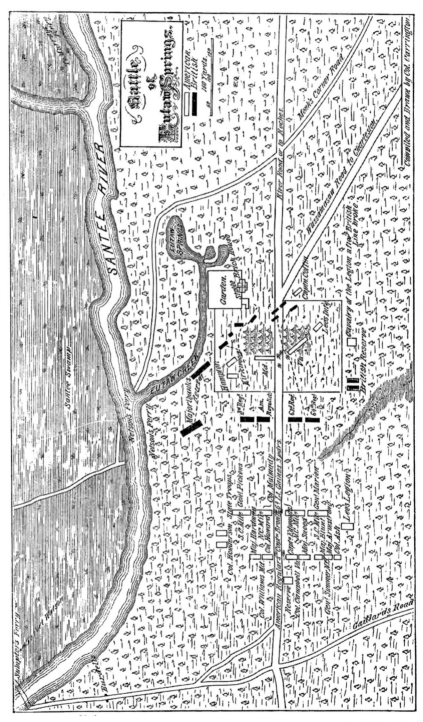

North Carolina troops suffered terribly at the Battle of Eutaw Springs in South Carolina.

Chapter 10
Evacuation and Revenge

In August 1781, General Griffith Rutherford of the North Carolina militia received instructions to assemble his troops for an attack on Wilmington. Driving the British from North Carolina's most important port had long been a goal of the Americans. With Cornwallis' army gone from the state and the threat of invasion over, they finally had the opportunity to make it possible.

The effort would be made by the state's militia, principally men from the western counties. The militia of the Cape Fear region had been in the field since January and were hard pressed to hold their own against Craig and the Loyalists. The state's newly raised Continental troops were not available, as they were with General Nathanael Greene's army in South Carolina.

Governor Thomas Burke, and later Governor Alexander Martin, had been working to organize weapons, ammunition, supplies, and material for the operation. In September news arrived in eastern North Carolina of the fierce battle at Eutaw Springs in South Carolina. The newly organized North Carolina Continental troops had fought there and done quite well in their first battle.[1]

The North Carolinians lost half their strength at Eutaw Springs, with 150 out of 350 becoming casualties. General Greene praised them for their performance. Among the North Carolina officers were many men from the coastal region of the state, including Brigadier General Jethro Sumner, Lieutenant Colonel John Baptista Ashe, and Major Redding Blount.

General Greene had repeatedly stated that retaking Wilmington was critical to securing North Carolina. He wrote in October 1781 that "The best way of silencing the Tories is by routing the Enemy from Wilmington." He had planned to send Lee's Legion, and some of his Maryland and Delaware troops to North Carolina to assist with besieging the British.[2]

In fact the troops had assembled, and preparations were made for transport and supplies. The men were ready to march when word arrived that a French fleet was due to arrive in North America to assist with the war effort. Greene changed course, anticipating that the French would assist with coastal operations and feeling that his troops were more effective in subduing South Carolina. As it turned out, this French fleet would assist with the siege of Yorktown that fall.[3]

George Washington agreed that Wilmington was a crucial target. He stated that its capture "would be of great Importance in the scale of future Negotiations; as it would in Effect, be the Liberation of another State." As the war wound down, both sides attempted to consolidate their control over territory with an eye towards peace talks.[4]

Rutherford began assembling his militia from western North Carolina at Robinson's Plantation, on Little River in Montgomery County on September 15th. His force consisted of 950 infantry and 200 cavalry, many of them from Guilford, Rowan, and Mecklenburg Counties. They trained for two weeks, as many were inexperienced. Those who had seen combat had fought at places like Cowan's Ford (near Charlotte), Trading Ford (near Salisbury), Kings Mountain, and Guilford Courthouse.[5]

On October 1st they left the Uwharrie Mountains, marching east towards the coast to liberate Cross Creek and eventually Wilmington. In Campbelltown Rutherford linked up with General Butler's militia, and the united force continued the march east.[6]

In mid October they encountered a Loyalist force of 300-600 resting near McPhaul's Mill on Raft Swamp (near modern Red Springs). Rutherford, with about 1,500 men, was at Monroe's Bridge on Drowning Creek. He sent Major Graham forward with cavalry to attack them on the 15th. The Loyalists decided to fall back in the face of the larger enemy.[7]

Loyalist commanders Cols. Duncan Ray, Archibald McDougald, and Hector McNeil had about 600 men at Raft Swamp. Hector McNeil had been killed in the ambush at Lindley's Mill, and another man of the same name put in his place. The slain McNeil had been a popular commander, and Loyalist

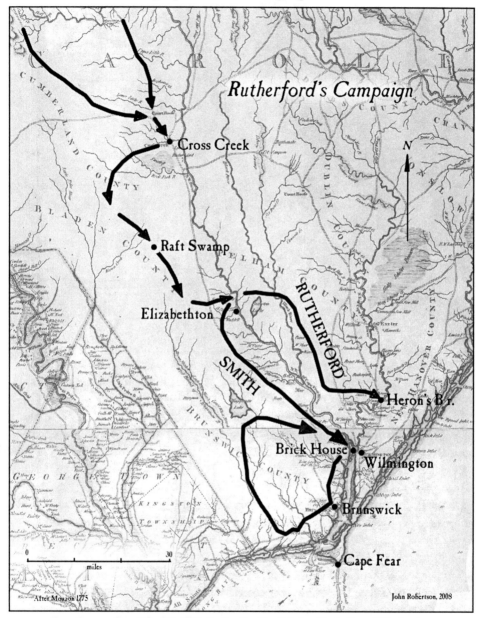

Gen. Greene dispatched Griffith Rutherford to dislodge Craig from Wilmington.

leaders hoped that the men would not learn the news, as it would demoralize them.

Colonel Ray felt that if the men did not know of the popular McNeil's death they would continue to fight. Fanning and Maj. John Elrod joined them. Together the Loyalists crossed Little Raft Swamp and took position on a hill on the northeast side of modern Lowry Road, about three miles southeast of the

The waters of Little Raft Swamp became a death trap for Loyalists caught by Rutherford.

town of Red Springs. Scouts were sent ahead to patrol in front of their camp, south along the modern Lowery Road.[8]

Here the Loyalists made a stand. Rutherford's army attacked from two sides: one force under Graham from the north and one under Martin from the south. Graham provides a detailed and vivid description of this little known battle: *"The enemy broke and fled as fast as they could...After their first fire, the enemy thought of no further resistance, but endeavoured to make their escape, and aimed for a branch of Raft Swamp in their front, over which there was a causeway two hundred yards wide. Our troops entered the causeway with them, using saber against all they could reach. As soon as it was felt, the Tories would throw themselves off to each side into the ditch, quitting their horses and making off in the swamp; the dragoons near the front fired their pistols at them in their retreat. By the time the Whigs got halfway through, the causeway was crowded with dismounted ponies for twenty steps before them, so that it was impossible to pass. Two or three stout men dismounted, and commenced pushing them over into the ditch, out of the way. When it was a little cleared, the dragoons rushed over, the front troop, now scattered, pursued the Tories in all directions."*[9]

It was a scene of utter confusion, and for the Loyalists, sheer terror. They knew that the Americans were in the neighborhood but had no idea they were so close. The Loyalist scouts went reeling back at full speed toward their camp, many being cut down or falling into the swamp as Graham mentioned.

Some Loyalists tried to make a stand, but it was no use. Many who had jumped off the causeway and waded into the swamp to get away became stuck in the mud and were shot. Above the swamp on high ground, about thirty-five Loyalists tried to hold a line, but were overrun, with many shot while trying to surrender. Farther back modern Lowery Road at Raft Swamp, a Loyalist rear guard held out, enabling the rest to escape.[10]

Rallying the troops was David Bethune, who played "The Campbell's Are Coming" on his bagpipes. Wrote one witness, "This encouraged the Tories so much that they extricated themselves from the surging crowd of Whigs and succeeded in assembling across the swamp in an old field where the little piper had begun his tune."[11]

As the Loyalists fled, chaos broke out. The Loyalists were not fighting as a unit anymore, but as individuals. The American cavalry was now in amongst them, and the horsemen were unstoppable. Here, above the swamp, William Watson was cut down while running from the Whig horsemen. A few yards away his brother John was also killed. Another relative, Thomas Watson, was mortally wounded, dying a week later. An unnamed Highlander was flushed out of his hiding place in the woods and killed. Many of the bodies were left unburied, scattered over the length of the battle site along the road and in swamps and woods, many wounded men having died after crawling away from the battle.[12]

Raft Swamp was the last battle in the area, and it ended Loyalist control of the region. In the 1800s workers repairing Lowery Road found bones and military artifacts from the battle.[13]

Many of the battles discussed here can be characterized as "running fights," engagements that begin at one point but which moved as troops advanced and stayed in contact. Often these small battles covered large distances. In the case of Raft Swamp, the fight probably went on for over four miles southeast of the town of Red Springs.

Rutherford intended to punish the Loyalists, and Raft Swamp illustrated his swift and decisive use of force. General Nathanael Greene warned him that "You are treating the Inhabitants...with great severity driving them indiscriminately from their dwellings without regard to age or Sex and laying waste their possessions destroying their produce and burning their houses." Greene warned him to not be so harsh on the Loyalists.[14]

The next day the Americans moved down the east side of Raft Swamp, where they were ambushed. Rutherford decided to fan out his troops and root the Loyalists from out of the area's numerous swamps. The effort was exhausting, with men "worn down" and "torn with bamboos and other briars, many had waded up to their middle in mud." In the meantime the Loyalists had fled.[15]

Col. James Martin wrote that "We made our way with much difficulty through bogs and morasses and some of the men and horsemen got mired...But we found no Tories or any body else save several camps which we supposed had been made by them."[16]

The American force next moved through Brown Marsh, fifteen miles southeast of Elizabethtown, where an earlier battle had been fought. Here Governor Alexander Martin, acting in place of the captured Burke, met with Rutherford and discussed the operation to retake Wilmington. He reviewed the troops and offered his encouragement.[17]

Closing in on Wilmington on October 23rd, Rutherford divided his force, sending the Legion of Capt. Robert Smith with 100 cavalry and 200 mounted infantry down the west bank of the Cape Fear. With the main force, Rutherford crossed the Cape Fear at Waddell's Ferry. Smith was to proceed down opposite to Wilmington, while Rutherford headed down the Negro Head Point Road and then over to Heron's Bridge. Together they would have the British surrounded.[18]

Craig had withdrawn his small force at Heron's Bridge as it was too isolated to support, being ten miles from Wilmington. He now was trapped within the land-side defenses of the city and the post on Eagles Island.[19]

On his way down towards Eagle's Island, Smith captured two Loyalists and learned of a British plan to cross the Cape Fear and attack Rutherford's force at Brown Marsh. Apparently nothing came of the plan as Craig never made the attempt.[20]

Across from Wilmington on Eagles Island (near the modern-day *USS North Carolina*'s parking lot) was a fortified brick house. The British had barricaded the doors and windows, and put up an abatis around the home (entanglements of sharpened stakes and brush meant to impede an attacker). Fifty men guarded the house.[21]

While pausing at this point, Smith sent Major Graham with ninety men to attack a Loyalist force at A. More's Plantation, about a mile away. On November 14th, while approaching the plantation, a force of Loyalists rode up to the Americans, mistaking them for their own men. It was a mistake that became all too common in warfare during which neither side had uniforms. Too late they tried to raise their weapons, but they were surrounded and disarmed.[22]

Moving on, Graham's force got to within 300 yards of the Loyalist camp by sunrise, where they spread out and took position. Two unarmed soldiers came out for firewood, and were taken prisoner without firing a shot. Seeing that about 100 Loyalists were camped at More's Plantation, Graham decided to attack.[23]

He divided his forces with one group under Capt. Kennedy, and another under Burke thirty steps to the right, while Capt. Bethel's Guilford Militia took

Graham's men used a fence to steady their aim during the attack at More's Plantation.

up position on the left. In the rear Capt. Polk's Mecklenburg cavalry waited on the road eighty yards away.

While getting into position, a Loyalist officer spotted them and gave warning. The Americans attacked immediately and their sudden strike caused great confusion in the camp. The Loyalists could not properly form a line of defense.

Some of Graham's men took up position on a causeway opposite the home, 140 yards from the enemy, where they could rest their weapons on a fence and fire with ease. The Loyalists returned fire but were not properly formed for action. They soon broke in confusion, and Polk's dragoons charged in. The Loyalists fled in all directions, most going into a nearby marsh, but not before many were cut with sabers.

The Loyalists lost twelve killed and thirty wounded, while Graham lost none. It was an incredible victory. In addition to scattering the enemy, the Americans collected badly needed weapons, horses, and supplies in the camp. They then returned back to the main force near the brick house.[24]

Smith's troops reconnoitered the house, and they reported back on its strong defenses: abatis, doors and windows barricaded with timber, and the fact that reinforcements were coming from across the water from Wilmington. Smith then marched back to above Livingston Creek.[25]

Polk's dragoons broke the Loyalists.

His men were upset that they did not attack, and it became a "constant subject of conversation." Possibly inspired by the successful attack at More's Plantation, the men grew restless over not attacking the brick house. Prodded by the men and officers, Smith conceded and moved back two days later to try and take the fortified home on the 15th. Early in the morning he sent a flag of truce to the Loyalist commander, Captain Kennedy, asking the garrison to surrender in ten minutes. "I disregard your orders: I don't surrender," Kennedy replied.

Smith then prepared his men for the attack. One force advanced under the cover of woods along the bank of the river on the left. The remainder attacked head on. Loyalist defenders, assisted by Hessian Jaegers (German riflemen) defended from every window. Those on the upper story were particularly effective. After an hour Smith broke off the attack and withdrew. Several men had clothes torn from moving through the brush. Smith lost one man killed and several wounded in the unsuccessful effort. They returned to their previous position to the northwest.[26]

The brick house stood until the 1850s, and its walls were pockmarked from musket balls. It sat on the north side of the road running across Eagle's Island, and was within sight of the town across the river.[27]

The next day, November 16th, Graham and Polk moved with their force of about ninety men down the river road, over Town Creek, past the destroyed town of Brunswick. They captured a few Loyalists, then camped at Seven Creeks, near the South Carolina state line.

It was a cold, rainy night, and the men took boards from nearby homes to make shelters. At eleven o'clock a Loyalist force of eighty men led by Col. Micajah Gainey surrounded the camp and attacked. One man had musket balls pass through a pumpkin he was using for a pillow. Quickly the Americans rose and defended their position, forming a line thirty steps behind their camp. They made their escape, losing only one man killed, Lt. Clarke. The Loyalists lost one killed as well. In addition Graham lost four horses killed, and several wounded. Graham noted that he thought Gainey was under truce with Col. Francis Marion (the Swamp Fox) in South Carolina, "but it appears he did not consider it binding in North Carolina." This action has been recorded as the Battle of Seven Creeks (in the vicinity of modern Nakina in Columbus County). The Americans fell back, passing Lake Waccamaw, and rejoined Smith's force outside Wilmington.[28]

Back at Rutherford's campsite above Heron's Bridge, a messenger arrived with startling news that changed the course of the campaign. Lt. Col. "Lighthorse" Henry Lee rode into the camp, having come straight from Yorktown, Virginia. He brought news of the defeat of Cornwallis one month earlier. He also said that General Washington was sending General Lafayette with troops from Virginia to assist with retaking Wilmington. It turned out that Lafayette's men would not be needed. Rutherford immediately issued orders for a "feu de joie," a volley of musket fire to celebrate the victory (the phrase is French for "fire of joy"). In the meantime Lee went on to deliver the good news to Smith's detachment above Livingston Creek.[29]

The next day Rutherford's army crossed the river and marched on Wilmington. Smith and Graham's forces broke camp and moved to Schaw's Plantation, just four miles from town. That same day Craig's garrison was preparing to evacuate. With less than 300 men, he could not hope to hold out against Rutherford's 1,000. He also had only two week's worth of flour, and his forces could not enter the countryside to forage due to Rutherford's and Smith's troops blocking the way.[30]

Forage for the horses was nonexistent, and the British moved all but twenty horses from the city to Eagles Island, where they had room to roam and find fodder. Food, clothing, and medicine were all in short supply.[31]

To lessen the supply burden on his garrison, Craig had expelled all women and children who were Whig sympathizers. The women were permitted "to carry with them nothing but their wearing apparel." It was pointed out by one that many Loyalists in the city opposed these measures and "strove to mitigate our sufferings."[32]

Wilmington's population, both civilian and military, were suffering from severe shortages of food and medicine. One civilian wrote that "every article to be sold in Wilmington is at least three Times as high...as usual." Governor Thomas Burke, held captive in a private home, agreed, noting that "if I may judge from such as I see daily passing by my window to the spring for water, who might well be taken for skeletons..." Craig himself wrote that he was "oblig'd to give a more unfavourable report of the healthiness of our men than I have hitherto done—we have more sickness here and lost more men within this month past than during the whole time of our being here before."[33]

The decision to defend Wilmington was out of Craig's hands. His small force could not face the larger number of Americans surrounding him, and orders arrived telling him that the garrison would be evacuated to Charleston, SC.

The British army boarded their transports early on the morning of November 18th. One witness recalled the ships lining the wharves, and the great amount of baggage taken on board. The redcoats marched down to the riverrfront to the sound of fifes and drums.

At Schaw's plantation Graham and Smith's men boarded boats and floated down river to the town. Rutherford's force had arrived an hour earlier. In the distance they could see the British fleet moving down river, headed back to Charleston. Rutherford made his headquarters at the home of Mr. Hill.[34]

The Americans were not about to let Craig's force go without one last strike. During the evacuation one witness reported that: "I was standing near where the old Court house used to stand, just as the sun was rising; and looking

up Market Street in the direction of the old church; when I saw a cloud of dust
arising on the hill; in a moment the trampling of horses was heard all around me.
It was the Whig light horse, who came thundering down the street, and at full
speed. There was a noted Tory who had lagged behind the embarking columns,
not dreaming of danger. He seemed petrified with fear as the cavalry
approached, and in a state of apparent mental hallucination walked forth with his
hand strechd out, as if to salute the troop. A young man left the ranks, drew his
hanger [sword], rushed upon him, and with one blow by a vertical cut laid his
head open, the divided parts falling on each shoulder."

It turns out that this Loyalist had hung the father of the cavalryman,
Thomas Tyler. As the Whig cavalry dashed into a group of British troops, they
hacked with sabres, and the British fired on them. Each side had some men
slightly wounded. At this point the British ships fired their guns on the town,
scattering the American cavalry, who quickly retreated up Market Street and out
of town. The remaining British troops quickly boarded and the fleet departed,
heading south out to sea.[35]

The fall of Wilmington had been a swift and relatively smooth campaign
for Rutherford's army. Col. James Martin wrote that, "We thought it very good
luck that by their vacating the town we were released from the danger of
fighting."[36]

Ironically, Captain Matthew Ramsey made his escape from the British
prison in Wilmington just two days before they evacuated. Ramsey had been
held as a prisoner for five months, and was appalled at the conditions. He wrote
that the guards "indiscriminately flung" officers, slaves, and soldiers into the
crowded jail.[37]

Onboard the British ships were a mix of people caught up in the
evacuation: runaway slaves, Loyalist refugees, British soldiers and sailors, camp
followers (wives and children of the soldiers), and the sick and wounded of
Cornwallis' army who could not march. The transports were crowded with their
human and material cargo.

One runaway slave, Lavinia, had been a house servant of William
Hooper. Her brother John remained with Hooper's estate, but Lavinia took her
chances with the British. Some friends of Hoopers saw her at the riverfront and
managed to force her, "much against her will," off a ship and took custody of
her, returning her to Hooper after the evacuation.[38]

Among those leaving with the British was James Rogers, who hosted
Captain Alexander MacLeod in his home on the night before the attack on
Moores Creek Bridge. Rogers had lived in relative peace until June 1781 when
he was arrested. He was going to be hung when David Fanning came upon him
and freed him from the Whig militia. He then moved to the safety of British-
held Wilmington, and had no choice but to flee with them when they left.[39]

Another Loyalist refugee fleeing with the royal army was merchant Joseph Titley. He took "all the books, notes, bonds & other Securities belonging to the Copartnership" that he had shared with John Gordon, who had been killed that summer at the head of his Loyalist cavalry.[40]

The following February, Margaret Gordon, his widow, petitioned Governor Thomas Burke for a flag of truce so she could go to Charleston to settle her late husband's debts. The Governor let her leave Wilmington but did not allow her to return.[41]

Refugee Janet Murchison also evacuated the city with Craig's forces. Her husband John was captured at Moores Creek, taken to Philadelphia, and returned in 1780 with British forces in South Carolina. She joined him shortly before the Battle of Camden, where he died of wounds. She remained with the British army and accompanied it on its marches through Carolinas. By the spring of 1781 she was sick and left at Wilmington when Cornwallis moved on. She lost all the property she had in Anson and Cumberland Counties.[42]

Loyalist Rigdon Brice wrote that "by the hurry and confusion of this evacuation, I lost most of my Baggage & Effects." Grocer John Mackay got his belongings on board, but fared no better, claiming that "Goods and Effects of considerable value, part of which he was obliged to leave on the wharfs, and what he put on board the Transports was Plundered & destroyed by the Soldiers, Sailors, and Negroes, on the passage." Arthur Benning recalled that he and his wife and children left "without anything, but their wearing Apparel."[43]

For the Loyalists of Wilmington, it must have been unreal. Just two months earlier the rebel governor had been captured and brought in as a prisoner, and British and Loyalist troops scoured the surrounding countryside. Now an American army had come and driven them from the city without a major fight.

Upon arriving in the city, the Americans took military stores left by the British. Their wagons from Heron's Bridge came down, and were loaded with salt. Some of this precious commodity was sent to the civilians, while the rest was used to pay the men. It was considered more valuable than a receipt for service.[44]

The suffering was not over for the residents of Wilmington. After Rutherford's militia occupied the town, many looted and stole from the civilians. General Rutherford placed guards to deter the plundering.[45]

William Hooper urged leniency towards the Loyalists who remained in the area, stating that "there will be a time, and I hope it is not of a great distance, when the distinction of Whig and Tory will be lost" and grudges will "die away."[46]

With the British now removed from the Cape Fear violence did subside, but not end. On December 10th about 300 American militia under Col. Elijah Isaacs began to raid Loyalist homes along the Deep River. Fanning's force kept out of reach of this larger army. Yet Fanning soon launched his own raid, striking at the home of Captain John Cox.[47]

Cox was not home and his house was quickly destroyed. Fanning then moved on to the home of his father Robert, at the forks of Big Juniper and McLendon's Creek, near modern Carthage. Three Whigs - John Cox, Robert Lowe - and William Jackson, heard the Loyalists approaching and fled. Finding the dwelling abandoned, Fanning's men torched it.[48]

Returning to watch, the three crept back to what they thought was a safe vantage point to observe the Loyalists. A guard discovered them and reported it to Fanning, who ordered them seized. Realizing they had been seen, the three men fled. Cox got away, but Jackson was shot and killed by Fanning near Juniper Creek. Lowe was wounded and overtaken, and brought back to the burning home.[49]

Lowe was in trouble and he knew it. He had previously served under Fanning and had switched sides. Immediately recognized, Fanning ordered his men to execute Lowe. Their volley wounded him further but he lingered, so Fanning used his own pistol to end his life. Fanning continued on to visit several other Whig homes before halting to rest. They soon learned the news of the British evacuation of Wilmington, and it was a severe blow. It meant the end of nearby British support and supplies, and for all of them, the end of any hope of winning the war.[50]

After Craig's reluctant evacuation, Americans once again held sway in Wilmington. Loyalists who remained behind suffered for their allegiance to the British. Many were rounded up and tried in court. Those accused of treason and sentenced to death were later exchanged for American prisoners held by the British. For the time being, Loyalist prisoners were held in a pen made of rails near St. James Church, where they were taunted by citizens.[51]

For Craig, his tenure on the Cape Fear was a lost opportunity. He continually complained of not enough men. In truth, had he been reinforced he probably could have done a great deal more damage to the American war effort in the state. He wrote that "had I the 4 or 500 more men I had so long wished for I would hope to give this Province a blow they would not easily recover."[52]

Major James Craig was harsh during his period of control in Wilmington, but he was thrust into a situation that was already volatile. The bitter civil war raging in the countryside around Wilmington did not give much room for political maneuver. He was also affected by actions over which he had no control.

For the ten months that he held Wilmington, Craig was in a unique situation. He had his own theater of the war, and operated with relative freedom from superiors. He also had the ability to impact the war effort of an entire state, cutting North Carolina off from its major port, raiding its inland towns, and supporting the raid on the capital at Hillsboro.

While the British had been fairly successful in southeastern North Carolina, their victories in battles here were overshadowed by other campaigns at same time. Ninety-Six, in South Carolina, and Yorktown, in Virginia are better known, and have received more attention from historians. The actions in and around Wilmington have been largely forgotten. Craig made the most of his opportunities in Wilmington, and had he had more men, probably would have had a bigger impact on the war as a whole.[53]

Craig rose to the rank of Major General in 1794, and served throughout the British empire: India, South Africa, and Italy. In 1807 he became Governor of Canada, and served until 1811. He passed away early in 1812, just missing the second British war with America.[54]

Starting on January 1st, 1782, sale of Loyalist property began in towns like Edenton, Halifax, Salisbury, Hillsboro, New Bern, and Wilmington. The armies had departed the state, and many Loyalists had fled with the British. Knowing they were not coming back, their property was now up for grabs.[55]

James Devane was one militiaman who escorted Loyalist women to Wilmington after the British evacuation. He wrote that he was "ordered to collect wives, children of the Tories and escort them to Wilmington." He found the task "so disagreeable" that he wrote he would rather have disobeyed orders and face disciplinary action. Although he avoided the duty at "all hazards," he had to carry out the assignment.[56]

That year twenty-one women of the Cape Fear area petitioned to stop the expulsion of the "helpless and innocent" wives and children of Wilmington's Loyalists. Tensions ran high, however, and the petition was ignored. Many of the women who prepared the petition had been expelled during the British occupation, and tried to prevent a similar fate for the Loyalist women. In their petition they refer to Major Craig's conduct during the occupation, noting he alone "is to be imputed the inhuman edicts, for even the British Soldiers were shocked at it." They argued that extending this treatment to the Loyalists, many of whom had no say in British policy, would serve no purpose.[57]

The following women signed this petition: Anne Hooper, wife of William, a signer of the Declaration of Independence; Mary Allen; Sarah Nash, widow of Brig. Gen. Francis Nash; Mary Nash, wife of the governor in 1781; Ann Towkes; M. Hand; S. Wilkings, Mary Moore, widow of Col. James Moore; E. Nash; Sarah Moore; M. Loyd; Catherine Young; J.M. Drayton; E. Wilkings; M. Lord; Isabella Read; Sally Read; Mary Grainger; Jane Ward; Hannah Ward; and Kitty Ward.[58]

After the British evacuation Middleton Mobley, a Loyalist leader from modern Sampson County, was arrested in Martin County. He had organized Loyalists in the summer of 1781 and skirmished with militia near Clinton and the Black River. Considered dangerous, he was taken to Wilmington, tried, and executed.[59]

Another incident in March shows the violent nature of the civil war that divided area residents. Major John Eliot (or Elrod), a Loyalist officer from the forks of the Yadkin, visited Wilmington with two companions while it was still occupied by Craig's forces. While there he saw that an old friend, Col. Thomas Dugan, was on a prison ship in the Cape Fear and about to be hung. Eliot interceded and had Dugan freed.

Later while returning home, Eliot and his companions encountered some paroled Whig militiamen who were clearly in arms, in violation of their parole. A soldier on parole was honor bound not to take up arms and actively serve. While it was not uncommon for both sides to violate paroles, it sent Eliot into a rage. They beat and killed one of the soldiers named Henry Johnson. Eliot broke his sword over Johnson's head, then knocked him down. Another Loyalist shot him. The other Whig barely made his escape.

Learning of this, Dugan set out for revenge at the head of a militia company. They caught up to Eliot and the Loyalists, had them tied to trees, and shot. Their bodies were left as a message to other Loyalists.[60]

In March 1782 David Fanning led a raid against American militia along the Deep River in the central part of the state. On the 10th he set out "in order to give them a small scourge." Indeed he did. The raid proved so successful that the Whig militia agreed to a temporary truce. It was six months after the surrender at Yorktown and the closest British soldiers were in Charleston, SC.[61]

Fanning's men raided several Whig homes. At the plantation of Col. Andrew Balfour, near modern Asheboro, the Loyalists struck with fury. The Colonel's sister Margaret recalled the attack six months later in a letter: *"...about twenty-five Ruffians came to the house with the intention to kill my brother. Tibby and I endeavoured to prevent them, but it was all in vain. The wretches cut and bruised us both a great deal, and dragged us from the dear man then before our eyes. The worthless, base, horrible Fanning shot a bullet into his head, which soon put a period to the life of the best of men, and the most affectionate and dutiful husband, father, son and brother. The sight was so shocking, that it is impossible for tongue to express any thing like our feelings, but the barbarians, not in the least touched with our anguish, drove us out of the house, and took everything that they could carry off except the negroes..."*[62]

Governor Burke sent an expedition into the region to engage and conquer Fanning, but it was unsuccessful. He also increased the guards in Hillsboro to prevent another raid on the capital. The British army had been gone from the state for five months, and Cornwallis had surrendered six months ago, but Fanning was still able to not only operate but fight effectively against the Whigs.[63]

Peace negotiations between England and the United States began that spring, and intensified over the summer. Armies in the field knew that the end was near, and active campaigning ground to a halt. The British clung to their garrisons in St. Augustine, Savannah, Charleston, New York, and Canada. With the writing clearly on the wall, British commanders made preparations for evacuating.

Although the war was winding down, for David Fanning there was no peace. In April 1782, he was to be wed to Sarah Carr in a triple ceremony along with two friends, Captain William Hooker and Captain William Carr. The day before the wedding American militia found and killed Hooker. Fanning was wed with only Carr. Afterwards they "Kept two Days merriment." Then they hid both wives in the woods while American militia were in the area.[64]

Soon after, he wrote, "I concluded within myself that it was Better for me to try and settle myself being weary of the disagreeable mode of Living I had Bourne with for some Considerable time." He had been at war, and on the move, for seven years. Learning of "truce land in Peedee, South Carolina," Fanning and his bride moved there to leave the violence behind them.[65]

The Truce Land had been established in June 1781 by joint consent of Francis Marion (the Swamp Fox) and Loyalist officer Col. Micajah Gainey (also spelled Ganey). It included modern Marlboro, Dillon, Marion, and Horry Counties of South Carolina. The Truce Land attracted many refugees of both sides who sought relief from the violence and turmoil of the war.[66]

Fanning attempted to negotiate his own Truce Land in North Carolina, writing that he hoped to establish an area twenty miles by thirty miles wide. He promised that "All back plundering shall be void," and that free trade and commerce would be unimpeded. Fanning also insisted that any Loyalists who committed crimes would be turned over to the Whigs, but also reserved the right to punish anyone caught plundering in his area. The state government refused his offer of setting up what was essentially a Loyalist reservation in Cumberland County.[67]

Soon he learned that the British were evacuating their garrison from Charleston, and decided to go with them to move to East Florida. Later, when this territory was given to Spain, Fanning moved to New Brunswick, and eventually Nova Scotia.[68]

Small outbreaks of violence continued, though the war was practically over. In September raiders disrupted a court session at the Bladen County Courthouse in Elizabethtown. Captain Robert Raiford, at the head of thirty Continental troops, rushed into the courtroom, and attacked Archibald MacLaine with a sword. MacLaine was defending a Loyalist who was on trial. After also beating the court's clerk, Raiford led his men on a raid through the county hunting down Loyalists. His actions had not been sanctioned, and he was later arrested for the deeds, though he was acquitted. MacLaine lost a great deal of property himself.[69]

For the residents of the Cape Fear region, both Whig and Loyalist, the war was finally over. A long, slow, and difficult healing process began. Tensions remained high as neighbors who had fought on opposites sides, and often raided each others homes, now attempted to live side by side again. The bitterness lasted for generations.

Chapter 11
Aftermath

The state legislature passed an Act of Pardon and Oblivion in 1783 to put closure on the violence and upheaval of the war. It refused to pardon anyone who served in the British military, anyone named in the earlier Confiscation Acts, anyone who left the state with the British at the end of the war, and those guilty of murder, robbery, or house burning. Only three individuals were specifically mentioned by name in the act: David Fanning, Peter Mallet, and Samuel Andrews.[1]

Mallet was a Loyalist who fled but later returned to Wilmington. Samuel Andrews was a lieutenant at Moores Creek. After his capture he took the oath of allegiance to the state, but joined the British again in 1780 in South Carolina. He fought at Hillsboro and Lindley's Mill in 1781. He evacuated Wilmington with Craig. Fanning, of course, was the most famous, and hated, Loyalist of all.[2]

In Wilmington twenty-four men were indicted for treason in Superior Court during 1782 and 1783. Of those present, seventeen were freed. In the years after the war, sales of confiscated or abandoned Loyalist property raised hundreds of thousands of dollars.[3]

Former Loyalists were often denied the right to vote. In 1785 the Bladen County sheriff refused to allow nearly four hundred men to vote; they those who had not supported the Revolutionary government. intimidation also kept many from voting or holding office. not only disrupted the economy and the courts, but it also ormous amount of legal, financial, and political turmoil. The state and local courts were still settling accounts for years afterwards. In 1788, for example, the state finally paid James Devane and Richard Herring for the muskets they produced in their gunworks in 1776.[4]

In 1787, the Federal Government sent military officers to examine the accounts of North Carolina and analyze the state's war debts. It was literally a mountain of paperwork. Financial records were in a state of chaos.[5]

People felt the disruption in many ways. Their affairs were in disorder, many lost land and goods. Others suffered from wounds or disease. The war also uprooted people and caused massive migrations. Thousands of Loyalists fled North Carolina for British Canada, while hundreds of slaves ran away and ended up in far flung places like Florida, Canada, England, and Africa. The movement of armies brought Germans, Africans, English, Scottish, and Americans from every colony to the Lower Cape Fear. Some remained to re-settle here. Few residents escaped any effect of it.

Ann Field of Guilford County, wife of Robert who fought at Moores Creek, sought permission for her banished husband to return. He had moved to England after the war. In 1785 the General Assembly rejected her plea, but two years later it was granted.

That same year Loyalist refugee Isaac DuBois returned to Wilmington to claim some of his property. He was immediately seized and jailed. Authorities ordered that he be banished, and remain in jail until the arrangements were completed.[6]

The war not only ruined fortunes but lives as well. Take Polly Rutledge, who in the summer of 1781 was Polly Rivenbark, and was engaged to one of the Americans killed at Rouse's Tavern. Distraught at the news of his death, she went into deep mourning. While visiting his grave, two Loyalist soldiers came upon her and forced her with them to Wilmington.[7]

There she met and apparently married a British officer named Rutledge. During the evacuation he abandoned her, and she was stranded without any means of support. In the years afterward local residents noted that she drifted through the area, spinning wool and linen to earn her keep, but living in poverty and often with a "wild and frightened" appearance.[8]

Like all wars, the Revolution brought unbounded prosperity to some, misery to others, and affected all who experienced it. Wilmington, and the Lower Cape Fear region of North Carolina, played a prominent role in the conflict from start to finish.

Slowly the area's residents recovered. Some found enterprising ways to get back on their feet. Loyalist Alexander McKay transferred ownership of his land to his Whig son, John. Thus after the war Alexander could reclaim it.[9]

In 1782 John Collet, the map maker and former commander of Fort Johnston, filed a claim for expenses he incurred while trying to maintain the fort. The North Carolina Assembly refused his petition.[10]

It is fitting that not only the opening acts of the Revolution occurred in the Cape Fear region, but also its concluding events as well. In 1789 the state's Constitutional Convention met in Fayetteville, the town formerly known as Cross Creek, and now renamed in honor of Marquis de Lafayette (the first city in America to be named for him). North Carolina was bitterly divided over the proposed Constitution, and in fact was the second to last state to ratify it. In finally doing so, it concluded the transfer of power and creation of government that began along the banks of the Cape Fear in the protests of the 1760s, some twenty years earlier.[11]

The state's General Assembly met in Fayetteville for many years. Here important decisions were made in the early national period: North Carolina ceded its western land (letting go of what would be come the state of Tennessee), the Assembly chartered the University of North Carolina, and the state named its first two Senators for Congress. The Assembly continued to meet there until the 1790s when the capital moved to Raleigh. In fact, Fayetteville aspired to become the state capital, and barely lost the vote.[12]

In the years that followed the war, Wilmington regained its status as the state's leading port. Merchants, including some former Loyalists, returned. Trade increased, and both Wilmington and Fayetteville prospered. By 1788 North Carolina's exports were double those of 1769, and the bulk of that trade passed through Wilmington.[13]

Shortly after the war one merchant wrote that "From Wilmington before the War I believe more Pitch, Tar & Turpentine was shipped than from all America...and it will be the Case again in a few years, that is as soon as the People can recover from the Damage they have sustained by the War..." He went on to note its importance as a port, declaring, "I assure you upon my Word is better than that of Charleston."[14]

In 1791, ten years after the siege of Yorktown effectively ended the war, President George Washington went on a tour of the Southern States. The nation's new president intended to visit each state to acquaint himself with the people and their concerns, and build a sense of nationalism.

That fall Washington visited Wilmington, arriving from the north on the post road (modern US 17). The former general left New Bern on April 23rd, riding south. He noted in his diary, "The whole road from New Bern to Wilmington passes through the most barren country I have ever beheld...especially in the parts nearest the latter, which is no more than a bed of white sand."

Washington stayed overnight just outside of Wilmington (in the Hampstead area), and arrived on the outskirts of town the following day. Here a troop of local militia cavalry greeted him, along with volleys of cannon fire and trumpets.

He spent the night at the home of Mrs. John Quince, at the corner of Dock and Front Streets, which he described as "very good lodgings." The next day, the 25th, he attended a procession through the streets of town, and dined at Dorsey's Tavern with city leaders. The tavern stood on Toomer Alley, between Front and Second Streets, now the site of a parking garage. A ball followed with dancing at the town hall. Bonfires lit the streets, and ships in the water were illuminated with lanterns.

John Quince's home in Wilmington. (NHCPL)

Washington described Wilmington in his journal: *"It has some good houses pretty compactly built. The whole under a hill; which is formed entirely of sand. The number of Souls in it amount...to about 1000...Wilmington, unfortunately for it, has a Mud bank miles below, over which not more than 10 feet of water can be brought at common tides, yet it is said vessels of 20 Tons have come up. The qu'ty of Shipping, which load here annually, amounts to about 1200 Tonns. The exports consist chiefly of Naval Stores and lumber. Some Tobacco, Corn, Rice, and flax seed with Porke. It is at the head of the tide navigation, but inland navigation may be extended 115 miles farther to and above Fayettesville which is from Wilmington 90 miles by land..."*

The next day he departed, crossing the river to Brunswick County. He noted that he was escorted by an "elegantly decorated revenue barge manned by six American Captains of ships, attended by boats from the harbor, and proceeded to the firing of cannon to 'Belvidere,' the plantation of Colonel Benjamin Smith..." He continued riding south towards modern Shallotte, and eventually on to Charleston. Washington had an eye for detail and his diary mentions numerous things like Wilmington's population, the impressive port facilities, its exports, and other details.[15]

In 1790 President Washington authorized ten cutters to be built to protect American ports and shipping. One of those ten, the *Diligence*, was assigned to Wilmington, and today its modern equivalent with the US Coast Guard still calls Wilmington home.[16]

Even before the turn of the century, Americans were celebrating holidays like July 4th, Washington's Birthday, and others associated with the Revolution. A Wilmington newspaper recorded in 1795 that, *"Saturday last, being the anniversary of the declaration of independence, the day was celebrated by the citizens of this town, in a manner which proved that they still prize freedom as the first boon of heaven.*

"Captain Martin's artillery ushered in the auspicious day, by a federal salute from the cannon on Fort Hill. At noon captain Walker's volunteer infantry company assembled at their parade, and marched from thence to the new court-house, where they fired three volleys, which were answered by an equal number of cheers, from the numerous spectators of all descriptions. In the afternoon the volunteer infantry again paraded, and marched round the town with the cap of liberty elevated and borne before them; on this occasion they fired a volley at each corner of the town.

"As harmony and order presided through the day, the evening was no less distinguished by civic fraternity and social festivity."[17]

The effects of the Revolution were felt for decades, though with each passing year the events of the 1770s and 1780s became more distant and blurred. Wives of soldiers were still filing pensions for compensation, based on the service of their husbands, into the 1850s, 1860s, and even 1870s. Some Revolutionary veterans of the lower Cape Fear were still alive to watch young men march off to another war in 1861.[18]

The Diligence was the first in a long line of US Coast Guard vessels calling Wilmington home.

Epilogue

T he land healed, but in places the war left a permanent mark on the landscape of the Lower Cape Fear. Devastated fields of crops and damaged homes would recover, but the movement of armies impacted the ground. Earthworks remained at Moores Creek until the early twentieth century, along with other locations along the Cape Fear River. The armies left a trail of graves in their wake: those who succumbed to battle deaths or disease, reminders of the passage of the armies. Scattered across eastern North Carolina are signs of their passage. Graves, battlefields, and campsites remain, though not always marked or easily accessible. Running across Duplin County, for example, is Cornwallis Road, approximately following the route of the British army in 1781.

The Community of Seventy-First in Cumberland County is another. It was created as a township in 1821, named after the British Highland Regiment that marched through the area in 1781, and it illustrates its ties to the area's Scottish settlers. Citizens created a school in the early 1900s, and today Seventy-First is a school in the Cumberland County school district.[1]

It is hoped that readers never see Wilmington, or the towns around it, the same way again. When driving past the National Cemetery on Market Street, think about Craig almost being ambushed. Remember those who suffered in the Bull Pen prison located between Second and Third Streets. Remember the captives who languished on prison ships in the Cape Fear River. Picture the American cavalry riding down Market Street to harass the British as they

, shooting in the streets. Imagine the protests at the courthouse site,
w... lliam Houston resigned, at the intersection of Front and Market Streets.
Remember Rouse's Tavern on US 17 near Middle Sound Loop, where eleven
American soldiers were bayoneted. When driving I-40 out of Wilmington, look
to the right and remember Heron's Bridge, site of two fierce battles.

That small part of downtown Wilmington that comprised the colonial
town, bounded by the river, Fourth Street, Orange Street, and Chestnut Street
was the center of much activity. Along Market, Water, and Front streets walked
Cornelius Harnett, James Moore, Richard Caswell, William Hooper, Alexander
Lillington, Robert Howe, David Fanning, Banastre Tarleton, Lord Cornwallis,
James Craig, Josiah Martin, William Tryon, George Washington, and hundreds
of others who were caught up in the events of the Revolution.

Important sites abound beyond Wilmington as well: protests at
Brunswick Town, naval battles along the Cape Fear, the American campsite at
Corbett's Ferry, Fort Johnston at Southport, the British raids into Duplin County,
the battle at Rockfish Creek near Wallace, and so many more.

Many lesser known sites exist throughout the region, such as
Lillington's grave in Pender County. Markers call attention to battle sites at
Rockfish Creek, McPhaul's Mill, Raft Swamp, the old town of Cross Creek, and
elsewhere. The places remain but the events are forgotten or obscured.

Sometimes myth grows out of memory. Stories are embellished or
altered over time. An example is the George Washington Tree in Hampstead.
Records indicate that during his 1791 presidential visit Washington slept in a
tavern near a prominent tree. In 1925 a local chapter of the Daughters of the
American Revolution planted a live oak to commemorate his stop. Some
sources now claim this is the tree visited by Washington, others that the tavern
was nearby. Sources also disagree on whether the general stayed overnight or
simply stopped for a meal. One account even claimed that Washington stopped
here with his generals during the war, when in fact he never visited North
Carolina until 1791. The truth is the site may be near the long-gone tavern, but it
is not the tree, nor is it at the exact site of his stop.[2]

As time advances the generation that fought the Revolution becomes
more distant, and more foreign to us today. The landscape has changed, their
written accounts are few, we have limited illustrations and graphics of the
period, and their experiences of daily life do not mirror ours.

Yet links to the past remain for us: monuments and memorials, historic
sites and homes, battlefields, and grave sites. Three Revolutionary War soldiers
are buried in Wilmington's Oakdale Cemetery. Historic markers are scattered
throughout the downtown historic district. Battle sites and important events are
marked across the region. With a little effort, it is possible to get a glimpse of
their lives and experiences.

Wilmington is well known for its historic district and well preserved architecture. This is no accident: the city has benefited from the hard work of many individuals and organizations. It is hoped that readers will be inspired to support the preservation and interpretation of the area's extensive Revolutionary War history.

The Revolutionary generation faced its challenges. It is up to their descendents to take up the duty and responsibility of preserving and remembering the sites and events of the past. Catherine Bisher, a prominent North Carolina historian, summarized it clearly, noting that the state "will undergo overwhelming changes that will alter the whole landscape irretrievably in the next generation. Change is accelerating beyond my ability to imagine its impact...How we are going to hang onto some vestiges of the hundreds of years of rural life that have passed...It will take powerful thought, and powerful effort."[3]

Appendix A
Historic Sites

Anumber of historic sites, monuments, and markers exist in the Lower Cape Fear to call attention to its role in the Revolution. Some are lost to development or to nature, others are noted by markers or preserved and open to the public. This list explains where these sites are and what may be seen at each.

Alamance Battleground State Historic Site - Located near Burlington, this is the only battle site of the Regulator War.

John Ashe Marker - On Highway 117 north of Rocky Point.

Samuel Ashe Marker - On Highway 117 north of Rocky Point.

Bald Head Island - Here the British built a small earthwork known as Ft. George, which the Americans attacked in the fall of 1776. Nothing remains of it today.

Black River Presbyterian Church - near Ivanhoe in Sampson County. Militia assembled here in 1776, and fought nearby at Moores Creek.

Black River Weapons Factory - Located near Clear Run in Sampson County, it produced 100 muskets before Loyalists destroyed it. Nothing remains today. A historic marker stands on Route 41 at the Black River bridge west of Harrells.

Brunswick Town State Historic Site - One of the region's most important historic sites, today it preserves the ruins of the town and has an excellent museum.

Brown Marsh - The battle site was near Clarkton on Red Hill Road.

Burgwin-Wright House - Cornwallis' headquarters in 1781, the home is located in downtown Wilmington. It is one of the only remnants of colonial Wilmington that survives. Tours are offered February through December.

Cape Fear Museum - Preserves the history of Wilmington and the Lower Cape Fear, located on Market Street.

Cape Fear River - The reason for Wilmington's being, and still a vital route for trade.

Cool Springs Tavern - Built just after the Revolution, this Fayetteville tavern hosted delegates to the state's Constitutional Convention. It stands near the site where the Loyalist army gathered for its march to Moores Creek in 1776.

Corbett's Ferry - Here militia under Col. Richard Caswell intended to stop General MacDonald's army in 1776. The Loyalists found another way across the river, forcing Caswell to retreat. The ferry was near the bridge over the Black River at Ivanhoe.

Cross Creek - The Scottish settlement stood in what is today downtown Fayetteville. Here the Loyalist army gathered for the march to Moores Creek in 1776. The town was an important supply depot for the Continental Army during the war. The British army also occupied the town in 1781.

Dollison's Landing - Here General James Moore's forces landed, having come down the Cape Fear River from Elizabethtown. They marched overland to Moores Creek, arriving just after the battle. The landing is inaccessible.

Fayetteville Transportation Museum - This museum has excellent exhibits about the early history of Fayetteville, especially its roads and waterways.

Fort Johnston - The fort guarded the entrance to the Cape Fear River. It was the oldest active military post in the nation, serving under the flags of three nations, and staying in use from 1748 through 2004. Historic markers stand on the waterfront in Southport to mark its location. Nothing remains of the fort today except the Garrison House.

Gov. Richard Caswell State Historic Site - Kinston burial site of the state's first governor and one of the commanders at Moores Creek.

Great Duplin Road - Leading north from Wilmington, the road crossed the Northeast Cape Fear River at Heron's Bridge and went straight north towards Duplin County. Modern US 117 closely parallels the road.

Guilford Courthouse National Military Park - The Battle of Guilford Courthouse, fought March 15, 1781, severely weakened the British army, though they won the field. It forced Cornwallis to leave the piedmont and find supplies on the coast.

Harmony Hall - Historic home of patriot leader John Richardson in White Oak, Bladen County. Built before the war, the home is open to the public.

Harmony Hall - Historic home of Richard Caswell, in Kinston. Open for tours.

Harnett Monument - One of Wilmington's most active Revolutionary War leaders, Harnett is virtually forgotten today. Hundreds of vehicles drive by his marker, and gravesite, in downtown Wilmington. The marker stands in the median at the intersection of Fourth and Market Streets. His grave is nearby in the cemetary at St. James Episcopal Church.

Heron's Bridge - Perhaps the most important Revolutionary War site in Southeastern North Carolina that is not preserved. The site of the drawbridge, campsite, and both Revolutionary and Civil War battles lies to the east of I-40 as it crosses the Northeast Cape Fear River. The land on both sides of the river is private property. A historical marker for the bridge is on Highway 117 at the border with Pender County. By the time of the Revolution it was also called Big Bridge or Blueford's Bridge (after a later owner). The bridge was over 400 feet long, and was one of two drawbridges in colonial America. The best place to view the site is from the state wildlife area off of Highway 117 in Castle Hayne.

Hooper's House - William Hooper's downtown home stood between Second and Third Streets, currently the site of a bank parking lot. Standing until the 1880s, it was the oldest house in Wilmington, and was lost in a fire. Two historic markers identify the site.

House in the Horseshoe State Historic Site - Site of one of Col. David Fanning's most famous battles. The home is open for tours, where bullet holes may still be seen in the walls.

Howe's Point - Birthplace of Gen. Robert Howe, raided by the British in the spring of 1776. The site is now part of Sunny Point Military Ocean Terminal.

Liberty Hall - Home of Col. James Kenan in Kenansville. Open for tours.

Lillington Cemetery - The family cemetery is located on Shaw Highway Road near Holly Shelter in Pender County.

Lindley's Mill Battlefield - A marker stands at the site where the battle began on Lindley Mill Road in lower Alamance County.

Alfred Moore Historical Marker - On NC 133 in Belville.

James Moore Historical Marker - On Highway 117 in Rocky Point.

Moores Creek National Battlefield - Site of the first Revolutionary War battle in North Carolina. The park features a museum, reconstructed earthworks, and a walking trail through the battlefield. Throughout the year the park offers tours and special events.

Museum of the Cape Fear - The museum has exhibits on the history of Fayetteville and Cumberland County.

Negro Head Point (Point Peter) - Landing site opposite Wilmington, where slave ships unloaded their human cargo in the eighteenth century. The site is inaccessible today.

Negro Head Point Road - In Pender County the old road is mostly preserved as modern Slocumb Trail and Blueberry Road. Both armies used this road to reach Moores Creek in 1776.

New Hanover County Courthouse Site - The courthouse, the scene of many pre-war protests, sat in the intersection of Front and Market Streets. A marker identifies the site.

North Carolina Maritime Museum - Located in downtown Southport, it chronicles the naval history of the region.

North Carolina Room, New Hanover County Public Library - This research room contains many important books, periodicals, and archival materials on local history. It is a tremendous asset for the people of southeastern North Carolina.

Northeast Cape Fear River - Winding its way north of Wilmington, it formed a natural defensive line above the city. It empties into the Cape Fear at Negro Head Point. The existence of this river is why Heron's Bridge was so important, as it was one of the few ways to cross into the lower part of New Hanover County and access Wilmington.

Old Smithfield Burying Ground - Burial place of General Robert Howe of the Continental Army, and Gov. Benjamin Smith, located in Southport.

Orton Plantation - Ancestral home of the Moore family. It is one of the few colonial era plantations in North Carolina open to the public.

Rockfish Creek (Cumberland County) - Here General James Moore built fortifications to stop General Donald MacDonald's Loyalist army in 1776. The site today is inaccessible.

Rockfish Creek (Duplin County) - Site of a British victory in 1781, a historic marker stands on Route 117 just south of Wallace.

Russellborough - Site of armed resistance to the Stamp Act, the ruins of the governor's house here are part of the Brunswick Town State Historic Site.

Sloop Point - Built in 1728 by Samuel Ashe, it is one of the oldest homes in North Carolina. Located near Hampstead, it is a private home.

Smith's Ferry - On the Cape Fear near Averasboro, the scene of the final surrender of the Loyalist survivors of Moores Creek. The site is private property today.

St. James Episcopal Church - The current building in Wilmington sits one block east of its wartime location on Fourth Street.

Tory Hole Park - Site of the Battle of Elizbethtown, where Loyalists forces were surrounded and cut off at the battle's end. Much of the fighting actually took place in what is now the modern downtown.

Tryon Palace - Located in New Bern, this was the royal governor's home. The palace is reconstructed and open for tours.

Tryon House Marker - At the corner of Water and Market Streets in downtown Wilmington. Here he was sworn in as governor in April 1765, but then shortly moved to Russelborough.

Wilmington Riverfront - Here ships docked to unload supplies and take on cargo. During the war troops from both sides landed here.

👑 Appendix B: 👑
Prisoners on the British *Forbay*

The *Forby* was a British prison ship stationed in Charleston harbor and in the Cape Fear River. This list names the prisoners held on the ship in May 1781.

Axson, William, Jr.
Ash, Samuel
Arthur, George
Anthony, John
Atmore, Ralph
Barnwell, Edward, Captain
Barnwell, John, Major
Barnwell, Robert
Baddily, Joh, Major
Bonnethean, Peter, Captain Lieutenant
Bembridge, Henry
Black, John, Lieutenant
Branford, William
Ball, Joseph
Blumdell, Nathaniel
Bricken, James
Bailey, Francis
Baoqum, William
Buie, Daniel, Captain
Clarke, Jonathan
Cockran, Thomas
Cohen, Jacob
Cooke, Thomas
Calhoon, John
Cray, J. Captain
Conyers, Norwood
Cox, James
Cummins, Richard
Cohen, Jacob
Dorain, John
Dewar, Robert

Desaussure, William
Dunlap, Joseph
Edmunds, Rever
Eveleigh, Thomas
Edwards, John, Jr.
Edwards, John Warren
Elliott, Thomas, Sr.
Elliot, Joseph, Jr.
Elliott, William
Evans, John
Eberly, John
Ezan, John
Guerrard, Benjamin
Guerard, Peter
Gibbons, John
Grayson, Thomas
Graves, John
Graves, William
Geir, Christian
Gadsden, Philip
Glover, Joseph
Grott, Francis
George, Mitchel
Holmes, William
Hughes, Thomas
Heward, James
Harris, Thomas
Hornby, William
Harvey, William, Lieutenant
Henry, Jacob
Hamilton, David
Holmes, John B.

Jones, George
Jonathan, Morgan
Jacobs, Daniel
Kent, Charles
Kain, John
Lockhart, S., Captain
Libby, Nathaniel
Liston, Thomas
Lee, Stephen, Lieutenant
Legare, Thomas
Lessene, John
Legbert, Henry
Magdalen, Charles
Marriett, Abraham
Meyers, Philip
Minoth, John, Jr.
Miche, John
Minott, John, Sr.
Moncrief, John
Miller, Samuel
Miller, Solomon, Lieutenant
Moore, Stephen, Colonel
Murphy, William
Monks, George
Moss, George, Dr.
Neufville, John, Jr.
Owen, John
Prioleau, Samuel, Sr.
Prioleau, Philip
Pinkney, Charles, Jr.
Pogas, James
Palmer, Job

Robinson, Joseph
Revin, Thomas
Rhodes, Daniel
Righton, Joseph
Sayle, William
Scott, John, Sr.
Scotton, Samuel
Seavers, Abraham
Shrewsbury, Stephen
Singleton, Rippily
Smith, Samuel
Snelling, William
Snyder, Paul
Stephenson, John, Jr.
Stephens, Daniel
Tonsiger, James
Tanders, John
Tayloe, Paul
White Sime, Lieutenant
Wigg, William
Williams, James
Warham, Charles,
   Adjutant
Waring, Thomas, Sr.
Waring, Richard
White, Isaac
Welch, George
Wheller, Benjamiin
Watirs, John, Jr.
Wilcocks, William
Warham, David
Wilkie, William
Yore, Thomas
Yeadon, Richard

👑 Appendix C: 👑
Sauthier Maps of Colonial N.C.
(Sauthier maps of Wilmington and Brunswick are located elsewhere in the text)

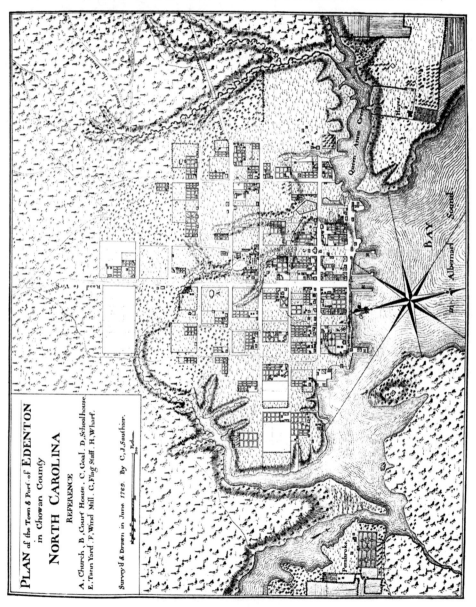

C.J. Sauthier's map of Edenton.

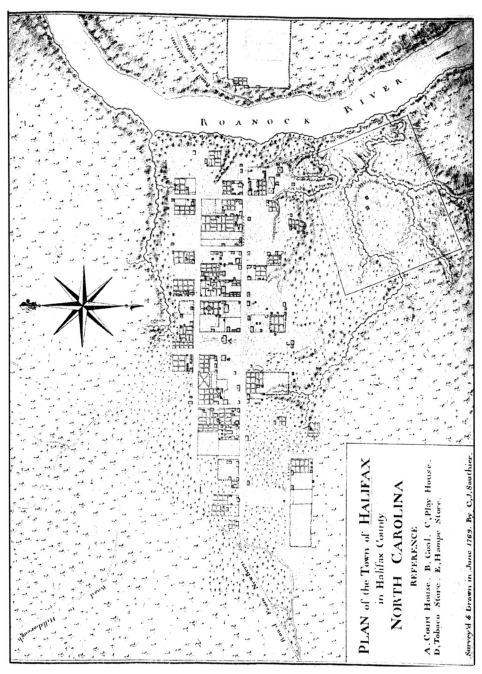

C.J. Sauthier's map of Halifax.

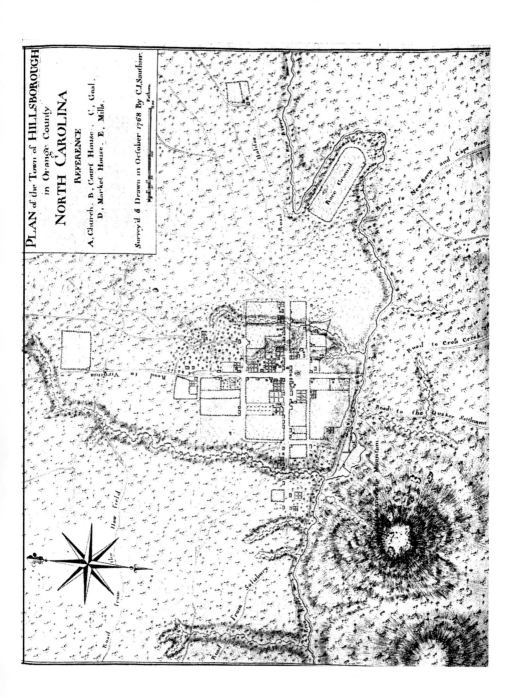

C.J. Sauthier's map of Hillsborough.

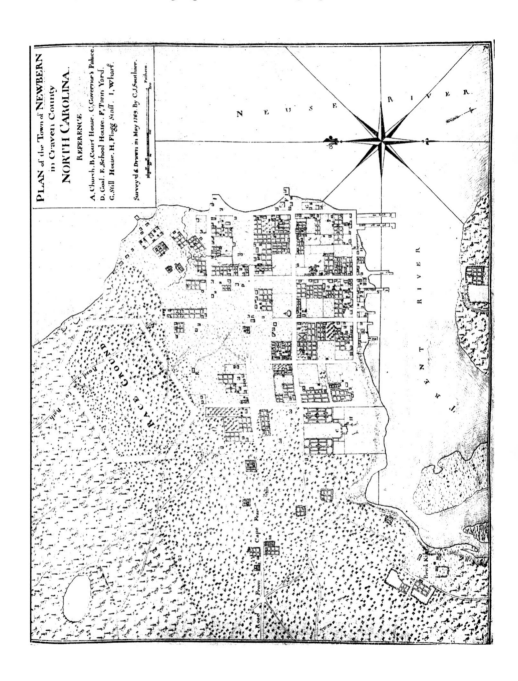

C.J. Sauthier's map of New Bern.

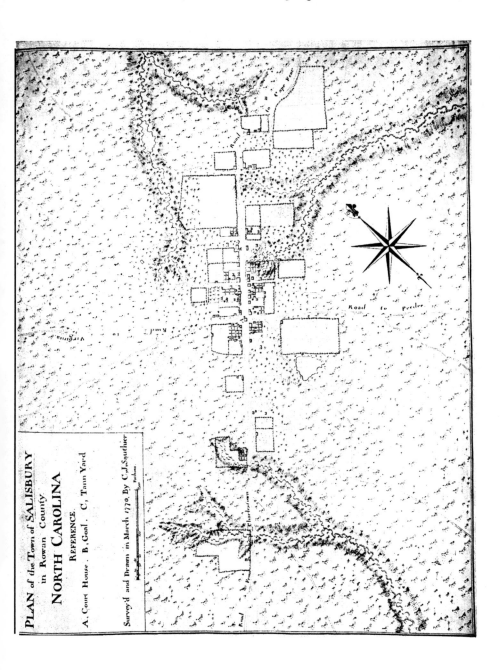

C.J. Sauthier's map of Salisbury.

👑 Appendix D: 👑
Revolutionary War Actions in N.C.

The following is a list of Revolutioanry War actions in North Carolina.

Key:

B-Battle, S-Skirmish, A-Attack, DA-Defensive Action, R-Raid, NR-Naval Raid.

1775 - 1779
- 16 May 1771 – Battle of Alamance – B
- 18 July 1775 – Ft. Johnston – A
- 16-21 Nov 1775 – Ft. Johnston – DA
- 27-28 Jan 1776 – Ft. Johnston – NS
- 10 Feb 1776 – Ancrum's Plantation – R
- 27 Feb 1776 – Moores Creek – B
- 8-12 Mar 1776 – Ft. Johnston – S
- 29 Mar 1776 – Cross Creek – R
- 6-27 April 1776 – Brunswick Town – S
- 14-17 April 1776 – Ocracoke Inlet – NS
- 1-3 May 1776 – Ft. Johnston – NS
- 11 May 1776 – Orton Mill/Kendal Plantation – S
- 17 May 1776 – Brunswick Town – S
- 23 May 1776 – Ft. Johnston – S
- July 1776 – Quaker Meadows – S
- 3-12 July 1776 – McDowell's Station – Seige
- 15 August 1776 – Roanoke Inlet – S
- 6-7 Sept 1776 – Ft. George (Bald Head Island) - S
- 19 Sept 1776 – Coweecho River – B
- 27 Oct 1776 Neowee Creek – S
- 12 May 1778 – Topsail Inlet – NR
- July 1778 – Salisbury – S
- 15 Nov 1778 – Currituck Inlet – NR
- May 1779 – Haw Fields – S
- 27 June 1779 – Cape Hatteras – S

1780
- 7 June 1780 – Cape Hatteras – NS
- 20 June 1780 – Ramsour's Mill – B
- 21 July 1780 – Colson's Mill – S
- Sept 1780 – Graham's Fort – S
- 9 Sept 1780 – Anson County – S
- 10 Sept 1780 – Mask's Ferry – S
- 12 Sept 1780 – Cane Creek – S
- 21 Sept 1780 – Wahab's Plantation – S
- 26 Sept 1780 – Charlotte Town – S
- Sept 1780 – Yadkin River – S
- 3 Oct 1780 – Richmond Town – R
- 3 Oct 1780 – Battle of the Bees – S
- 7 Oct 1780 – King's Mountain – B
- 8 Oct 1780 – Richmond Town – R
- 9 Oct 1780 – Polk's Mill – S
- 13 Oct 1780 – Charlotte Town – S
- 14 Oct 1780 – Shallow Ford – S
- Oct 1780 – Myhand's Bridge – S
- 3 Nov 1780 – Great Swamp – S

1781
- 30 Jan 1781 – Heron's Bridge – S
- Feb 1781 – Chestnut Mountain – S
- 1 Feb 1781 – Cowan's Ford – S
- 1 Feb 1781 – Tarrant's Tavern – S
- 4-5 Feb 1781 – Trading Ford – S
- 4 Feb 1781 – Grant's Creek – S
- Feb 1781 – Shallow Ford – S
- 8 Feb 1781 – Reedy Creek/Shallow Ford – S
- 12 Feb 1781 – Summerfield – S
- 13 Feb 1781 – Speedwell Furnace – S
- 17 Feb 1781 – Hart's Mill – S
- 25 Feb 1781 – Pyle's Defeat (Massacre) – S
- 26 Feb 1781 - Dickey's Farm – S
- 2 Mar 1781 – Fletcher's Mill – S

- 4 Mar 1781 – Clapp's Mill – S
- 5 Mar 1781 – Clapp's Mill – S
- 5 Mar 1781 – Alamance River – S
- 6 Mar 1781 – Wetzel's Mill – S
- 7 Mar 1781 – near Wetzel's Mill – S
- 7 Mar 1781 – Alamance River – S
- 7 Mar 1781 – Reedy Fork – S
- 13 Mar 1781 – Bull Run Creek – S
- 15 Mar 1781 – New Garden Meeting House – S
- 15 Mar 1781 – Guilford Courthouse – B
- 15 Mar 1781 – Alamance – S
- 19 Mar 1781 – Ramsey's Mill – S
- 25 Mar 1781 – Stewart's Creek – S
- Mar 1781 – Rouse's Tavern – S
- 15-16 April 1781 – Big Glades – S
- 29 April 1781 – Barbecue Church – S
- 6 May 1781 – Swift Creek/Fishing Creek – S
- 7 May 1781 – Halifax – S
- 9 May 1781 – Deep River – S
- 11 May 1781 – Coharie Swamp – S
- 11-12 May 1781 – Buffalo Ford – S
- 13 May 1781 – Legat's Bridge – S
- 13 May 1781 – Myhand's Bridge – S
- 16 May 1781 – Portevent's Mill – S
- June 1781 – Edenton – S
- 8 June 1781 – Cox's Mill – S
- July - Wyanoke Ferry – R
- 8 July 1781 – New Berne – S
- 17 July 1781 – Chatham Courthouse – R
- 26 July 1781 – Stuart's Creek – S
- 29 July 1781 – House in the Horseshoe – S
- 30 July 1781 – Cox's Mill – S
- 2 Aug 1781 – Rockfish Creek – S
- 3 Aug 1781 – Piney Bottom – S
- 4 Aug 1781 – Beatti's Bridge – S
- 9-12 Aug 1781 – Richmond/Cumberland Counties – R
- 14 Aug 1781 – Cumberland County Courthouse – R
- 16 Aug 1781 – Kingston – S
- 17 Aug 1781 – Robeson's Plantation – R
- 17 Aug 1781 – Webber's Bridge – S
- 19 Aug 1781 – New Berne – S

- 21 Aug 1781 – Kingston – S
- 27 Aug 1781 – Tory Hole (Elizabethtown) – B
- 28 Aug 1781 – Fanning's Mill – S
- Sept 1781 – Hood's Creek – S
- 1 Sept 1781 – Little Raft Swamp – B
- Sept 1781 – Beck's Ford – S
- 12 Sept 1781 – Hillsboro – S
- 12 Sept 1781 – Kirk's Farm – S
- 13 Sept 1781 – Lindley's Mill – B
- 23 Sept 1781 – Livingston's Creek – S
- Sept 1781 – Brown Marsh – S
- Oct 1781 – Brush Creek – S
- 15 Oct 1781 – Raft Swamp – S
- Oct 1781 – Bear Creek – S
- Nov 1781 – Mill's Station – R
- 14 Nov 1781 – More's Plantation – S
- 15 Nov 1781 – The Brick House – S
- 16 Nov 1781 – Seven Creeks – S
- 18 Nov 1781 – Evacuation of Wilmington – S
- Nov 1781 – Chatham County – S
- 10 Dec 1781 – Cox' Mill – R
- Dec 1781 – Big Juniper Creek – R

1782
- 11 Feb 1782 – Deep River – S
- 7-10 Mar 1782 – Randolph County – S
- 11 Mar 1782 – Balfour's Plantation - R
- 4-17 April 1782 – Beaufort – Siege
- Sept 1782 – Bladen County Courthouse – R

Bibliography

• *Account of Sundries furnished...for his Majesty's Service in North Carolina.* Public Records, Audit Office, 13/3, ERD 7795, 94. Public Records Office, Kew, Surry, England.

• Anderson, Fred. *Crucible of War*. New York: Alfred A. Knopf, 2000.

• Angley, Wilson. *A History of Fort Johnston*. Southport, NC: Southport Historical Society, 1996.

• Asbury, R.V., Ida B. Kellam, and Edward F. Turberg, ed. *The Schenck Diary*. Wilmington, NC: Wilmington Public Library, 1998.

• Ashe, Samuel. *The History of North Carolina*. Vol. I. Spartanburg, SC: The Reprint Co., 1971.

• Babits, Lawernce, and Joshua Howard. *Fortitude and Forbearance*. Raleigh: North Carolina Department of Archives and History, 2004.

• Baker, Elisha. *Federal Pension Application*. R 411. Washington, DC: National Archives.

• Bannerman, George. *Federal Pension Application*. S 8055. Washington, DC: National Archives.

• Barefoot, Daniel. *Touring North Carolina's Revolutionary War Sites*. Winston Salem, NC: J.F. Blair, 1998.

• Bezzant, Brock. *Federal Pension Application*. S 16791. Washington, DC: National Archives.

• Bivins, John Jr. *Wilmington Furniture*. Wilmington, NC: St. Johns Museum of Art, 1989.

• Bizzell, Virginia and Oscar. *Revolutionary War Records of Duplin and Sampson Counties, North Carolina*. Newton Grove, NC: Sampson County Historical Society, 1997.

• Boykin, Beverly and William Kern, ed. *Historic Cemeteries of Fort Bragg, Camp MacKall, and Pope Air Force Base*. Fort Bragg, NC: Department of the Army, 2007.

• Bloodworth, Mattie. *History of Pender County*. Richmond, VA: Dietz Press, 1947.

• Block, Susan. *The Wrights of Wilmington*. Wilmington, NC: Wilmington Printing Co., 1992.

• Brock, Bezzant. *Federal Pension Application*. 16791. Washington, DC: National Archives.

• Brown, Joseph. *The Commonwealth of Onslow*. New Bern, NC: The Owen G. Dunn Co., 1960.

• Brown, Thomas. *Federal Pension Application*. W 9745. Washington, DC: National Archives.

• Bullard, Thomas. *Federal Pension Application*. S 6770. Washington, DC: National Archives.

• Burke, James C. *Deconstructing Historic Text for Geographic References - The Plan of the Unnamed Colonel*. Unpublished research paper, 2008.

• Butler, Carol. *Treasures of the Longleaf Pine*. Shalinar, FL: Tarkel Publishing, 1998.

• Butler, Lindley S. *North Carolina and the Coming of the American Revolution*. Raleigh: Department of Archives and History, 1976.

• Ibid., ed. *Narrative of David Fanning*. Davidson, NC: Briarpatch Press, 1981.

• *Cape Fear Mercury* (Wilmington, NC), August 11, 1775; November 24, 1769; December 29, 1773; October 13, 1770; January 13, 1773; September 22, 1773.

• Carr, James O., ed. *The Dickson Letters*. Raleigh: Edwards and Broughton, 1901.

• Ibid., *"The Battle of Rockfish in Duplin County,"* North Carolina Booklet, Vol. 6, No. 3, Jan 1907, 177-84

• Caruthers, Eli. *The Old North State in 1776*. Philadelphia: Hayes and Zell, 1854.

• *Claim of Arthur Benning*. Public Records Office, Audit Office, 13/117.

• *Claim of Rigdon Brice*. Public Records Office, Audit Office, 13/117.

• *Claim of John Mackay*. Public Records Office, Audit Office, 13/117.

• Clark, Jonathan. *Federal Pension Application*. S 2438. Washington, DC: National Archives.

• Clark, Walter, ed. *State Records of North Carolina*. Vols. XI, XV, XVI, XXII. Raleigh, NC, 1905.

• Clark, William, ed. *Naval Documents of the American Revolution*. Washington, DC: US Government Printing Office, 1968.

• Clayton, Alexander and W. Keats Sparrow. *First of Patriots and the Best of Men: Richard Caswell in Public Life.* Kinston, NC: Lenoir County Colonial Commission, 2007.

• *Clinton, Sir Henry* to Lord Charles Cornwallis. 30 April, 1781. Cornwallis Papers, Public Records Office, 30/11/5/30.

• Ibid. to George Martin. 10 May, 1781. Sir Henry Clinton Papers, Vol. 263, Miscellaneous Correspondence, 1776-1782, University of Michigan, William L. Clements Library.

• Ibid. *The American Rebellion: Sir Henry Clinton's Narrative of His Campaigns, 1775-1782, with an Appendix of Original Documents.* William B. Wilcox, ed. New Haven, CT: Yale University Press, 1954.

• *Colvin Family Papers*. Park Archives. Moores Creek National Battlefield, Currie, NC.

• Connor, R.D.W. *History of North Carolina*. Vol. I. Chicago: Lewis Publishing Co., 1919.

• Conrad, Dennis, ed. *The Papers of Nathanael Greene*. Vol. VIII, IX, X. Chapel Hill: University of North Carolina Press, 1997.

• Conser, Walter H., Jr. *A Coat of Many Colors*. Lexington: University of Kentucky Press, 2006.

• Coombs, Edwin L. III. *"Trading in Lubberland: Maritime Commerce in Colonial North Carolina."* *North Carolina Historical Review*, Vol. LXXX, #1 (January 2003), 1-27.

• *Cornwallis, Lord Charles* to Sir Henry Clinton. 10 April, 1781. Cornwallis Papers, 30/11/5/207. Public Records Office, Kew, Surry, England.

• Ibid. Proclamation. 18 March, 1781. Cornwallis Papers, 30/11/101, ff 24-31. Public Records Office, Kew, Surry, England.

• Ibid. to Lord George Germain. 18 April, 1781. Cornwallis Papers, 30/11/5/ 254. Public Records Office, Kew, Surry, England.

• Ibid. to Lord George Germain. 23 April, 1781. Cornwallis Papers, 30/11/5/ 215. Public Records Office, Kew, Surry, England.

• Ibid. to Sir Henry Clinton. 23 April, 1781. Cornwallis Papers, 30/11/5/219. Public Records Office, Kew, Surry, England.

• *Craig, James* to Lt. Col. Balfour. 4 February, 1781. C.O. 5/101, fo. 248. Colonial Office, Public Records Office, Kew, Surry, England.

• Ibid. to Lord Charles Cornwallis. 10 February, 1781. Cornwallis Papers, 30/ 11/5/179, Public Records Office, Kew, Surry, England.

• Ibid. to Lt. Col. Balfour. 18 February, 1781. Cornwallis Papers, 30/11/5/34. Public Records Office, Kew, Surry, England.

• Ibid. to Lord Charles Cornwallis. 6 April, 1781. Cornwallis Papers, 30/11/5/ 181. Public Records Office, Kew, Surry, England.

• Ibid. to Lord Charles Cornwallis. 12 April, 1781. Cornwallis Papers, 30/11/5/ 305. Public Records Office, Kew, Surry, England.

• Ibid. to Lt. Col. Balfour. 22 October, 1781. Cornwallis Papers, 30/11/6/391-398. Public Records Office, Kew, Surry, England.

• Crary, Catherine. *The Price of Loyalty.* New York: McGraw Hill Book Co., 1973.

• Crawford, C.E. *A History of Bladen County.* Elizabethtown, NC: Bladen County Historical Society, 1987.

• Crow, Jeffery. *The Black Presence in the American Revolution*. Raleigh: North Carolina Department of Archives and History, 1977.

• Ibid. "Liberty Men and Loyalists" in Ronald Hoffman and Thad Tate, ed., *An Uncivil War: The Southern Backcountry.* Charlottesville: University Press of Virginia, 1985.

• Davis, Burke. *The Cowpens-Guilford Courthouse Campaign*. Philadelphia: University of Pennsylvania Press, 2003.

• DeMond, Robert O. *The Loyalists in North Carolina During the American Revolution*. Baltimore: Clearfield Co., 2002.

• De Van Massey, Gregory. "The British Expedition to Wilmington, North Carolina, January-November, 1781." MA Thesis, East Carolina University, 1987.

• Devane, James. *Federal Pension Application*. S 8317. Washington, DC: National Archives.

• *Diary of Sergeant Von Koch*.

• Dill, Alonzo. *"Eighteenth Century New Bern," North Carolina Historical Review* 23: 325-351.

• Dudley, Guilford. *"A Sketch of the Military Services Performed by Guilford Dudley, Then of the Town of Halifax, North Carolina, During the Revolutionary War." Southern Literary Messenger* (March–June 1845).

• Dunkerly, Robert M. **Bravery and Sacrifice: Women on the Southern Battlefields**. Charleston, SC: History Press, 2007.

• Ibid. **The Battle of Kings Mountain: Eyewitness Accounts**. Charleston, SC: History Press, 2007.

• Earley, Lawrence. **Looking for Longleaf**. Chapel Hill: University of North Carolina Press, 2004.

• Edge, John. **Federal Pension Application**. R 3232. Washington, DC: National Archives.

• Ellet, Elizabeth. **The Women of the Revolution**. New York: Baker and Scribner, 1849.

• Elzas, Barnett A. **The Jews of South Carolina**. Philadelphia: J.B. Lippincott Co., 1905.

• Fanning, David. **The Narrative of Colonel David Fanning**. Spartanburg, SC: The Reprint Co., 1973.

• Flowers, John Braxton. *"Did Polly Slocumb Ride to the Battle of Moores Creek Bridge?" Lower Cape Fear Historical Society Bulletin* Vol. XIX, No. 2 (February 1976).

• Fonvielle, Chris E. **Historic Wilmington and the Lower Cape Fear**. San Antonio, TX: Historical Publishing Network, 2007.

• Fowler, John. **Federal Pension Application**. S 16809. Washington, DC: National Archives.

• Frech, Laura. *"The Wilmington Committee of Public Safety and the Loyalist Rising of February, 1776." North Carolina Historical Review* 41 (1968): 21-33.

• Fryar, Jack E., Jr., ed. **"Benson J. Lossing's Pictorial Field-Book of the Revolution in the Carolinas & Georgia**. Wilmington, NC: Dram Tree Books, 2005.

• Graham, William. *General Joseph Graham and his Revolutionary Papers*. Raleigh, NC: Edwards and Broughton, 1904.

• Green, William. *Federal Pension Application*. S 3413. Washington, DC: National Archives.

• Grinsley, George. *Federal Pension Application*. R 4333. Washington, DC: National Archives.

• Hall, Wes. *"An Underwater Archaeological Survey of Heron's Colonial Bridge Crossing Site over the Northeast Cape Fear River near Castle Hayne, North Carolina."* Masters Thesis, East Carolina University, 1992.

• Hairr, John. *Colonel David Fanning: The Adventures of a Carolina Loyalist*. Erwin, NC: Averasboro Press, 2000.

• Ibid. *North Carolina Rivers*. Charleston, SC: The History Press, 2007.

• Ibid. *"Commanding Presence" Our State*, Vol. 75, No. 5 (October, 2007), 29-32

• Hatch, Charles. *The Battle of Moores Creek Bridge*. Washington, DC: National Park Service, 1969.

• Haywood, Marshall. *Governor William Tryon*. Raleigh, NC: E. M. Uzell, 1902.

• Hewlett, Crockette W. and Mona Smalley. *Between the Creeks, Revised, Masonboro Sound, 1735-1895*. Wilmington: New Hanover Printing Co., 1985.

• *History of the George Washington Bicentennial Celebration*. Washington, DC: George Washington Bicentennial Commission, 1932.

• Howard, Jack. *A History of Hampstead*.

• Howell, Andrew J. *The Book of Wilmington*. Wilmington: The Wilmington Printing Co., 1930.

• Jackson, Claude. *Cape Fear-Northeast Cape Fear Rivers Comprehensive Study*. Kure Beach, NC: North Carolina Department of Archives and History, Underwater Archaeology Division, 1996.

• Johnson, Elijah. *Federal Pension Application*. S 1806. Washington, DC: National Archives.

• Johnston, Peter. *Poorest of the Thirteen*. Haverford, PA: Infinity Publishing, 2001.

• Johnstone, Mary Daniels. *The Heritage of Wayne County, North Carolina*. Winston-Salem, NC: Hunter Publishing Co., 1982.

• Jones, Elisha. *Federal Pension Application*. S 7084. Washington, DC: National Archives.

• [Jones, John D.] *"Cape Fear Sketches and Loafer Ramblings by the Author of the Wilmington Whistling Society, etc."* Folder 29, Benjamin Franklin Perry Papers, #588, Southern Historical Collection, Wilson Library, The University of North Carolina at Chapel Hill.

• *Journal of the Provincial Congress of North Carolina*. Office of the Secretary of State.

• *Journal of the Honourable Hessian Infantry Regiment von Bose*.

• Kaplan, Sidney and Emma Kaplan. *The Black Presence in the Era of the American Revolution*. Amherst: University of Massachusetts Press, 1989.

• Kay, Marvin, and William S. Price. *"To Ride the Woods Mare: Road Building and Militia Service in Colonial North Carolina, 1740-1775."* North Carolina Historical Review 57 (October 1980): 361-409.

• Keith, Alice, ed. *John Gray Blount Papers*. Raleigh, NC: Department of Archives and History, 1952.

• Kelly, Douglass and Caroline Kelly. *Carolina Scots*. Dillon, SC: 1739 Publications, 1998.

• Kemp, Allan. *The British Army in the American Revolution*. London, UK: Almark Publishing Co., 1973.

• Kierner, Cynthia A. *Southern Women in Revolution, 1776-1800*. Columbia: University of South Carolina Press, 1998.

• Lee, James. *Federal Pension Application*. S 7145. Washington, DC: National Archives.

• Lee, Lawrence. *The Lower Cape Fear in Colonial Days*. Chapel Hill: University of North Carolina Press, 1976.

• Lee, Robert E., ed. *The Revolutionary War Memoirs of General Henry Lee*. New York: Da Capo Press, 1998.

• Lee, Wayne E. *Crowds and Soldiers in Revolutionary North Carolina*. Gainesville: University of Florida Press, 2001.

• Lennon, Donald R. and Ida Brooks Kellman, ed. *Wilmington Town Book*. Raleigh: North Carolina Department of Archives and History, 1973.

• *London Chronicle*. March 20, 1766.

• *Lower Gullah Culture Special Resource Study*. Washington, DC: National Park Service, 2006.

• *Loyalist Diary*, author unknown. *Sir Henry Clinton Papers*, 14:10.

• MacDonald, Allan. Auditors Office, 13/122, 27. Public Records Office, Kew, Surry, England.

• MacLeod, Ruairidh H. *Flora MacDonald*. London: Shepheard-Walwyn, 1995.

• Maze, Terry. *John Grady and the Patriots Monument*. 1979. Research paper on file at Moores Creek National Battlefield, Currie, NC.

• McCaskle, Mary. Audit Office, American Loyalist Claims, American Series 13, Number 91. Public Records Office, Kew, Surry, England.

• McCrady, Edward. *History of South Carolina in the American Revolution*. New York: Russell & Russell, 1969.

• McEachern, Leora, and Isabel M. Williams, ed. *Wilmington-New Hanover Safety Committee Minutes*. Wilmington: Wilmington-New Hanover County American Revolution Bicentennial Association, 1974.

• Ibid. *Lower Cape Fear Revolutionary War Events 1776*. Wilmington: Wilmington-New Hanover County American Revolution Bicentennial Association.

• Ibid. *Lower Cape Fear Revolutionary War Events 1765-1774*. Wilmington: Wilmington-New Hanover County American Revolution Bicentennial Association.

• Ibid. *Lower Cape Fear Revolutionary War Events 1775*. Wilmington: Wilmington-New Hanover County American Revolution Bicentennial Association.

• McEachern, Leora, and Ruth Walker. *"Pensioners Remember The War,"* *Lower Cape Fear Historical Society Bulletin* Vol. XXIV, No. 2 (January 1991): 1-5.

• McGeachy, John A. *"Revolutionary Reminiscences from the "Cape Fear Sketches,"* North Carolina State University, 2001.

• McGowen, Faison Wells, ed. *Flashes of Duplin County's History and Government*. Raleigh, NC: Edwards and Broughton, 1971.

• McLean, Alexander. *Narrative of the Proceedings of a Body of Loyalists in North Carolina*. English Records, C.O., 5, Vol. 93, p. 297.

• McLean, Angus. *Highland Scots in North Carolina*. North Carolina Scottish Heritage Society, 1993.

• McRea, Duncan. Audit Office, American Loyalist Claims, American Series 13, Number 121. Public Records Office, Kew, Surry, England.

• Medley, Bryant. *Federal Pension Application*. S 8894. Washington, DC: National Archives.

• Merrens, Harry Roy. *Colonial North Carolina in the Eighteenth Century*. Chapel Hill: University of North Carolina Press, 1964.

• Merritt, Daniel. *Federal Pension Application*. S 16497. Washington, DC: National Archives.

• Moore, John. *Federal Pension Application*. R 7340. Washington, DC: National Archives.

• Moore, Louis T. *Stories Old and New of the Cape Fear Region.* Wilmington, NC: Broadfoot Publishing, 1999.

• Morgan, David T. *"Cornelius Harnett: Revolutionary Leader and Delegate to the Continental Congress,"* North Carolina Historical Review XLIX, No. 3 (July 1972): 229-241.

• Morgan, Edmund S. *The Challenge of the American Revolution.* New York: WW Norton, 1976.

• Ibid. *The Birth of the Republic.* Chicago: University of Chicago Press, 1992.

• Morrison, Alexander. Auditors Office, 13/122, Public Records Office, Kew, Surry, England.

• Morrissey, Brendan. *Boston.* Oxford, UK: Osprey, 1993.

• Moss, Bobby G. *Loyalists in the Battle of Moores Creek Bridge.* Blacksburg, SC: Scotia Hibernia Press, 1992.

• Ibid. *Patriots in the Battle of Moores Creek Bridge.* Blacksburg, SC: Scotia Hibernia Press, 1992.

• Ibid. and Michael Scoggins. *African American Loyalists in the Southern Campaign of the American Revolution.* Blacksburg, SC: Scotia Hibernia Press, 2005.

• Murphy, Hugh. *Federal Pension Application.* S 9044. Washington, DC: National Archives.

• Nash, Gary. *Forgotten Fifth.* Harvard: Harvard University Press, 2006.

• Newlin, Algie. *The Battle of Lindley's Mill.* Burlington, NC: Alamance Historical Association, 1975.

• Newsome, A.R. *"Twelve North Carolina Counties in 1810-1811,"* North Carolina Historical Review 5 (1928): 413-446.

• *North Carolina Gazette* (Wilmington, NC) February 22, 1766; February 12, 1766.

• Oates, John. *The Story of Fayetteville*. 1950.

• Odom, Nash. *"The Battle of Brown Marsh."* The Bladen Journal, September 15, 1973.

• Parker, Roy Jr. *Cumberland County: A Brief History*. Raleigh: North Carolina Department of Archives and History, 1990.

• Peckham, Howard, ed. *The Toll of Independence*. Chicago: University of Chicago Press, 1974.

• Pedlow, Franda D. *The Story of Brunswick Town and Fort Anderson*. Wilmington, NC: Dram Tree Books, 2005.

• Perkins, Betty. "A Patriots Return to Moores Creek," *State Magazine* (January 1975): 17-18.

• Peterson, John. *Federal Pension Application*. S 7303. Washington, DC: National Archives.

• *Petition To His Excellency Josiah Martin Esquire, Governor & Commander in Chief of the Province of North Carolina*. Cornwallis Papers, 30/11/5/201-203. Public Records Office, Kew, Surry, England.

• Powell, William S. *The War of the Regulation and the Battle of Alamance*. Raleigh: Department of Cultural Resources, 1975.

• Pridgen, William. *Federal Pension Application*. S8982. Washington, DC: National Archives.

• *Proclamation of Charles, Earl Cornwallis, Lieutenant General of His Majesty's Forces*. Cornwallis Papers, 30/11/5/256, Public Records Office, Kew, Surry, England.

• Quarles, Benjamin. *The Negro in the American Revolution*. New York: WW Norton, 1961.

• Quynn, Dorothy, *"Flora MacDonald in History,"* North Carolina Historical Review XVIII, 3 (July 1941), 236-58.

• Rankin, Hugh. *The Moores Creek Bridge Campaign*. Fort Washington, PA: Eastern National, 1998.

• Ibid. *The North Carolina Continentals*. Chapel Hill: University of North Carolina Press, 2005.

• Raphael, Ray. *The First American Revolution*. New York: The New Press, 2002.

• Reeves, Bill. *Southport (Smithville): A Chronology*. Vol. I. Wilmington, NC: Broadfoot Publishing, 1985.

• *Report on the Petition of Mr. DuBois*. 1803. Private Collection.

• Robinson, Blackwell P. *The Five Royal Governors of North Carolina*. Raleigh: Department of Archives and History, 1968.

• Rogers, James. Audit Office, American Loyalist Claims, American Series 13, Number 138. Public Records Office, Kew, Surry, England.

• Ross, Charles. *The Correspondence of Charles, First Marquis Cornwallis*. London: J Murray, 1859.

• Ross, Malcom. *The Cape Fear*. New York: Holt, Rinehart, and Winston, 1965.

• *Roster of Soldiers from North Carolina in the American Revolution*. Baltimore, MD: Clearfield Co., 2003.

• Russell, David Lee. *Victory on Sullivan's Island*. West Haverford, PA: Infinity, 2002.

• Sabine, Lorenzo. *Biographical Sketches of Loyalists of the American Revolution*. Port Wasington, NY: Kennikat Press, 1966.

• Salmon, Vincent. *Federal Pension Application*. R 9156. Washington, DC: National Archives.

• Saunders, William, ed. *Colonial Records of North Carolina*. Raleigh: State of North Carolina, 1886-1890.

• Schenck, David. *North Carolina 1780-81*. Bowie, MD: Heritage Books, 2000.

• Schaw, Janet. *Journal of a Lady of Quality.* Lincoln: University of Nebraska, 2005.

• Schriener, Mark. *"Martyred Patriot Remembered," Wilmington Morning Star*, 7 March 2002.

• Secrest, John. *Federal Pension Application*. S 3875. Washington, DC: National Archives.

• Shipman, James. *Federal Pension Application*. Washington, DC: National Archives.

• Siler, Walter D. *A History of Chatham County*. Chatham News, 1931. Available at www.rootsweb.com/~ncchatha/siler.htm.

• Sloan, Robert. *Federal Pension Application*. S 7523. Washington, DC: National Archives.

• Smith, John. *Federal Pension Application*. S 7540. Washington, DC: National Archives.

• Smith, John W. *"Wilmington's Legal Legacy 1759-1765: Chief Justice Charles Berry," Lower Cape Fear Historical Society Bulletin*, Vol. XLVIII, No. 1 (Late Winter, 2004).

• Ibid. *Legal Legacy of the Lower Cape Fear and the Development of the North Carolina Courts From the Revolutionary Period*. 2005.

• Smyth, John F. D. *A Tour of the United States of America*. Vol. I. London, 1784.

• Sprunt, James. *Chronicles of the Cape Fear River: 1660-1916*. Wilmington, NC: Dram Tree Books, 2005.

• Ibid. *The Story of Orton Plantation*. Wilmington, 1966.

• State Agency Records, Treasurer and Comptroller, Journal A, 1775-1776. North Carolina State Archives, Raleigh, NC.

• *State of the Troops that marches with the Army under the Command of Lieut. General Earl Cornwallis*. Cornwallis Papers, Public Records Office, 30/11/5/134.

• Steelman, Ben. *"Brunswick Map tells tales of coast's Colonial past."* *Wilmington Star Morning News*, December 12, 1983.

• Still, William N. Jr., *North Carolina's Revolutionary War Navy*. Raleigh: North Carolina Department of Archives and History, 1976.

• Stokes, Samuel, et. al. *Saving America's Countryside.* Baltimore: Johns Hopkins University Press, 1989.

• Stout, George F. *"The Second Man at Moore's Creek . . ."* *Pender Chronicle*, 1972

• Stumpf, Vernon O. *"The Radical Ladies of Wilmington and their Tea Party,"* *Lower Cape Fear Historical Society Bulletin* XVI #2 (February 1973).

• Sykes, Josiah. *Federal Pension Application*. S 7673. Washington, DC: National Archives.

• Tarleton, Banastre. *A History of the Campaigns of 1780 and 1781 in the Southern Provinces of North America*. North Stratford, NH: Ayer Co., 2001.

• Taylor, Thomas. *Federal Pension Application*. S 7675. Washington, DC: National Archives.

• Troxler, Caroline W. *The Loyalist Experience in North Carolina*. Raleigh: North Carolina Department of Archives and History, 1976.

• Troy, Robert E. *"Cain's Account."* *The Fayetteville Observer*, March 12, 1845.

• Tucker, David. *Federal Pension Application*. W6318. Washington, DC: National Archives.

• *University Magazine* Vol. 4 (November 1854), 139-40.

• Van Massey, Gregory D. *"The British Expedition to Wilmington, North Carolina, January-November, 1781."* Masters Thesis, East Carolina University, 1987.

• Waddell, Alfred Moore. *A Colonial Officer and His Times*. Spartanburg, SC: The Reprint Co., 1973.

• Wade, Joseph. *Federal Pension Application*. S 7826. Washington, DC: National Archives.

• Walker, Alexander. *New Hanover County Court Minutes, 1738-1769*. Bethesda, MD: Alexander Walker, 1958.

• Ibid., *New Hanover County Court Minutes, 1771-1785*. Bethesda, MD: Alexander Walker, 1959.

• Ward, Christopher. *The War of the Revolution*. Vol. 2. New York: Macmillan Co., 1952.

• Ward, William. *Federal Pension Application*. S 7809. Washington, DC: National Archives.

• Walker, John W., and Jerry W. Lee. *A Study of Historic, Topographic, and Archaeological Data Pertaining to the Revolutionary Period Earthworks at Moores Creek National Battlefield, North Carolina*. Tallahassee, FL: Southeast Archaeological Center, 1988.

• *"Washington Slept Here -Two Nights,"* Wilmington's 250th Anniversary, *Star News*, 23 July 1989.

• Watson, Alan D. *"Wilmington: A Town Born of Conflict, Confusion, and Collusion,"* Lower Cape Fear Historical Society Bulletin Vol. XXX No. 2 (February 1988): 1-5.

• Ibid. *Society in Colonial North Carolina*. Raleigh: North Carolina Department of Archives and History, 1996.

• Ibid. *"The Committees of Safety and the Coming of the American Revolution in North Carolina, 1774-1776."* North Carolina Historical Review. Vol. LXXIII No. 2 (April 1996), 131-155.

• Ibid. *"Women in Colonial North Carolina: Overlooked and Underestimated."* North Carolina Historical Review. Vol. LVIII (1981), 1-22.

• Ibid. *Wilmington: Port of North Carolina*. Columbia: University of South Carolina Press, 1992.

• Ibid., Dennis R. Lawson, and Donald R. Lennon. *Harnett, Hooper, Howe*. Wilmington, NC: Lower Cape Fear Historical Society, 1979.

• Watts, Gordon P., and Wesley K. Hall. *An Investigation of Blossom's Ferry on the Northeast Cape Fear River*. Greenville, NC: East Carolina University, 1986.

• Weynette, Haun. *North Carolina Revolutionary War Accounts, Secretary of Treasury and Comptroller Papers, Journal "A."*

• Wheeler, E. Milton. *"Development and Organization of the North Carolina Militia,"* North Carolina Historical Review No. 68 (1941): 307-323.

• Wheeler, John. *Historical Sketches of North Carolina*. New York: Frederick Hitchcock, 1925.

• Wickwire, Franklin and Mary. *Cornwallis and the American Adventure*. Boston: Houghton and Mifflin Co., 1970.

• *Wilmington Chronicle*, July 19, 1795

• *Wilmington Messenger, "A Revolutionary Story"* August 4, 1905.

• *Wilmington Star*, January 22, 1980.

• Wilmington Town Commissioner Meeting Minutes, 14 April, 1772; 1 March, 1774; 4 April, 1774.

• Williams, Isabel and Leora McEachern. *Salt*. Wilmington, NC, 1973.

• Wilson, David K. *The Southern Strategy*. Columbia: University of South Carolina Press, 2005.

• Wood, Bradford J. *This Remote Part of the World*. Columbia: University of South Carolina Press, 2004.

• Ibid. *"Politics and Authority in Colonial North Carolina: A Regional Perspective,"* North Carolina Historical Review LXXXI (January 2004): 1-37.

• Ibid. *"Formation of a Regional Colonial North Carolina: The Lower Cape Fear."* Ph.D. Dissertation. Johns Hopkins University, 1999.

• Wood, William. *Federal Pension Application.* S 7809. Washington, DC: National Archives.

• Wright, Robert. *The Continental Army.* Washington, DC: Government Printing Office, 1989.

• Wyatt, Lillian Reeves. *The Reeves, Mercer, and Newkirk Families.* Jacksonville, FL: Cooper Printing, 1956.

• www.sfhs.ccs.k12.nc.us

• wilmingtonforsale.com/Hampstead.asp hampsteadchamber.com

• www.uscg.mil/lantarea/cutter/dilligence

• www.royalprovincial.com/military/rhist/blkpion/blkhist.com

Notes

Chapter 1

1 Alan D. Watson, *Society in Colonial North Carolina* (Raleigh: North Carolina Department of Archives and History, 1996), 10.

2 C.E. Crawford, *A History of Bladen County* (Elizabethtown, NC: Bladen County Historical Society, 1987), 14; John Hairr, *North Carolina Rivers* (Charleston: History Press, 2007), 51, 53, 54.

3 Hairr, 59, 62.

4 Ibid., 64. The name "Negro Head Point" appears on a 1781 map, and is referred to in documents as early as the 1740s.

5 Gordon P. Watts and Wesley K. Hall, *An Investigation of Blossom's Ferry on the Northeast Cape Fear River* (Greenville, NC: East Carolina University, 1986), 2.

6 Janet Schaw, *Journal of a Lady of Quality* (Lincoln: University of Nebraska Press, 2005), 145; Lawrence Lee, *The Lower Cape Fear in Colonial Days*, (Chapel Hill: University of North Carolina Press, 1976), 171, 178.

7 Lorena McEachern and Isabel M. Williams, ed, *Lower Cape Fear Revolutionary War Events 1775* (Wilmington: Wilmington-New Hanover County American Revolution Bicentennial Association).

8 Harry Roy Merrens, *Colonial North Carolina in the Eighteenth Century* (Chapel Hill: University of North Carolina Press, 1964), 100. 116, 159-60; Roy Parker, *Cumberland County: A Brief History* (Raleigh: North Carolina Department of Archives and History, 1990), 13-17. Evidence shows that most of western North Carolina's trade went through Charleston, SC, but some did come up through the Cape Fear, via Cross Creek.

9 Parker, 1-12.

10 Ibid.

11 Schaw, 159.

12 Lawrence Earley, *Looking for Longleaf* (Chapel Hill: University of North Carolina Press, 2004), 1-2.

13 Schaw, 174-5, 158, 163.

14 Ibid., 148, 319-20.

15 Merrens, 86.

16 Earley, 1-2, 40.

17 Ibid., 42.

18 Lee, 6-7.

19 Ibid., 101, 107.

20 Bradford Wood, *This Remote Part of the World* (Columbia: University of South Carolina Press, 2004), 21, 17.

21 Lee, 109, 114-5.

22 Alan D. Watson, Dennis Lawson, and Donald R. Lennon, *Harnett, Hooper, Howe* (Wilmington, NC: Lower Cape Fear Historical Society, 1979), 9.

23 James Sprunt, *The Story of Orton Plantation* (Wilmington, NC, 1966), 3; Merrens, 27.

24 Wood, 38, 65.

25 Ibid., 99, 177, 181.

26 *Lower Gullah Culture Special Resource Study* (Washington, DC: National Park Service, 2006); Lee, 191.

27 Lee, 191-2.

28 Edwin L. Coombs, III, *"Trading in Lubberland: Maritime Commerce in Colonial North Carolina."* North Carolina Historical Review Vol. LXXX, #1 (January 2003): 13, 21.

29 Ibid., 16; Wood, 190.

30 Coombs, 17, 18, 21; Wood, 190. Ship arrival was key, and storms, bad harvest, weather, and epidemics like smallpox all affected trade.

31 Wood, 185.

32 Earley, 99.

33 Carol Butler, *Treasures of the Longleaf Pine* (Shalinar, FL: Tarkel Publishing, 1998), 10-12.

34 Lee, 149-50.

35 Alan D.Watson, *"Wilmington: A Town Born of Conflict, Confusion, and Collusion,"* Lower Cape Fear Historical Society Bulletin Vol. XXX No. 2 (February 1988): 5; Franda Pedlow, *The Story of Brunswick Town and Fort Anderson* (Wilmington, NC: Dram Tree Books, 2005), 5; Schaw, 142; Bill Reeves, *Southport (Smithville): A Chronology, Vol. I.* (Wilmington, NC: Broadfoot Publishing, 1985), 2-3, 5.

36 Pedlow, 5.

37 Ibid., 109-11, 58, 11.

38 Ibid., 109-11, 58.

39 Walter H. Conser, Jr., *A Coat of Many Colors* (Lexington: University of Kentucky Press, 2006), 49; Schaw, 278.

40 Conser, 36.

41 Ibid., 37, 70.

42 Pedlow, 17, 19; Conser, 49.

43 Schaw, 144; Lee, 140.

44 Pedlow, 8, 48, 107.

45 Ibid., 58.

46 Ibid., 51; Sprunt, 17.

47 Pedlow, 53, 55, 109.

48 Ibid., 57-9, 66.

49 Schaw 279; Merrens, 151-2.

50 Chris E. Fonvielle, *Historic Wilmington and the Lower Cape Fear* (San Antonio TX: Historical Publishing Network, 2007), 20.

51 Schaw, 283; Merrens, 90, 1.

52 Schaw, 285; R.V. Asbury, et. al, *The Schenck Diary* (Wilmington, NC: Wilmington Public Library, 1998), 2.

53 Donald R. Lennon and Ida Brooks Kellman, ed., *Wilmington Town Book* (Raleigh: North Carolina Department of Archives and History, 1973), xvii; Susan Block, *The Wrights of Wilmington* (Wilmington, NC: The Wilmington Printing Co., 1992), 25-26.

54 Watson, et. al., *Harnett, Hooper, Howe*, 6.

55 Lee, 136-7.

56 Ibid., 134-5.
57 Lee, 121, 125; *Report on the Petition of Mr. DuBois*, 1803.
58 Conser, 52.
59 Watts and Hall, 2; Wesley Hall, *"An Underwater Archaeological Survey of Heron's Colonial Bridge Crossing Site over the Northeast Cape Fear River near Castle Hayne, North Carolina."* (Masters Thesis, East Carolina University, 1992), 36, 37, 33.
60 Schaw, 202.
61 Watts and Hall, 13.
62 Lee, 141; Crawford, 4-5, 27.
63 Crawford, 6.
64 Butler, 3, 4; Merrens, 53.
65 Wood, 35; Watson, *Society in Colonial North Carolina*, 12, 20.
66 Alan D. Watson, *"Women in Colonial North Carolina: Overlooked and Underestimated."* North Carolina Historical Review Vol. LVIII (1981).
67 Merrens, 57; Conser, 61.
68 Conser, 53-4, 61; Watson, *Society in Colonial North Carolina*, 19.
69 Wood, 133.
70 Ibid., 62; Merrens, 27.
71 Pedlow, 5.
72 Coombs, 4-7, 13.
73 Ibid.
74 Pedlow, 35.
75 Wood, 179.
76 Ibid., 178, 180; Merrens, 88; Pedlow, 33.
77 Merrens, 93, 6, 8, 100.
78 Coombs, 12-13.
79 *North Carolina Gazette*, February 22, 1766; September 22, 1773.
80 *Cape Fear Mercury*, October 13, 1770.
81 Watson, *Society in Colonial North Carolina*, 11; Fonvielle, 21-22; Block, 28. Burgwin broke his leg playing "blind mans bluff" and had to seek proper medical treatment in England. He took the oath of allegiance to the state in 1775, but like many merchants, secretly supported the Highlanders at Cross Creek in 1776. Bugwin seems to have used his connections among both sides to his advantage: after the war he petitioned the state to reclaim his house, and also filed for losses with the British government (for materials he supplied MacDonald's army in 1776).
82 *Cape Fear Mercury*, January 13, 1773; September 22, 1773.
83 Coombs, 24; Schaw, 144, 314.
84 Ibid.
85 Isabel Williams and Leora McEachern, *Salt* (Wilmington, NC, 1973), 164.
86 Coombs, 16-17; Schaw, 324-5.
87 *North Carolina Gazette*, February 12, 1766; Wood, 233; *Cape Fear Mercury*, September 22, 1773.
88 John Bivins, Jr., *Wilmington Furniture* (Wilmington, NC: St. Johns Museum of Art, 1989), 12-15.
89 Schaw, 321.
90 Coombs, 17.

91 *Cape Fear Mercury*, November 24, 1769; December 29, 1773.
92 Wood, 172.
93 Ibid.
94 Lindley Butler, *North Carolina and the Coming of the American Revolution* (Raleigh: Department of Archives and History, 1976), 1-2.
95 Ibid., 2; E. Milton Wheeler, *"Development and Organization of the North Carolina Militia,"* North Carolina Historical Review No. 68 (1941): 309.
96 Wheeler, 316-7; Marvin Kay and William S. Price, *"To Ride the Woods Mare: Road Building and Militia Service in Colonial North Carolina, 1740-1775."* North Carolina Historical Review 57 (October 1980).
97 Wheeler, 319.
98 Bradford J. Wood, *"Formation of a Regional Colonial North Carolina: The Lower Cape Fear,"* PhD. Dissertation, Johns Hopkins University, 1999, 319.

Chapter 2

1 Fred Anderson, *The Crucible of War* (New York: Alfed A. Knopf, 2000), 214, 226, 228-9.
2 Edmund S. Morgan, *The Challenge of the American Revolution* (New York: WW Norton, 1976), 104; Anderson, 562, 580; Brendan Morrissey Boston (Oxford, UK: Osprey, 1993), 8. Americans paid 6 pence compared to 25 shillings for British citizens; in other words, Americans were paying 6 pence while their British cousins paid about 300 pence.
3 Butler, 12.
4 Morgan, 1-40; Edmund S. Morgan, *The Birth of the Republic* (Chicago: University of Chicago, 1992), 52.
5 Williams and McEachern, 163.
6 Watson, et. al., 71, 92; Predlow, 110, 80.
7 Watson, et. al., 72, 74, 75.
8 Ibid., 78,80, 82, 92.
9 Morgan, Challenge, 230-4; Reeves, 4.
10 Fonvielle, 23; Morgan, Challenge, 231, 233-4.
11 Watson, et. al., 22.
12 Schaw, 178; Ibid., 6.
13 Morgan, Challenge, 235-6, 240; Watson, et. al., 14, 16, 17.
14 Hairr, 29-30.
15 Ibid., 30-32.
16 Butler, 10.
17 Ibid., 11.
18 Ibid., 15.
19 Leora McEachern and Isabel M. Williams, *Lower Cape Fear Revolutionary War Events 1765-1774.* Wilmington: Wilmington-New Hanover County American Revolution Bicentennial Association.
20 Blackwell P. Robinson, *The Five Royal Governors of North Carolina* (Raleigh:

Department of Archives and History, 1968.), 44-46; Lee, 199. Despite their great difference in age, Justina seems to have been a devoted wife who cared for her elder husband until his death.

21 Robinson, 47.

22 Ibid., 48.

23 Ibid., 50-51.

24 Lee, 36.

25 Butler, 17.

26 Lee, 36, 239.

27 Ibid., 36.

28 Ibid., 37.

29 Ibid.

30 Lorena McEachern and Isabel M. Williams, ed, *Lower Cape Fear Revolutionary War Events 1775.*

31 Lee, 37.

32 Ibid; *London Chronicle*, March 20, 1766.

33 James Sprunt, *Chronicles of the Cape Fear* (Wilmington: Dram Tree Books, 2005), 101-3.

34 John W. Smith, *"Wilmington's Legal Legacy 1759-1765: Chief Justice Charles Berry,"* Lower Cape Fear Historical Society Bulletin, Vol. XLVIII, No. 1 (Late Winter, 2004), 29; Jack E. Fryar, Jr., ed., *Benson J. Lossing's Pictorial Field-Book of the Revolution in the Carolinas & Georgia* (Wilmington, NC: Dram Tree Books, 2005), 5.

35 Smith, 1; Fryar, 5-6, 22.

36 Robert DeMond, *The Loyalists in North Carolina During the American Revolution* (Baltimore: Clearfield Co., 2002), 12; Lee, 38.

37 Lee, 38.

38 DeMond, 12; Butler, 20; Lee, 247.

39 Lee, 38.

40 Ibid.

41 Ibid.

42 Ibid., 40.

43 Smith, 29; DeMond, 12-13; Butler, 20; Alfred Moore Waddell, *A Colonial Officer and His Times* (Spartanburg, SC: 1973), 94, 118, 120.

44 DeMond, 13-14; Waddell, 120.

45 Lee, 40; Butler, 21; Schaw, 315.

46 Lee, 40; Butler, 21; *North Carolina Gazette*, February 22, 1766.

47 Lee, 13, 41.

48 Butler, 23.

49 Lee, 41.

50 Butler, 23.

51 Ibid., Lee, 13-14.

52 Leora McEachern and Isabel M. Williams, *Lower Cape Fear Revolutionary War Events 1765-1774.*

53 Ibid., Butler, 23; Sprunt, Orton, 21.

54 Pedlow, 71.

55 Butler, 23.

56 DeMond, 15-16; Sprunt, *Orton*, 16; Butler, 25.

57 Sprunt, *Orton*, 20.

58 DeMond, 18-19.

59 Ibid., 19.

60 *Cape Fear Mercury*, November 24, 1769.

61 Ibid.

62 Butler, 30.

63 William S. Powell, *The War of the Regulation and the Battle of Alamance* (Raleigh: Department of Cultural Resources, 1975), 5; Butler, 32.

64 Butler, 33.

65 Powell, 6-7.

66 Ibid., 34.

67 Ibid.

68 Butler, 37.

69 Pedlow, 75.

70 Powell, 11-12.

71 Butler, 38; Powell, 14.

72 Powell, 9, 14; Robinson, 56.

73 Powell, 15-16.

74 Ibid., 16.

75 Ben Steelman, *"Brunswick Map tells tales of coast's Colonial past."* *Wilmington Star Morning News*, December 12, 1983.

76 Butler, 39; Robinson, 59.

77 Powell, 19-20.

78 Predlow, 76; Powell, 40.

79 John Hairr, *"Commanding Presence"* Our State, Vol. 75, No. 5 (October, 2007), 31.

80 Powell, 24; Robinson, 62.

81 Pedlow, 77; Fryar, 27.

82 Robinson, 62-74; Watson, et. al., 10; Butler, 47. The boundary between the two colonies was re-surveyed in 1773 and the current upper part of South Carolina was transferred from North to South Carolina; it was known as the New Acquisition District.

83 Lennon and Kellman, 209, 223; *Wilmington Town Commissioner Meeting Minutes*, 14 April, 1772, 1 March 1774.

84 Lennon and Kellman, 223; *Wilmington Town Commissioner Meeting Minutes*, 4 April, 1774.

85 Leora McEachern and Isabel M. Williams, *Lower Cape Fear Revolutionary War Events 1765-1774.*

86 Watson, et. al., 35-37.

87 Ibid., 37-38; *Wilmington Star*, January 22, 1980; Crockette W. Hewlett and Mona Smalley, *Between the Creeks, Revised, Masonboro Sound, 1735-1895* (Wilmington, New Hanover Printing Col, 1985), 12.

88 Watson., 42-43, 51-53.

89 Ibid., 56, 61.

90 Pedlow, 79.

91 Sprunt, Orton, 7; Pedlow, 79.

92 Leora McEachern and Isabel M. Williams, *Lower Cape Fear Revolutionary War Events 1765-1774.*

93 Ibid.

94 Ibid.

95 Ibid.

96 Ibid.

97 Ibid.; Alan D. Watson, *"The Committees of Safety and the Coming of the American Revolution in North Carolina, 1774-1776."* North Carolina Historical Review. Vol. LXXIII No. 2 (April 1996), 133.

98 Leora McEachern and Isabel M. Williams, *Lower Cape Fear Revolutionary War Events 1765-1774.*

99 Ibid.

100 Williams and McEachern, 65; Eli Caruthers, *The Old North State in 1776* (Philadelphia: Hayes and Zell, 1854), 28; Alexander Clayton and W. Keats Sparrow, *First of Patriots and the Best of Men: Richard Caswell in Public Life* (Kinston, NC: Lenoir County Colonial Commission, 2007), xv.

101 Clayton and Sparrow, 108.

102 Ibid., xvii, xix.

103 Ibid., xxi. The Franklin controversy arose from western settlers who lived beyond the mountains in modern Tennessee. Isolated from the rest of North Carolina, they felt neglected by the state's eastern government and hoped to create their own state, named in honor of Benjamin Franklin. Caswell firmly negotiated with the western leaders and helped quell the unrest, preventing the loss of North Carolina's western lands at the time.

104 Leora McEachern and Isabel M. Williams, *Lower Cape Fear Revolutionary War Events 1765-1774.*

105 Ibid., Watson, *Committees of Safety*, 134; Watson, et. al., *Harnett, Hooper, Howe*, 61.

106 Williams and McEachern, 102.

107 Ibid., 105.

108 DeMond, 19; Gregory D. Van Massey, *"The British Expedition to Wilmington, North Carolina, January-November, 1781"* Masters Thesis, East Carolina University, 1987, 23.

109 Vernon O. Stumpf, *"The Radical Ladies of Wilmington and their Tea Party,"* Lower Cape Fear Historical Society Bulletin XVI #2 (February 1973), 1.

110 Ibid., 3.

111 Leora McEachern and Isabel M. Williams, *Lower Cape Fear Revolutionary War Events 1765-1774.*

112 Watson, *Committees of Safety*, 131-2.

113 Leora McEachern and Isabel M. Williams, *Lower Cape Fear Revolutionary War Events 1765-1774.*

Chapter 3

1 Ray Raphael, *The First American Revolution* (New York: The New Press, 2002), 1-3.

2 Ibid.

3 Watson, *Committees of Safety*, 134-5, 142, 150.
4 Ibid., Raphael, 1-3, 66-67, 86.
5 Williams and McEachern, xxii; Lorena McEachern and Isabel M. Williams, ed, *Lower Cape Fear Revolutionary War Events 1775*; Watson, *Committees of Safety*, 138.
6 Watson, *Committees of Safety*, 140-1; Williams and McEachern, 6, 7.
7 Williams and McEachern, ix.
8 Ibid., 3.
9 Ibid., 164.
10 Lorena McEachern and Isabel M. Williams, ed, *Lower Cape Fear Revolutionary War Events 1775*; Schaw, 149.
11 Watson, *Committees of Safety*, 139.
12 Ibid., 143; Lorena McEachern and Isabel M. Williams, ed, *Lower Cape Fear Revolutionary War Events 1775*.
13 Schaw, 156.
14 Ibid., 155; Stumpf, 3.
15 Stumpf, 3.
16 Williams and McEachern, 100.
17 William N. Still, Jr., *North Carolina's Revolutionary War Navy* (Raleigh: North Carolina Department of Archives and History, 1976), 1.
18 David Lee Russell, *Victory on Sullivan's Island* (West Haverford, PA: Infinity, 2002), 36; Pedlow, 83. By April nearly 20,000 New England militia had surrounded and trapped the British garrison in Boston.
19 Butler, 58.
20 Schaw, 156.
21 Ibid., 156, 179, 188.
22 Russell, 36; Reeves, 5; Butler, 58.
23 Leora McEachern and Ruth Walker, *"Pensioners Remember The War,"* Lower Cape Fear Historical Society Bulletin Vol. XXIV, No. 2 (January 1991), 3.
24 Laura Frech, *"The Wilmington Committee of Public Safety and the Loyalist Rising of February, 1776."* North Carolina Historical Review 41 (1968), 22.
25 Lorena McEachern and Isabel M. Williams, ed, *Lower Cape Fear Revolutionary War Events, 1775*.
26 Ibid.
27 Frech, 27.
28 Roy Parker Jr., *Cumberland County: A Brief History* (Raleigh: North Carolina Department of Archives and History, 1990), 19-20.
29 Russell, 42.
30 Ibid., 41-42.
31 Wayne E. Lee, *Crowds and Soldiers in Revolutionary North Carolina* (Gainesville: University of Florida Press, 2001), 147.
32 Ibid.
33 Lorena McEachern and Isabel M. Williams, ed, *Lower Cape Fear Revolutionary War Events, 1775*.
34 Schaw, 190.
35 Ibid., 191.

36 Lorena McEachern and Isabel M. Williams, ed, *Lower Cape Fear Revolutionary War Events, 1775*; Steelman.

37 Lorena McEachern and Isabel M. Williams, ed, *Lower Cape Fear Revolutionary War Events, 1775*; Reeves, 5; *Watson, Committees of Safety*, 145.

38 Frech, 24, 30-31.

39 Ibid., 25.

40 Lorena McEachern and Isabel M. Williams, ed, *Lower Cape Fear Revolutionary War Events, 1775*.

41 Butler, 59; Russell, 40.

42 Russell, 42.

43 Caruthers, 12.

44 Watson, *Committees of Safety*, 145.

45 *Journal of the Provincial Congress of North Carolina*, 186; Bobby Moss, and Michael Scoggins, *African American Loyalists in the Southern Campaign of the American Revolution* (Blacksburg, SC: Scotia Hibernia Press, 2005), 204.

46 Russell, 47.

47 Hugh Rankin, *The North Carolina Continentals* (Chapel Hill: University of North Carolina Press, 2005), 17.

48 *Journal of the Provincial Congress*, 186-209.

49 Lorena McEachern and Isabel M. Williams, ed, *Lower Cape Fear Revolutionary War Events, 1775*.

50 Schaw, 199.

51 Wayne E. Lee, 144.

52 Caroline W. Troxler, *The Loyalist Experience in North Carolina* (Raleigh: North Carolina Department of Archives and History, 1976), 3-4.

53 Ibid., 4.

54 Schaw, 196, 193.

55 Virginia and Oscar Bizzell, *Revolutionary War Records of Duplin and Sampson Counties, North Carolina* (Newton Grove, NC: Sampson County Historical Society, 1997), 128; Bobby Moss, *Patriots in the Battle of Moores Creek Bridge*. Blacksburg, SC: Scotia Hibernia Press, 1992), 212; Louis T. Moore, *Stories Old and New of the Cape Fear Region* (Wilmington, NC: Broadfoot Publishing, 1999), 103; Claude Jackson, *Cape Fear-Northeast Cape Fear Rivers Comprehensive Study* (Kure Beach, NC: North Carolina Department of Archives and History, Underwater Archaeology Division, 1996), 105, 141, 26.

56 Lorena McEachern and Isabel M. Williams, ed, *Lower Cape Fear Revolutionary War Events, 1775*.

57 Watson, *Committees of Safety*, 134-5.

58 Lorena McEachern and Isabel M. Williams, ed, *Lower Cape Fear Revolutionary War Events, 1775*.

59 *Cape Fear Mercury*, August 11, 1775.

60 Schaw, 180.

61 Russell, 54-57.

62 Ibid., 63.

63 Schaw, 210-12.

64 Lee, 148.
65 Ruairidh H. MacLeod, *Flora MacDonald* (London: Shepheard-Walwyn, 1995), 152, 161.
66 Russell, 56, 64, 71.
67 Ibid., 71.
68 Ibid., 70-71.
70 Walter Clark, X, 314-15.
71 Alexander McLean, *Narrative of the Proceedings of a Body of Loyalists in North Carolina, English Records*, C.O., 5, Vol. 93, p. 297.
72 Lorena McEachern and Isabel M. Williams, ed, *Lower Cape Fear Revolutionary War Events, 1775.*
73 Ibid.
74 Ibid.
75 Ibid.
76 Williams and McEachern, 93.
77 William Clark, ed. *Naval Documents of the American Revolution* (Washington, DC: US Government Printing Office, 1968), Vol. 3, 408.
78 Lorena McEachern and Isabel M. Williams, ed, *Lower Cape Fear Revolutionary War Events, 1775.*
79 Ibid.
80 Ibid.
81 Ibid.

Chapter 4

1 Russell, 108.
2 MacLeod, 163.
3 Ibid., 166.
4 Lorena McEachern and Isabel M. Williams, ed., *Lower Cape Fear Revolutionary War Events 1776* (Wilmington: Wilmington-New Hanover County American Revolution Bicentennial Association).
5 Ibid.
6 William Clark, Vol. 3, 1232.
7 Alexander McLean, 4; Caruthers, 12.
8 Lorena McEachern and Isabel M. Williams, ed. *Lower Cape Fear Revolutionary War Events 1776.*
9 Ibid.
10 Ibid; Charles Hatch, *The Battle of Moores Creek Bridge* (Washington, DC: National Park Service, 1969), 16.
11 Lorena McEachern and Isabel M. Williams, ed. *Lower Cape Fear Revolutionary War Events 1776.*
12 Ibid.
13 Ibid., William Clark, Vol. 3, 1372.
14 Lorena McEachern and Isabel M. Williams, ed. *Lower Cape Fear Revolutionary War Events 1776*; James Shipman, *Federal Pension Application* (Washington, DC: National Archives).

15 Williams and McEachern, 82; Lorena McEachern and Isabel M. Williams, ed. *Lower Cape Fear Revolutionary War Events 1776.*

16 MacLeod, 168; Alexander McLean; *Loyalist Diary*, author unknown Sir Henry Clinton Papers, 14:10.

17 McLean.

18 Williams and McEachern, 83.

19 Ibid.

20 Caruthers, 10.

21 Diary; John F. D. Smyth, *A Tour of the United States of America* (London, 1784), Vol. I, 226-33.

22 Diary.

23 Russell, 112, 173.

24 James Lee, Federal Pension Application, S 7145 (Washington, DC: National Archives); John Fowler, Federal Pension Application, S 16809 (Washington, DC: National Archives).

25 State Agency Records, Treasurer and Comptroller, Journal A, 1775-1776. North Carolina State Archives, Raleigh, NC.

26 Ibid.

27 Ibid.

28 Walter Clark, ed. *State Records of North Carolina* (Raleigh, NC, 1905), Vol. XI, 444.

29 Pedlow, 84.

30 MacLeod, 154.

31 William Clark, Vol. 3, 1232, 102.

32 Alexander McLean.

33 Walter Clark, XI, 429.

34 Russell, 112; Alexander McLean; MacLeod, 174-5.

35 *Account of Sundries furnished . . . for his Majesty's Service in North Carolina* (Public Records, Audit Office, 13/3, ERD 7795, 94. Public Records Office, Kew, Surry, England); McLeod, 176.

36 Bobby Moss, *Loyalists in the Battle of Moores Creek Bridge* (Blacksburg, SC: Scotia Hibernia Press, 1992), 63.

37 Diary; Doroth Quynn, *"Flora MacDonald in History,"* North Carolina Historical Review XVIII, 3 (July 1941), 242.

38 Edward McCrady, *History of South Carolina in the American Revolution* (New York: Russell & Russell, 1969), 182.

39 Ibid., 181; Smyth, 226-33.

40 Walter Clark, XI, 13; Rankin, 42.

41 Moss, *Loyalists*, 64.

42 Alexander McLean.

43 Christopher Ward, *The War of the Revolution* (New York: Macmillan Co., 1952), Vol. 2, 663; Caruthers, 29; Journal A.

44 Caruthers, 29-30.

45 Lorena McEachern and Isabel M. Williams, ed. *Lower Cape Fear Revolutionary War Events 1776.*

46 Ibid.

47 Caruthers, 15; DeMond, 94; Journal A; John Oates, *The Story of Fayetteville* (1950), 788.

48 Moss, *Loyalists*, 60; Diary.

49 Moss, *Loyalists*, 9; Russell, 114.

50 Moss, *Loyalists*, 9.

51 Ibid., 130.

52 James DeVane, Federal Pension Application, S 8317 (Washington, DC: National Archives); James Lee, Federal Pension Application, S 7145 (Washington, DC: National Archives).

53 Journal A.

54 Ibid.

55 Ibid.; Smyth, 226-33.

56 Alexander McLean; Diary.

57 William Clark, Vol. 3, 71-73, 105.

58 Lorena McEachern and Isabel M. Williams, ed. *Lower Cape Fear Revolutionary War Events 1776.*

59 Ibid.; Journal A.

60 Bizzell. This is from a sampling of 376 soldiers from Duplin, New Hanover, Bladen, and Sampson Counties. Some men were in their mid-60s, others were teenagers. Most were in their mid 20s.

61 Alexander McLean.

62 Ibid.; Diary.

63 Journal A.

64 Diary.

65 Ibid.

66 Ibid.; Colvin Family Papers, Park Archives, Moores Creek National Battlefield, Currie, NC.

67 Colvin.

68 Moss, *Loyalists*, 74, 40, 16, 17.

69 Moss, *Patriots*, 41, 31, 65, 69, 143, 88, 237, 23.

70 Ibid., 74, 114, 223.

71 Moss, *Loyalists*, 20-21.

72 Alexander McLean; Diary.

73 John W. Walker and Jerry W. Lee, *A Study of Historic, Topographic, and Archaeological Data Pertaining to the Revolutionary Period Earthworks at Moores Creek National Battlefield, North Carolina* (Tallahassee, FL: Southeast Archaeological Center, 1988), 19, 63; Elisha Baker, Federal Pension Application, R 411 (Washington, DC: National Archives). Archaeology done in the 1930s at Moores Creek revealed the original height and depth of the earthworks. There were still traces of the original defenses at this time, faint and shallow depressions in the ground. Today reconstructed earthworks at the site suggest their location, not their true depth and scale.

74 Hugh Murphy, Federal Pension Application, S 9044 (Washington, DC: National Archives; William Ward, Federal Pension Application, S 7809 (Washington, DC: National Archives).

75 Caruthers, 20; Moss, *Loyalists*, 23.

76 Walter Clark, XI, 341; Caruthers, 19.

77 Elijah Johnson, Federal Pension Application, S 1806 (Washington, DC: National Archives); Baker, Federal Pension Application.

78 Diary.

79 Ibid.

80 Ibid.

81 Alexander McLean; Diary; James Rogers, Audit Office, American Loyalist Claims, American Series 13, Number 138 (Public Records Office, Kew, Surry, England). In his claim for losses during the war, James Rogers stated that McLeod stayed in his home the night before the battle. This may be the house referred to in the account.

82 Alexander McLean.

83 Ibid.

84 Diary.

85 Caruthers, 20.

86 Ibid., Moss, *Loyalists*, 60.

87 Josiah Sykes, Federal Pension Application, S 7673, (Washington, DC: National Archives); Caruthers, 20; University Magazine Vol. 4 (November 1854), 139-40.

88 Elisha Baker, Federal Pension Application, R 411 (Washington, DC: National Archives; Bryant Medley, Federal Pension Application, S 8894 (Washington, DC: National Archives).

89 Walter Clark, XI, 321.

90 Caruthers, 21. This, along with Loyalist accounts, confirms that the Highlanders did have bagpipes at Moores Creek.

91 Ibid.

92 Duncan McRea, Audit Office, American Loyalist Claims, American Series 13, Number 121 (Public Records Office, Kew, Surry, England); Moss, *Loyalists*, 56.

93 Moss, *Loyalists*, 3, 8, 74, 62; Journal A.

94 Moss, *Loyalists*, 73.

95 Walter Clark, XI, 285; Alexander McLean.

96 Moss, *Loyalists*, 162, 11.

97 Bloodworth, 53; *Wilmington Messenger*, *"A Revolutionary Story"* August 4, 1905; Lillian Reeves Wyatt, The Reeves, Mercer, and Newkirk Families (Jacksonville, FL: Cooper Printing, 1956), 2803. Different versions of the story disagree over who owned the sword. Most agree that Joseph Rhodes, brother in law of Newkirk, ended up with it.

98 William Green, Federal Pension Application, S 3413 (Washington, DC: National Archives); Caruthers, 26-7; Terry Maze, *John Grady and the Patriots Monument* (Research paper on file at Moores Creek National Battlefield, Currie, NC, 1979); Moss, *Patriots*, 107; Betty Perkins, *"A Patriots Return to Moores Creek,"* State Magazine (January 1975): 17-18. Two eyewitnesses mention his killing: James Holland and Richard Harrell. Capt. James Love said Grady was buried with his sword, research has not turned up where. There has been considerable debate about whether Grady was buried under the monument at Moores Creek. Evidence does not confirm that his remains were found and interred there, despite efforts to do so. Records indicate an effort to find his grave, but nothing says it was located. Grady died on March 2nd, four days after the battle, and the army had moved on by that time. He was buried either at

Long Creek, where the army was on March 2nd, in Wilmington, where he may have been sent for treatment, or on the field at Moores Creek, if he had been left there to be treated. Interestingly, the monument was first placed (in 1857) at the site believed to be where he was hit (it has since been moved to the park's walking trail).

99 George F. Stout, *"The Second Man at Moore's Creek . . ."* *Pender Chronicle*, 1972.

100 Moss, *Patriots*, 86.

101 Hugh Rankin, *The Moores Creek Bridge Campaign* (Fort Washington, PA: Eastern National, 1998), 37.

102 Lee, 270-1; Lorena McEachern and Isabel M. Williams, ed. *Lower Cape Fear Revolutionary War Events 1776.*

103 Alexander McLean.

104 Diary.

105 Ibid.; Walter Clark, XI, 282; Moss, *Patriots*, 51.

106 Alexander and Sparrow, 108.

107 Troxler, 7.

108 Bizzell, 21-2; Rankin, *Moores Creek*, 42; Moss, *Patriots*, 50.

109 Caruthers, 21.

110 Diary.

111 Marshall Haywood, *Governor William Tryon* (Raleigh, NC: E. M. Uzell, 1902), 182.

112 Ibid; Thomas Taylor, Federal Pension Application S 7675 (Washington, DC: National Archives).

113 Caruthers, 20.

114 Moss, *Loyalists*, 60.

115 Cynthia Kierner, *Southern Women in Revolution, 1776-1800* (Columbia: University of South Carolina Press, 1998), 136-7.

116 Caruthers, 24.

117 Mary McCaskle, Audit Office, American Loyalist Claims, American Series 13, Number 91. Public Records Office, Kew, Surry, England.

118 Walter Clark, XI, 392.

119 Rankin, *Moores Creek*, 20.

120 Smyth, 226-33.

121 Angus McLean, *Highland Scots in North Carolina* (North Carolina Scottish Heritage Society, 1993), 199.

122 Ibid., 200; Moss, *Loyalists*, 35.

123 Allan MacDonald, Auditors Office, 13/122, 27. Public Records Office, Kew, Surry, England; Dorothy Quynn, *"Flora MacDonald in History,"* North Carolina Historical Review XVIII, 3 (July 1941), 249, 255.

124 Catherine Crary, *The Price of Loyalty* (New York: McGraw Hill Book Co., 1973), 51; Robert M. Dunkerly, *Bravery and Sacrifice: Women on the Southern Battlefields,* (Charleston, SC: History Press, 2007), 42.

125 Alexander Morrison, Auditors Office, 13/122, Public Records Office, Kew, Surry, England.

126 McCleskle.

127 Moss, *Loyalists*, 5, 30, 51-2, 65.

128 Walter Clark, XI, 766.

129 Watson, *Committees of Safety*, 137.
130 Lorena McEachern and Isabel M. Williams, ed. *Lower Cape Fear Revolutionary War Events 1776.*
131 Bizzell, 124, 148.
132 Moss, *Loyalists*, 54.
133 Walter Clark, XI, 492.
134 John Edge, Federal Pension Application R 3232 (Washington, DC: National Archives).
135 Lorena McEachern and Isabel M. Williams, ed. *Lower Cape Fear Revolutionary War Events 1776*; Col Rec X, 539; Walter Clark, XV, 785, 788, XVI, 168.
136 Walter Clark, XVI, 476.
137 Caruthers, 23.

Chapter 5

1 Russell, 130.
2 Walter Clark, XI, 491.
3 James Shipman, Federal Pension Application,(Washington, DC: National Archives).
4 George Grinsely, Federal Pension Application, R 4333 (Washington, DC: National Archives);Lorena McEachern and Isabel M. Williams, ed. *Lower Cape Fear Revolutionary War Events 1776.*
5 James Lee, Federal Pension Application, S 7145 (Washington, DC: National Archives; Shipman, Federal Pension Application; William Pridgeon, Federal Pension Application, S8982 (Washington, DC: National Archives); Walter Clark, XV, 785.
6 Robert Wright, *The Continental Army* (Washington, DC: Government Printing Office, 1989), 300-1; Rankin, *Continentals*, 64-5.
7 Rankin, *Continentals*, 65.
8 Walter Clark, XI, 582, 619, 301, 610; Ibid., 83, 59.
9 Walter Clark, XI, 301-2; Asbury, 6.
10 Russell, 138-9.
11 William Clark, Vol. 5-131; Benjamin Quarles, *The Negro in the American Revolution* (New York: WW Norton, 1961), 177-78; Gary Nash, *Forgotten Fifth* (Harvard: Harvard University Press, 2006), 183; Sidney and Emma Kaplan, *The Black Presence in the Era of the American Revolution* (Amherst: University of Massachusetts Press, 1989), 86; Jeffrey Crow, *The Black Experience in Revolutionary North Carolina* (Raleigh: North Carolina Department of Archives and History, 1977), 70; www.royalprovincial.com; Bobby G. Moss, *African American Loyalists in the Southern Campaign of the American Revolution* (Blacksburg, SC: Scotia Hibernia Press, 2005), 240, 280; Sir Henry Clinton to George Martin, 10 May, 1776, Sir Henry Clinton Papers, Vol. 263, Miscellaneous Correspondence, 1776-1782, University of Michigan, William L. Clements Library. It is not known how many runaway slaves joined the British that spring, but it was likely over a hundred. Many served as guides and scouts, being familiar with the area. Among those we know of are: Thomas Peters, owned by William Campbell; Moses Campbell, owned by John Campbell of Wilmington; Caesar, owned by Mr. Izard; John Archer and Thomas Payne, slaves of John Gerald of Wilmington; Leslie Abraham, owned by Richard Quince; London, a baker owned by Isaac DuBois; Samuel, owned by

Captain Fisher of Holly Shelter; Saris, a female; David Saunders, slave of John Inman; Scipio; Cyrus Sperr of Cross Creek; Murphy Steele, slave of Stephen Daniel of Lockhart's (Lockwood's) Folly; Tom, owned by Roger Davis of Brunswick County; Joseph Moore, Thomas Moore, and Sherry Moore, slaves of Hunting Moore of Lockart's (Lockwood's) Folly; Daniel Moore, owned by John Moore; Morris of Town Creek in Brunswick County; Patience; Peggy; Nancy Watson, owned by Patrick Quince; and Ned Zanger and Drury London, property of William Lord of Lockharts (Lockwood's) Folly.

12 Lorena McEachern and Isabel M. Williams, ed. *Lower Cape Fear Revolutionary War Events 1776.*

13 R.D.W. Connor, *History of North Carolina, Vol. I.*, (Chicago: Lewis Publishing Co., 1919), 398.

14 Lorena McEachern and Isabel M. Williams, ed. *Lower Cape Fear Revolutionary War Events 1776.*

15 Ibid.

16 Ibid.; Williams and McEachern, 167; Mattie Bloodworth, *History of Pender County* (Richmond, VA: Dietz Press, 1947), 237-8.

17 Reeves, 6; Russell, 142-3.

18 Lorena McEachern and Isabel M. Williams, ed. *Lower Cape Fear Revolutionary War Events 1776.*

19 Ibid.

20 McEachern and Walker, "Pensioners," 4; Howard Peckham, *The Toll of Independence* (Chicago: University of Chicago Press, 1974), 15-17.

21 Peter Johnston, *Poorest of the Thirteen*, (Haverford, PA: Infinity Publishing, 2001), 94; Moss, *African Americans*, 159, 230. In 1779 Howe's slave Patty, fourteen years old at the time, fled with her six month old son, eventually reaching the British.

22 Russell, 147, 61; William Clark, Vol. 5, 131.

23 Russell, 156.

24 Ibid.

25 Ibid., 150.

26 Lorena McEachern and Isabel M. Williams, ed. *Lower Cape Fear Revolutionary War Events 1776*; William Clark, Vol. 5, 80.

27 Ibid.

28 Ibid; William Clark, Vol. 5, 139.

29 Russell, 150.

30 Ibid., 154.

31 William Clark, Vol. 5, 131, 9; Forster, 51-2; Russell, 161.

32 John Peterson, Federal Pension Application, S 7303 (Washington, DC: National Archives); McEachern and Walker, *"Pensioners,"* 4; Bizzell, 262.

33 Forster, 55.

34 Ibid. There is no evidence that this was done.

35 Russell, 162-3.

36 Lorena McEachern and Isabel M. Williams, ed. *Lower Cape Fear Revolutionary War Events 1776*; Petition of DuBois, DuBois' bakery was described as "the only one at that time in that part of America."

37 Ibid.

38 Ibid.; Watson, *Society in Colonial North Carolina*, 67.
39 Lorena McEachern and Isabel M. Williams, ed. *Lower Cape Fear Revolutionary War Events 1776*; Connor, 410.
40 Williams and McEachern, 8.
41 Mark Schriener, *"Martyred Patriot Remembered," Wilmington Morning Star*, 7 March 2002.
42 Still, 3; Lorena McEachern and Isabel M. Williams, ed. *Lower Cape Fear Revolutionary War Events 1776.*
43 Lorena McEachern and Isabel M. Williams, ed. *Lower Cape Fear Revolutionary War Events 1776*; William Saunders, ed., *Colonial Records of North Carolina* (Raleigh: State of North Carolina, 1886), X, 498.
44 Lorena McEachern and Isabel M. Williams, ed., *Lower Cape Fear Revolutionary War Events 1776*; Robinson, 73-4.

Chapter 6

1 DeMond, 101.
2 Ibid.; Lee, 170-1; Walter Clark, XI, 663-5.
3 Demond, 101.
4 Rankin, *North Carolina Continentals*, 68.
5 Ibid., 88; Walter Clark, XI, 329; John Moore, Federal Pension Application, R 7340 (Washington, DC: National Archives).
6 Saunders, X, 841.
7 Rankin, *North Carolina Continentals*, 81; Walter Clark, XI, 832.
8 Rankin, *North Carolina Continentals*, 84; Walter Clark, XI, 833.
9 William Clark, Vol. 7, 1148-9.
10 Walter Clark, XI, 576, 366.
11 Still, 6.
12 Ibid., 14.
13 Ibid., 13.
14 Rankin, *North Carolina Continentals*, 185.
15 Ibid., 89; Walter Clark, XI, 834.
16 DeMond, 181.
17 Rankin, *North Carolina Continentals*, 88; Walter Clark, XI, 454.
18 DeMond, 105.
19 Walter Clark, XI, 347.
20 Still, 3. 14; Lee, 275.
21 William Clark, Vol. 8, 1054-5, 1033.
22 Malcom Ross, *The Cape Fear River* (New York: Holt, Rinehart, and Winston, 1965), 135, 109-14; Lorena McEachern and Isabel M. Williams, ed. *Lower Cape Fear Revolutionary War Events 1776.*
23 Wright, 302.
24 Williams and McEachern, 9; Walter Clark, XI, 533, 560.
25 Ibid.
26 Williams and McEachern, 9.
27 Walter Clark, XI, 546, 591; DeMond, 104-5.

28 Walter Clark, XVI, 479.

29 Alexander Walker, *New Hanover County Court Minutes, 1771-1785* (Bethesda, MD: Alexander Walker, 1959), 42, 44, 48, 50, 21, 63, 64.

30 Walter Clark, XI, 755, 774, 760. 804; Crow, 67. Among the Randolph's crew were several local slaves who served in the Continental Navy.

31 Ibid., 749.

32 William Clark, Vol.9, 789.

33 Walter Clark, XI, 585, 610.

34 Rankin, *North Carolina Continentals*, 147.

35 Walter Clark, XI, 685-6.

36 Still, 22.

37 William Clark, Vol. 11, 274.

38 Lennon and Kellman, 232.

39 Ibid., 234.

40 Still, 23.

41 Lennon and Kellman, 233, 237; Conser, 50; Moss, *African Americans*, 230.

42 Kierner, 167.

43 Lee, 275; Still, 3; Alonzo Dill, *"Eighteenth Century New Bern,"* North Carolina Historical Review 23: 342-3.

44 Williams and McEachern, 9.

45 Ibid., 11.

46 Ibid., 13-15.

47 Ibid., 17-18.

48 Dennis Conrad, ed., *The Papers of Nathanael Greene* (Chapel Hill: University of North Carolina Press, 1997), Vol. VII, 236; Jeffrey Crowe, *"Liberty Men and Loyalists,"* in Ronald Hoffman and Thad Tate, ed., *An Uncivil War: The Southern Backcountry* (Charlottesville: University Press of Virginia, 1985), 148.

49 David K. Wilson, *The Southern Strategy* (Columbia: University of South Carolina Press, 2005), xi, xxiii-xv, 3.

50 Kierner, 28; Rankin, *North Carolina Continentals*, 218.

51 DeMond, 18; Frech, 32.

52 Troxler, 8.

53 Ibid.

54 Joseph Brown, *The Commonwealth of Onslow* (New Bern, NC: The Owen G. Dunn Co., 1960), 27.

55 Ibid.

56 Bizzell, 180.

57 Faison Wells McGowen, ed., *Flashes of Duplin County's History and Government.* (Raleigh: Edwards and Broughton, 1971), 57.

58 Troxler, 9, 29.

59 McGowen, 47-8.

60 Troxler, 9.

Chapter 7

1 Gregory De Van Massey, *"The British Expedition to Wilmington, North Carolina,*

January-November, 1781." (MA Thesis East Carolina University, 1987), 18-19.

2 Ibid., 20.

3 Ibid., 21.

4 Ibid., 22.

5 Walter Clark, XI, 582, 619; Rankin, *North Carolina Continentals*, 59, 83; Conrad, VII, 572.

6 Massey, 26.

7 John Hairr, *Colonel David Fanning: The Adventures of a Carolina Loyalist* (Erwin, NC: Averasboro Press, 2000), 92.

8 Wes Hall, *"An Underwater Archaeological Survey of Heron's Colonial Bridge Crossing Site over the Northeast Cape Fear River near Castle Hayne, North Carolina."* (Masters Thesis, East Carolina University, 1992), 39; Massey, 26; Petition of DuBois.

9 Allan Kemp, *The British Army in the American Revolution* (London, UK: Almark Publishing Co., 1973), 67.

10 Claude Jackson, *Cape Fear-Northeast Cape Fear Rivers Comprehensive Study* (Kure Beach, NC: North Carolina Department of Archives and History, Underwater Archaeology Division, 1996), 82; Massey, 25. No contemporary sources indicate where Ellis's Plantation was. It may be the home of Robert Ellis, whose property was just north of Sugar Loaf, opposite Brunswick Town, in modern Carolina Beach State Park

11 Ibid., 40; Conrad, VII, 236.

12 Massey, 28, 30; Conrad, VII, 236.

13 William Green, Federal Pension Application, S 3413 (Washington, DC: National Archives).

14 Thomas Brown, Federal Pension Application, W 9745 (Washington, DC: National Archives).

15 Ross, 143; Watson, Lawson, and Lennon, 19; Brown, 35.

16 Massey, 31, 32; Hewlett and Smalley, 13.

17 Massey, 32.

18 Bizzell, 241.

19 Massey, 29-30.

20 Ibid., 23; Conrad, VII, 236; Block, 29. According to family tradition, Major Craig occupied the house before Cornwallis did in 1781.

21 Ibid.

22 James Craig to Lt. Col. Balfour, 4 February, 1781, C.O. 5/101, fo. 248 (Colonial Office, Public Records Office, Kew, Surry, England).

23 Ibid.

24 Ibid.

25 Ibid.

26 Ibid.

27 Ibid.

28 Ibid.; Massey, 34.

29 Ibid.; Massey, 35.

30 Hall, 43; Craig to Balfour, 4 February, 1781.

31 Hall, 40-42.

32 Craig to Balfour, 4 February, 1781.

33 Ibid.

34 Massey, 45.

35 Ibid., 58.

36 James Craig to Lord Charles Cornwallis, 10 February, 1781 (Cornwallis Papers, 30/11/5/179, Public Records Office, Kew, Surry, England).

37 James Craig to Lt. Col. Balfour, 18 February, 1781 (Cornwallis Papers, 30/11/5/34. Public Records Office, Kew, Surry, England); William Graham, *General Joseph Graham and his Revolutionary Papers* (Raleigh NC: Edwards and Broughton, 1904), 353-4.

38 Craig to Balfour, 18 February, 1781.

39 James Craig to Lord Charles Cornwallis, 6 April, 1781 (Cornwallis Papers, 30/11/5/181. Public Records Office, Kew, Surry, England).

40 Massey, 40.

41 Ibid., 42.

42 Ibid., 51.

43 Moss, *Loyalists*, 67.

44 Ibid., 66; Massey, 42.

45 Conrad, VIII, 210; 51; Petition of DuBois.

46 Massey, 42-43.

47 Walter D. Siler, *A History of Chatham County* (Chatham News, 1931), available at www.rootsweb.com/~ncchatha/siler.htm; Walker, *New Hanover County Court Minutes, 1771-1785*, 64.

48 Massey, 44.

49 Ibid., 45.

50 Ibid., 46.

51 Ibid., 47.

52 Ibid., 48-9.

53 Ibid., 50.

54 Ibid., 51.

55 Ibid., 52.

56 Ibid., 52-53.

57 Ibid., 52; Watson, Lawson, Lennon, 21.

58 Massey, 53.

59 Ibid., 59-60.

60 Fonvielle, 45-61.

61 Massey, 54-55; James Craig to Lord Charles Cornwallis, 12 April, 1781, Cornwallis Papers, 30/11/5/305, (Public Records Office, Kew, Surry, England); Thomas Bullard, Federal Pension Application, S 6770 (Washington, DC: National Archives).

62 Massey, 54-55; Craig to Cornwallis, 12 April, 1781; McEachern and Walker, *"Pensioners,"* 5.

62 Ibid.

64 Craig to Cornwallis, 12 April, 1781; Conrad, VII, 457.

65 Massey, 56; McEachern and Walker, *"Pensioners,"* 5; Bizzell, 222; Conrad, VII, 457.

66 Thomas Brown, Federal Pension Application, W 9745 (Washington, DC: National Archives); Bizzell, 144; John Edge, Federal Pension Application, R 3232 (Washington, DC: National Archives); Bezzant Brock, Federal Pension Application, 16791 (Washington, DC: National Archives).

67 Massey, 56-57; Bullard; Bizzell, 129.

68 Fowler.

69 Massey, 57; Conrad, VII, 457.

70 Conrad, VIII, 75, VII, 457.

71 Massey, 55.

72 Ibid.

73 Ibid., 55-56.

74 Ibid., 57-58.

75 McGowen, 65.

76 Mark Schriener, *"Martyred Patriot Remembered,"* *Wilmington Morning Star*, 7 March 2002.

77 Brown, Federal Pension Application.

78 George Bannerman, Federal Pension Application, S 8055 (Washington, DC: National Archives); Bizzell, 28.

79 Brown, Federal Pension Application.

80 Franklin and Mary Wickwire, *Cornwallis and the American Adventure* (Boston: Houghton and Mifflin Co., 1970), 315.

81 David Schenck, *North Carolina 1780-81* (Bowie, MD: Heritage Books, 2000), 86; Rankin, *North Carolina Continentals*, 289-91; Banastre Tarleton, *A History of the Campaigns of 1780 and 1781 in the Southern Provinces of North America* (North Stratford, NH: Ayer Co., 2001), 231-3; David Fanning, *The Narrative of Colonel David Fanning* (Spartanburg, SC: The Reprint Co., 1973), 34.

82 Bizzell, 191, 272; www.battleofcamden.org/sm8109518.htm. Lieutenant Colonel Stephen Lee of the North Carolina militia and Major John Barnwell of the South Carolina militia wrote a petition to General Nathanael Greene complaining about their conditions.

83 Williams and McEachern, 18, 164.

84 Andrew J. Howell, *The Book of Wilmington*, (Wilmington: The Wilmington Printing Co., 1930), 65.

85 Massey, 164.

86 Walter Clark, XV, 479; Lawrence Babits and Joshua Howard, *Fortitude and Forbearance* (Raleigh: North Carolina Department of Archives and History, 2004), 141.

87 Walter Clark, XXII, 1024.

88 Ibid., 1027.

89 Ibid.

90 Caruthers, 179.

Chapter 8

1 Burke Davis, *The Cowpens-Guilford Courthouse Campaign* (Philadelphia: University of Pennsylvania Press, 2003), 174, 119.

2 Tarleton, 231.

3 Wickwire, 311.

4 Ibid., 313.

5 Ibid. Since the care of prisoners was a burden that neither side could adequately handle during the war, paroles were convenient ways to deal with captured troops. The prisoners signed an agreement stating they would not take up arms until they were properly exchanged, and then let go.

6 Ibid., 314.

7 Ibid.

8 Lord Charles Cornwallis, Proclamation, 18 March, 1781 (Cornwallis Papers, 30/11/101, ff 24-31, Public Records Office, Kew, Surry, England).

9 *State of the Troops that marches with the Army under the Command of Lieut. General Earl Cornwallis*, (Cornwallis Papers, Public Records Office, 30/11/5/134)

10 Tarleton, 270, 280-1; Schenck, 374-5; Caruthers, 152-5.

11 Lord Charles Cornwallis to Sir Henry Clinton, 10 April, 1781 (Cornwallis Papers, 30/11/5/207. Public Records Office, Kew, Surry, England).

12 Ibid.

13 *Journal of the Honourable Hessian Infantry Regiment von Bose*, 53.

14 Cornwallis to Clinton, 10 April, 1781.

15 Wickwire, 316.

16 Cornwallis to Clinton, 10 April, 1781; Davis, 119.

17 Cornwallis to Clinton, 10 April, 1781.

18 Caruthers, 154; Tarleton, 281.

19 Caruthers, 154.

20 Ibid., 105-6.

21 Von Bose, 54.

22 Crow, 75; Caruthers, 154. Crow briefly describes the use of runaway slaves in running captured mills and foraging for the army. Caruthers has collected many stories of the British army's march across the state.

23 Lord Charles Cornwallis to Lord George Germain, 18 April, 1781 (Cornwallis Papers, 30/11/5/254. Public Records Office, Kew, Surry, England).

24 Tarleton, 281; Von Bose, 54.

25 Von Bose, 54.

26 Ibid., 55.

27 Wickwire, 317; Moore, 95; Block, 28, 34. Moore collected a story that a daughter of the Burgwin family fell in love with a British officer during their stay. The two carved their initials into a glass window pane. In the early 1900s a descendent of the British officer came to visit the home, and in the basement a search revealed the glass pane. He was allowed to take it home. No other evidence for this story exists. While there is no clear cut documentation, enough evidence from family tradition exists to state that it seems highly likely that Cornwallis did indeed use this home as his headquarters. Children who lived in the home at the time recalled the general staying there. Another witness, fourteen years old at the time, recalled seeing the general there, recounting his story while an eighty-five year old man in the 1850s.

28 Cosner, 77.

29 Conrad, VIII, 114.

30 Charles Ross, *The Correspondence of Charles, First Marquis Cornwallis* (London: J Murray, 1859), 85-89, 516-23.

31 Lord Charles Cornwallis to Lord George Germain, 18 April, 1781.

32 *Petition To His Excellency Josiah Martin Esquire, Governor & Commander in chief of the Province of North Carolina*, (Cornwallis Papers, 30/11/5/201-203. Public Records Office, Kew, Surry, England).

33 Fryar, 37.

34 Wickwire, 318.

35 Ibid., 319.

36 Tarleton, 284.

37 Wickwire, 319.

38 Lindley S. Butler, *Narrative of David Fanning* (Davidson, NC: Briarpatch Press, 1981), x; Lord Charles Cornwallis to Lord George Germain, 23 April, 1781 (Cornwallis Papers, 30/11/5/215. Public Records Office, Kew, Surry, England).

39 Von Bose, 55.

40 Ibid., 56.

41 Diary of Sergeant Von Koch.

42 Lord Cornwallis to Sir Henry Clinton, 23 April, 1781 (Cornwallis Papers, 30/11/5/219. Public Records Office, Kew, Surry, England).

43 Ibid.

44 Von Bose, 56; Hall, 44-46, 60; Tarleton, 285; Wickwire, 321.

45 Ibid.

46 Wickwire, 321; Talreton, 285. Like Guilford Courthouse, Hobkirk's Hill was a British victory, but also like Guilford, the army was so weakened that it abandoned the exposed post at Camden as it was too far to supply and reinforce from their main base at Charleston.

47 Sir Henry Clinton to Lord Charles Cornwallis, 30 April, 1781 (Cornwallis Papers, Public Records Office, 30/11/5/30).

48 Robert Sloan, Federal Pension Application, S 7523 (Washington, DC: National Archives).

49 McEachern and Walker, *"Pensioners,"* 5.

50 Bizzell, 38, 39; Joseph Wade, Federal Pension Application. S 7826)Washington, DC: National Archives).

51 Mary Daniels Johnstone, *The Heritage of Wayne County, North Carolina* (Winston Salem, NC: Hunter Publishing Co., 1982), 5-6; Von Bose, 57.

52 Johnstone, 6-7.

53 Ibid., 7; Guilford Dudley, *"A Sketch of the Military Services Performed by Guilford Dudley, Then of the Town of Halifax, North Carolina, During the Revolutionary War."* Southern Literary Messenger (March–June 1845).

54 McGowen, 59.

55 Bizzell, 82.

56 James C. Burke, *Deconstructing Historic Text for Geographic References - The Plan of the Unnamed Colonel*, Unpublished research paper, 2008.

57 Elizabeth Ellet, *The Women of the Revolution* (New York: Baker and Scribner, 1849, 304-8.

58 Ibid., 309-12.

59 Ibid.

60 John Braxton Flowers, *"Did Polly Slocumb Ride to the Battle of Moores Creek Bridge?"* Lower Cape Fear Historical Society Bulletin Vol. XIX, No. 2 (February 1976). There is no record of Ezekiel or Mary at Moores Creek. While her story states that she left her infant son to ride to the battle, records clearly show that their son was born four years later. His own pension statement claims that Ezekiel enlisted in 1780, and the only battle he mentions is Camden, in 1780. The story must have some basis in truth, but we may never know for sure where or when Mary Slocum made her midnight ride.

61 Tarleton, 286.

62 Johnstone, 7; Tarleton, 287.

63 Tarleton, 287, 289.

64 Von Bose, 56-57.

65 Tarleton, 290.

66 Alice Keith, ed., *John Gray Blount Papers* (Raleigh, NC: Department of Archives and History, 1952), 15.

Chapter 9

1 Hairr, Fanning, 5-10.

2 Ibid; Crow, *"Liberty Men,"* 131.

3 Fanning, 86, 94.

4 Conrad, VIII, 75, 114.

5 A.R. Newsome, *"Twelve North Carolina Counties in 1810-1811,"* North Carolina Historical Review 5 (1928), 435.

6 Bizzell, 212, 222; David Tucker, Federal Pension Application, W66318 (Washington, DC: National Archives); Newsome, 435.

7 Newsome, 435; William Wood, Federal Pension Application, S 7809 (Washington, DC: National Archives); Bizzell, 211. The mill stood at the mouth of Torkill Branch on the Six Runs, near Ingold (about ten miles south of Clinton).

8 Ibid.

9 Ibid.

10 Bizzell, 212, 287; John Smith, Federal Pension Application, S 7540 (Washington, DC: National Archives); Newsome, 435.

11 Bizzell, 317; Daniel Merritt, Federal Pension Application, S 16497 (Washington, DC: National Archives).

12 Sprunt, *Chronicles of the Cape Fear*, 114; Brown, 27. The Duplin jail was used throughout the war to hold local Loyalist prisoners.

13 Hairr, Fanning, 88.

14 Beverly Boykin and William Kern, ed., *Historic Cemeteries of Fort Bragg, Camp MacKall, and Pope Air Force Base* (Fort Bragg, NC: Department of the Army, 2007), 183; John Oates, *The Story of Fayetteville* (1950), 793; Caruthers 94-95

15 Douglass and Caroline Kelly, *Carolina Scots* (Dillon, SC: 1739 Publications, 1998), 123; Caruthers, 95.

16 DeMond, 120; Caruthers, 94-95.
17 Caruthers, 95-97; Kelly, 219.
18 Ross, 147; Caruthers, 41.
19 Lee, 192; Hairr, *Fanning*, 90, 93; *Fanning*, 24-5.
20 Hairr, *Fanning*, 93-94; Caruthers, 43.
21 Fanning, 23-24.
22 Caruthers, 38-39.
23 [John D. Jones], *"Cape Fear Sketches and Loafer Ramblings by the Author of the Wilmington Whistling Society, etc."* Folder 29, Benjamin Franklin Perry Papers, #588, Southern Historical Collection, Wilson Library, The University of North Carolina at Chapel Hill, 151-61; Bizzell, 164.
24 Jones, 151-61.
25 Ibid., Bizzell, 164; Elisha Jones, Federal Pension Application, S 7084 (Washington, DC: National Archives).
26 Ibid.; Conrad, VII, 114.
27 McGowan, 41.
28 Jones, 151-61.
29 McGowen, 41-42.
30 Jones, 151-61; 45-61.
31 Ibid., 151-61.
32 Howard Peckham, ed., *The Toll of Independence* (Chicago: University of Chicago Press, 1974), 88.
33 Jones, 45-61.
34 Ibid., 151-61.
35 Ibid.
36 DeMond, 127.
37 Walter Clark, XXII, 543.
38 Ibid.
39 Angus McLean, 241.
40 DeMond, 220; Caruthers, 165-68.
41 Angus McLean, 241.
42 Kelly, 219.
43 Caruthers, 44; Hairr, *Fanning*, 99-105.
44 Caruthers, 95-98; Angus McLean, 243.
45 Caruthers, 95-98.
46 Hairr, *Fanning*, 109; Walter Clark, XV, 496, 99, 535, 67.
47 Newsome, 436-37.
48 Bizzell, 170, 153; Massey, 118.
49 Bizzell, 170, 153.
50 Bizzell, 178, 129, 317; Massey, 118; Newsome, 437; McGowan, 65.
51 Bizzell, 178; McEachern and Walker, *"Pensioners,"* 5.
52 Caruthers, 181-2.
53 Massey, 119.
54 Ibid., 119-120; Conrad, IX, 154.
55 Clark, XV, 634-5.

56 Sprunt, *Chronicles of the Cape Fear*, 115; Brown, 28.

57 Sprunt, *Chronicles of the Cape Fear*, 115.

58 Ibid., Massey, 126.

59 Massey, 128.

60 Dill, 358.

61 McGowan, 47.

62 Dill, 357; Massey, 131.

63 Dill, 357; Massey, 131-2; Keith, 18.

64 Ibid.

65 Massey, 132.

66 Ibid., 135.

67 Ibid., 132.

68 Sprunt, *Chronicles of the Cape Fear*, 115; McGowan, 60.

69 McGowan, 62-3.

70 Brown, 29.

71 Hairr, *Fanning*, 107.

72 Ibid., 108.

73 Fanning, 30.

74 Sprunt, *Chronicles of the Cape Fear*, 117; *Daniel Barefoot, Touring North Carolina's Revolutionary War Sites* (Winston Salem, NC: J.F. Blair, 1998), 122; Crawford, 29; John Wheeler, *Historical Sketches of North Carolina* (New York: Frederick Hitchcock, 1925), 37-8.

75 Ibid.; Robert E. Troy, *"Cain's Account," The Fayetteville Observer*, March 12, 1845; www.usno.navy.mil.

76 Ibid.

77 Hairr, *Fanning*, 115; Sprunt, *Chronicles of the Cape Fear*, 115.

78 Caruthers, 98-101; Moss, *Loyalists*, 69; Sprunt, *Chronicles of the Cape Fear*, 117; Wheeler, *Sketches*, 37-39. Details are sketchy and the only published accounts of the battle were collected in the 1840s from veterans and witnesses.

79 Kelly, 295.

80 Caruthers, 42.

81 Hairr, 118-25; Caruthers, 29-43; Fanning, 52-3. There is still debate over the location of this battle site. While many sources place it just north of the modern US 401 bridge at the Lumber River, others place it near Pine Bluff. Based on local tradition, Fanning's account, and analysis of the terrain, this seems to be the more likely location.

82 Fanning, 31.

83 Hairr, Fanning, 122.

84 Caruthers, 41-2.

85 Crow, 132, 144.

86 Ibid., 144-45.

87 Ibid., 170.

88 Walter Clark, XV, 605.

89 James Craig to Lord Charles Cornwallis,12 April, 1781, 30/11/5/305 (Cornwallis Papers,Public Records Office, Kew, Surry, England).

90 Caruthers, 102-3; Craig to Cornwallis, 12 April.

91 Troxler, 26; Moss, Loyalists, 73.

92 Massey, 149.

93 Caruthers, 50.

94 Ibid., 51; Moss, *Loyalists*, 53.

95 Ibid. Local traditions maintain that McDougal threatened to kill the prisoners rather than see them retaken. No eyewitness accounts mention this, and the origin of the story remains unknown. McDougal may indeed have made such a threat under the circumstances, but it could easily be an exaggeration of Loyalist cruelty. Eli Caruthers collected stories about the battle in the mid 1800s from local residents, and his sources were often biased.

96 Caruthers, 51; Moss, *Loyalists*, 53; Algie Newlin, *The Battle of Lindley's Mill* (Burlington, NC: Alamance Historical Association, 1975), 13.

97 Newlin, 13.

98 Ibid.; Caruthers, 51.

99 Fanning, 207.

100 Hairr, *Fanning*, 163.

101 Ibid., 142.

102 Ibid., 147-9; Caruthers, 55.

103 Ibid.

104 Caruthers, 55.

105 Ibid.

106 James Shipman, Federal Pension Application. Washington, DC: National Archives.

107 Hairr, *Fanning*, 150-2; Caruthers, 91; DeMond, 61.

108 Caruthers, 91; Nash Odom, *"The Battle of Brown Marsh," The Bladen Journal*, September 15, 1973.

109 Massey, 154.

110 Ibid., 154-55.

111 Ibid., 157-8; 174-5.

112 Ibid., 175.

113 Bizzell, 105.

114 Ibid., 122, 153.

115 Ibid., 200-201.

116 Ibid., 230.

117 Ibid., 235.

118 Ibid., 298.

Chapter 10

1 Keith, 21.

2 Conrad, IX, 430, 166; Massey, 122.

3 Robert E. Lee, ed., *The Revolutionary War Memoirs of General Henry Lee* (New York: Da Capo Press, 1998), 446-8.

4 Conrad, IX, 504.

5 Hairr, *Fanning*, 156; Caruthers, 200; Walter Clark, XXII, 148.

6 Massey, 159; Hairr, *Fanning*, 157; William Graham, *General Joseph Graham and his Revolutionary Papers* (Raleigh NC: Edwards and Broughton, 1904), 357.

7 Hairr, *Fanning*, 157; Graham, 357.

8 Caruthers, 200-202; Angus McLean, 243.
9 Walter Clark, XXII, 149; Hairr, *Fanning*, 158.
10 Hairr, *Fanning*, 158-9.
11 Hairr, *Fanning*, 160; Angus McLean, 240.
12 Caruthers, 202.
13 Hairr, *Fanning*,160; Angus McLean, 240.
14 Walter Clark, XIX, 963.
15 Graham, 361-3.
16 Walter Clark, XXII, 149.
17 Samuel Ashe, *The History of North Carolina, Vol. I* (Spartanburg, SC: The Reprint Co., 1971), 700.
18 Ibid.; Graham, 363-4.
19 Massey, 164.
20 Graham, 365.
21 Ibid., 354.
22 Ibid.; Caruthers, 203.
23 Graham, 366.
24 Ibid., 367; Caruthers, 203.
25 Graham, 368.
26 Ibid., 369-70; Caruthers, 203; Jonathan Clark, Federal Pension Application, S 2438 (Washington, DC: National Archives).
27 Ashe, 701.
28 Graham, 369-73; Caruthers, 203; Clark, Federal Pension Application.
29 Lee, 518.
30 Sprunt, *Chronicles of the Cape Fear*, 115; Graham, 373; Craig to Balfour, October 22, 1781 (Cornwallis Papers, 30/11/6/391-398, Public Records Office, Kew, Surry, England).
31 Massey, 169.
32 Walter Clark, XVI, 467-9.
33 Massey, 164-5.
34 Graham, 373.
35 Jones, 45-61.
36 Walter Clark, XVII, 149.
37 Conrad, IX, 376.
38 Moss and Scoggins, *African American Loyalists*, 183.
39 Moss, Loyalists, 67; Rogers.
40 McGowan, 47.
41 Ibid.
42 Moss, *Loyalists*, 61-2.
43 Claim of Arthur Benning (Public Records Office, Audit Office, 13/117); Claim of Rigdon Brice (Public Records Office, Audit Office, 13/117); Claim of John Mackay (Public Records Office, Audit Office, 13/117).
44 Graham, 373.
45 Hairr, *Fanning*, 165; Ashe, 703.
46 Watson, et. al., 56.

47 Fanning, 39, 41; Hairr, *Fanning*, 168-9.
48 Hairr, *Fanning*, 170.
49 Ibid.
50 Ibid.; Caruthers, 56-7.
51 DeMond, 123; Walter Clark, XVI, 216, 220; Caruthers, 200-1; Hairr, *Fanning*, 164-5.
52 Massey, 168-9.
53 Ibid., 3-4.
54 Ibid., 173.
55 DeMond, 162; Alexander Walker, *New Hanover County Court Minutes, 1771-1785* (Bethesda, MD: Alexander Walker, 1959), 67.
56 Devane.
57 Kierner, 162, 168-70; Walter Clark, XVI, 467-8.
58 Walter Clark, XVI, 170-1.
59 Bizzell, 212.
60 Caruthers, 87-8; DeMond, 120.
61 Caruthers, 78-9; Hairr, *Fanning*, 174-9; DeMond, 123.
62 Hairr, *Fanning*, 176-7; Caruthers, 78-9.
63 Hairr, *Fanning*, 179-83.
64 Fanning, 56-7; Hairr, *Fanning*, 184.
65 Fanning, 60; Hairr, *Fanning*, 183, 187.
66 McLean, 254.
67 Crow, 172.
68 Fanning, 60; Hairr, *Fanning*, 183, 187.
69 DeMond, 127.

Chapter 11

1 Troxler, 30; Conor, 501.
2 Lorenzo Sabine, *Biographical Sketches of Loyalists of the American Revolution* (Port Wasington, NY: Kennikat Press), 1966, 44; Moss, *Loyalists*, 1.
3 Troxler, 24; DeMond, 172-73.
4 Walter Clark, XVI, 168; Crow, 176.
5 Haun Wynette, *North Carolina Revolutionary War Accounts*, Secretary of Treasury and Comptroller Papers, Journal "A.", ii.
6 Kierner, 137; Petition of Isaac DuBois.
7 Jones, 45-61.
8 Ibid.
9 Ross, 134.
10 Reeves, 7.
11 Parker, 24; Alan D. Watson, *Wilmington: Port of North Carolina* (Columbia: University of South Carolina Press, 1992), 33.
12 Parker, 24-26.
13 Watson, *Wilmington*, 30-33.
14 Alice Keith, ed. *John Gray Blount Papers* (Raleigh, NC: Department of Archives and History, 1952), 163.

15 *"Washington Slept Here-Two Nights,"* Wilmington's 250ᵗʰ Anniversary, *Star News*, 23 July 1989; *History of the George Washington Bicentennial Celebration* (Washington, DC: 1932), 133, 290.
16 www.uscg.mil/lantarea/cutter/dilligence.
17 *Wilmington Chronicle*, July 19, 1795. This paper, established after the war, was published at Second and Market Streets.
18 Bizzell, 86, 96, 310; Moss, *Patriots*, 169; Robert M. Dunkerly, *The Battle of Kings Mountain: Eyewitness Accounts* (Charleston, SC: History Press, 2007), 8-9.

Epilogue

1 www.sfhs.ccs.k12.nc.us; Parker, 21.
2 www.wilmingtonforsale.com/Hampstead.asp hampsteadchamber.com; Bloodworth, 204; Jack Howard, *A History of Hampstead*, 4.
3 Samuel Stokes, et. al., *Saving America's Countryside* (Baltimore: Johns Hopkins University Press, 1989), 1.

Appendix B

1 *Roster of Soldiers from North Carolina in the American Revolution* (Baltimore, MD: Clearfield Co., 2003), 632-3; Barnett A. Elzas, *The Jews of South Carolina* (Philadelphia: J.B. Lippincott Co., 1905), 93; Bizzell, 191, 272.

Index

About the Author

Robert M. Dunkerly

Robert M. Dunkerly is a historian, author, and speaker who is actively involved in historic preservation and research. He holds a degree in History from St. Vincent College and a Masters in Historic Preservation from Middle Tennessee State University. He has worked at nine historic sites, written six books and over twenty articles. His research includes archaeology, colonial life, military history, and historic commemoration. Dunkerly is currently Lead Park Ranger at Appomattox Court House National Historical Park. He has visited over 300 battlefields and over 600 historic sites worldwide. When not reading or writing, he enjoys hiking, camping, and photography.

LaVergne, TN USA
25 November 2009
165264LV00004B/70/P